The Dynamics of Language and Inequality in Education

NEW PERSPECTIVES ON LANGUAGE AND EDUCATION
Founding Editor: Viv Edwards, *University of Reading, UK*
Series Editors: Phan Le Ha, *University of Hawaii at Manoa, USA* and Joel Windle, *Monash University, Australia.*

Two decades of research and development in language and literacy education have yielded a broad, multidisciplinary focus. Yet education systems face constant economic and technological change, with attendant issues of identity and power, community and culture. This series will feature critical and interpretive, disciplinary and multidisciplinary perspectives on teaching and learning, language and literacy in new times.

All books in this series are externally peer-reviewed.

Full details of all the books in this series and of all our other publications can be found on http://www.multilingual-matters.com, or by writing to Multilingual Matters, St Nicholas House, 31-34 High Street, Bristol BS1 2AW, UK.

NEW PERSPECTIVES ON LANGUAGE AND EDUCATION: 77

The Dynamics of Language and Inequality in Education

Social and Symbolic Boundaries in the Global South

Edited by
Joel Austin Windle, Dánie de Jesus and Lesley Bartlett

MULTILINGUAL MATTERS
Bristol • Blue Ridge Summit

DOI https://doi.org/10.21832/WINDLE6942
Library of Congress Cataloging in Publication Data
A catalog record for this book is available from the Library of Congress.
Names: Windle, Joel A., editor. | Jesus, Dánie Marcelo de, editor. |
  Bartlett, Lesley, editor.
Title: The Dynamics of Language and Inequality in Education: Social and
  Symbolic Boundaries in the Global South/Edited by Joel Austin Windle,
  Dánie de Jesus and Lesley Bartlett.
Description: Bristol; Blue Ridge Summit: Multilingual Matters, [2020] |
  Series: New Perspectives on Language and Education: 77 | Includes
  bibliographical references and index. | Summary: 'This book contributes
  new perspectives from the global south on the ways in which linguistic
  and discursive boundaries shape inequalities in educational contexts,
  ranging from Amazonian missions to Mongolian universities, using
  critical ethnographic and sociolinguistic analyses' – Provided by
  publisher.
Identifiers: LCCN 2019037516 (print) | LCCN 2019037517 (ebook) | ISBN
  9781788926942 (hardback) | ISBN 9781788926935 (paperback) | ISBN
  9781788926959 (pdf) | ISBN 9781788926966 (epub) | ISBN 9781788926973
  (kindle edition)
Subjects: LCSH: Language and education – Developing countries – Case studies.
  | Educational equalization – Developing countries – Case studies.
Classification: LCC P40.85.D44 D96 2020 (print) | LCC P40.85.D44 (ebook)
  | DDC 306.44 – dc23
LC record available at https://lccn.loc.gov/2019037516
LC ebook record available at https://lccn.loc.gov/2019037517

British Library Cataloguing in Publication Data
A catalogue entry for this book is available from the British Library.

ISBN-13: 978-1-78892-694-2 (hbk)
ISBN-13: 978-1-78892-693-5 (pbk)

Multilingual Matters
UK: St Nicholas House, 31–34 High Street, Bristol BS1 2AW, UK.
USA: NBN, Blue Ridge Summit, PA, USA.
Website: www.multilingual-matters.com
Twitter: Multi_Ling_Mat
Facebook: https://www.facebook.com/multilingualmatters
Blog: www.channelviewpublications.wordpress.com

Copyright © 2020 Joel Austin Windle, Dánie de Jesus, Lesley Bartlett and the authors of individual chapters.

All rights reserved. No part of this work may be reproduced in any form or by any means without permission in writing from the publisher.

The policy of Multilingual Matters/Channel View Publications is to use papers that are natural, renewable and recyclable products, made from wood grown in sustainable forests. In the manufacturing process of our books, and to further support our policy, preference is given to printers that have FSC and PEFC Chain of Custody certification. The FSC and/or PEFC logos will appear on those books where full certification has been granted to the printer concerned.

Typeset by Riverside Publishing Solutions.
Printed and bound in the UK by the CPI Books Group Ltd.
Printed and bound in the US by NBN.

Contents

Contributors   vii

Introduction: The Dynamics of Language and Inequality   xi
Joel Windle, Dánie de Jesus and Lesley Bartlett

Section 1: The Shifting Boundaries of Linguistic Inequality

1 Across Linguistic Boundaries: Language as a Dimension of Power in the Colonization of the Brazilian Amazon   3
Dennys Silva-Reis and Marcos Bagno

2 Navigating Soft and Hard Boundaries: Race and Educational Inequality at the Borderlands   24
Joel Windle and Kassandra Muniz

3 Rural-Urban Divides and Digital Literacy in Mongolian Higher Education   44
Daariimaa Marav

Section 2: Language, Ideology and Inequality

4 A Cycle of Shame: How Shaming Perpetuates Language Inequalities in Dakar, Senegal   61
Teresa Speciale

5 The Role of Shame in Drawing Social Boundaries for Empowerment: ELT in Kiribati   71
Indika Liyanage and Suresh Canagarajah

6 Native-speakerism and Symbolic Violence in Constructions of Teacher Competence   84
Junia C.S. Mattos Zaidan

7 Knowledge Politics, Language and Inequality in Educational Publishing   100
Maria do Socorro Alencar Nunes Macedo, Daniele Alves Ribeiro, Euclides de Freitas Couto and André Luan Nunes Macedo

Section 3: Transgression and Agency

8 Decoloniality and Language in Education: Transgressing
   Language Boundaries in South Africa   115
   Carolyn McKinney

9 Queering Literacy in Brazil's Higher Education: Questioning
   the Boundaries of the Normalized Body   133
   Dánie de Jesus

10 'Saudi Women Are Finally Allowed to Sit Behind the Wheel':
   Initial Responses from TESOL Classrooms   141
   Osman Z. Barnawi and Phan Le Ha

   Multilingual Abstracts   158
   Index   165

Contributors

Marcos Bagno, PhD, is a Professor at the Institute for Modern Languages at the University of Brasília. He is a translator, fiction writer, poet, and author of children's literature. His research focuses on the sociology of language, the description of Brazilian Portuguese and the pedagogy of linguistic variation. He has translated more than a hundred books into Portuguese, including scientific and literary works. He has published, among other titles, *Preconceito Linguístico* (1999), *Gramática pedagógica do português brasileiro* (2012), *Dicionário crítico de sociolinguística* (2017) and *Objeto língua* (2019).

Osman (also written Othman) Barnawi is Associate Professor of TESOL/Applied Linguistics and critical education. His recent books are: *Neoliberalism and English Language Education Policies in the Arabian Gulf* (Routledge. 2017), and *Writing Centers in the Higher Education Landscape of the Arabian Gulf* (Palgrave Macmillan, 2017). His research interests include second language writing, teachers' identities, critical education, higher education studies, curriculum, and TESOL and Blackness. His works appear in journals such as 'Language and Education', 'Critical Studies in Education' and 'Language and Literacy'.

Lesley Bartlett, PhD in anthropology, is a Professor in Education Policy Studies at University of Wisconsin-Madison. Her research and teaching interests include migration and multilingual literacies. Her most recent book, authored with Frances Vavrus, is *Rethinking Case Study Research* (Routledge, 2017). She serves on the editorial boards of *Teachers College Record* and *Journal of Latinos in Education*.

Suresh Canagarajah is the Edwin Erle Sparks Professor and Director of the Migration Studies Project at Pennsylvania State University. He teaches World Englishes, Second Language Writing, and Postcolonial Studies in the departments of English and Applied Linguistics. He has taught before in the University of Jaffna, Sri Lanka, and the City University of New York. His most recent publication is *Translingual Practice: Global Englishes and Cosmopolitan Relations* (Routledge, 2013), which won the best book award from AAAL, BAAL and MLA.

He was formerly the editor of *TESOL Quarterly* and President of the American Association of Applied Linguistics.

Euclides de Freitas Couto, PhD in History, is an Assistant Professor at the Federal University of São João del Rey. He is currently Professor in the Postgraduate Program in History. His research and teaching interests include the areas of history and sociology of sport. His most recent book is *From Dictatorship to Dictatorship: A Social History of Brazilian Football.* (Editora da UFF, 2014).

Dánie de Jesus received his PhD in Applied Linguistic and Language Studies from the Pontifical Catholic University of São Paulo in 2007. He works at Federal University of Mato Grosso where he was coordinator of the Graduate Program of Language Studies in 2008. In 2013 and 2014 he undertook post-doctoral studies at University of São Paulo and the University of Illinois, USA. From 2014 to 2016, he served on the executive board of the Applied Linguistics Association of Brazil. His research focuses on queer perspectives on language education.

Indika Liyanage is Associate Professor in TESOL and Discipline Leader (TESOL/LOTE) at Deakin University, Australia. He is also an Honorary Professor at the Faculty of Education, Sichuan Normal University, and Researcher at the Research Centre for Multi-culture, Sichuan Province, People's Republic of China. Indika has been an English language teacher educator and doctoral supervisor for many years. He has published widely and worked as an international consultant on TESOL in the Pacific. He is the series editor for Springer's Multilingual Education Yearbook.

André Luan Nunes Macedo holds a PhD in History from the Federal University of Ouro Preto. He undertook his MA in History at the Federal University of São João del-Rei. His research focuses mainly on comparative history in Latin America, based on the relationship between historiographic and school knowledge in history textbooks. From 2016 to 2017 he was an assistant professor at the Federal University of Alagoas. His most recent book is *Between the Politician's Crisis and Revolutionary Nationalism: The History of the Brazilian and Venezuelan Textbooks* (Prismas, 2018).

Maria do Socorro Alencar Nunes Macedo, PhD in education, is Associate Professor at the Federal University of São João del Rey. In 2010 she undertook post-doctoral studies at King's College University of London. Her research and teaching interests include the fields of academic literacy, school literacy, literacy in urban and rural areas and also research methods in the humanities. She is the leader of GPEALE (Grupo de Pesquisa em Alfabetização e Letramento) and the coordinator of the

Postgraduate Program in Education. Her most recent book, authored with Claudia Mendes Gontijo, is *Literacy Policies and Practices* (Editora UFPE, 2017). She serves on the editorial board of the *Brazilian Journal of Literacy*.

Junia C.S. Mattos Zaidan, PhD in Linguistics, teaches English, applied linguistics and translation at the Department of Languages of the Federal University of Espírito Santo, in Brazil, where she coordinates the research and outreach program of the Observatory of Translation: Art, Media and Education. She is co-editor of *Marxismo e Modernismo em Época de Literatura Pós-Autônoma* (2015), *Cultura e Imperialismo Americano* (2016), *Literatura, Lacã e o Comunismo* (2017) and *Foi Golpe: o Brasil de 2016 em Análise* (2019). Her post-doctoral work focused on violence, critical literacy and translation. She is a founding member of the Fórum Capixaba de Lutas Sociais.

Daariimaa Marav is an Associate Professor at the School of Arts and Sciences, National University of Mongolia. She completed her PhD and MA degrees in language education at Monash University, Australia. Her research interests include educational inequalities, sociology of education, technology use in everyday and educational settings and English language education. Her research contributes to global perspectives on lived digital literacy practices by researching youth in Mongolia and extending global discussions on the application of Bourdieu's theories in the field of Literacy Studies.

Carolyn McKinney is Associate Professor of Language Education at the School of Education, University of Cape Town. She is a teacher educator, graduate student supervisor and convenor of the MEd programme in Language and Literacy Studies. Carolyn's research focuses on language ideologies; multilingualism as a resource for learning; critical literacy and relationships between language, identity/subjectivity and learning. She recently published *Language and Power in Post-Colonial Schooling: Ideologies in Practice* (2017, Routledge).

Kassandra Muniz holds a Masters and PhD in linguistics from the State University of Campinas (UNICAMP), and a BA from the Federal University of Pernambuco. She is Assistant Professor at the Federal University of Ouro Preto, where she is assistant coordinator of a professional development course that promotes racial equality in schools. She also coordinates the Research Group on Language, Culture and Identity, is a consultant for the Centre for Afro-Brazilian and Indigenous studies (UFOP), and is a member of the Identity Practices Working Group of the National Association of Postgraduate Programs in Linguistics and Literature. Her research, situated in the fields of linguistics and education, focuses on Afro-Brazilian culture.

Phan Le Ha (also written Phan Le-Ha, Le Ha Phan and Le-Ha Phan in some publications; Phan is the family name/last name), is Full Professor, Department of Educational Foundations, University of Hawaii at Manoa, Hawaii, USA. She has held appointments as well as visiting professorship positions at institutions in Vietnam, Australia, the UK, the US, Malaysia and Brunei. Phan Le Ha's expertise includes language-culture-identity-pedagogy studies, sociology of education and knowledge production, TESOL, academic and knowledge mobility, and the internationalisation of education in global contexts.

Daniele Alves Ribeiro holds an MA in education from Federal University of São João del-Rei and has been working as the editor of *Educação em foco*, the Journal of Minas Gerais State University.

Dennys Silva-Reis is Assistant Professor of French Literature at the Federal University of Acre. He holds a degree in French from the University of Brasília, a Master's degree in Translation Studies and a PhD from the Graduate Program in Literature at the same university. He specialises in the work of Victor Hugo, the history of translation in Brazil and intersemiotic theories, especially of the relations between literature and other arts. He is editor of the book *Literature and Other Arts in Latin America* (2019).

Teresa Speciale is a PhD candidate in Educational Policy Studies at the University of Wisconsin-Madison. Her work draws on and contributes to the fields of comparative and international education, language and education policy, and critical theories of education. Through this interdisciplinary lens, she explores how privilege and exclusion are culturally (re)produced through education for students from different socio-economic and linguistic backgrounds. She holds an MA in International Education from The George Washington University and a BA in Linguistics with a minor in French Language and Literature from Boston University.

Joel Windle is Assistant Professor at the Institute of Modern Languages of the Fluminense Federal University and Senior Adjunct Researcher at the Faculty of Education, Monash University. He coordinates the Centre for Critical Studies in Language, Education and Society, a research group of the Brazilian National Council for Scientific and Technological Advancement. His book *Making Sense of School Choice* (Palgrave, 2015) won the Raewyn Connell and Stephen Cook Prizes for best first book and best overall book in Australian sociology. His research focuses on educational inequalities, drawing on perspectives from sociology and applied linguistics.

Introduction: The Dynamics of Language and Inequality

Joel Windle, Dánie de Jesus and Lesley Bartlett

The concept of boundaries has long been central to the field of language studies, through classifications of linguistic forms and speakers. More recently, linguistic and discursive boundaries, along with boundary crossing and gatekeeping, have gained attention within work attending to the generation of inequalities, particularly through educational institutions (see, for example, Block, 2012; Heller & McElhinny, 2017). The present volume contributes new scholarship from the global south to this line of investigation. One motivation for (re)focusing attention on boundaries is a trend towards viewing geographical and linguistic divisions as of limited and fading importance, swept away by the currents of globalization and replaced by metaphors of flow and movement. Global flows, however, remain structured and articulated by boundaries, which do not merely stand in their way but help to constitute them (Gerrard & Sriprakesh, 2018; Stroud & Prinsloo, 2015). It is important, therefore, to show how, and where, linguistic inequalities continue to work through both old and new types of boundaries, contributing to the geopolitics of colonialism, capitalism and myriad, interwoven, forms of social life that structure both oppression and resistance.

Boundaries can be thought of as relational constructs that mark exclusion, as well as the terms upon which admission to groups, institutions, territories, identities or practices may be granted (Oommen, 1995). Boundaries are useful metaphors for analysing power because they draw attention to how difference is produced and enforced in externalised and durable ways, particularly through the establishment of a center-periphery relationship. Although boundaries may vary in rigidity and stability, it is at the moments of boundary crossing, or attempted crossings, that they are brought to life as central elements of social relations (Anzaldúa, 1987). Boundaries can be enacted through linguistic ideologies, language policies, curriculum choices, exclusionary identity constructions and communicative practices – topics examined in the chapters that follow.

Importantly, boundaries have the capacity of binding together both the included and the excluded, constituting an essential dimension of relations of expropriation, exploitation and domination. Boundaries and boundary-making may, indeed, hold strongest sway over those who are held outside of their limits, yet who remain part of the same social world as the priviledged centre, interpellated even as they are held apart (Feltran, 2011). As Feltran observes,

> Where there is a boundary, there is communication of an unequal and controlled kind. If there is a boundary, it is precisely to control communication between the sides … Where there is a boundary, there is conflict. Even if it is latent. If a boundary can be contested, it is common, particularly in extremely hierarchical and unequal societies, that latency gives way to violence. (2011: 15, our translation)

Those who are engaged in hybrid or boundary-crossing practices are often in the firing line of literal and symbolic border policing, considered subversive, dangerous and shameful. It is no accident that *Borderlands*, a book that described the US-Mexican border as '*una herida abierta* where the Third World grates against the first and bleeds' (Aznaldúa, 1987: 25), was banned in Arizona schools in 2012 as part of a xenophobic backlash against Latino studies.

The present volume focuses on the divisions produced by linguistic inequalities in settings in the Global South that are strongly shaped by imperialism, including chapters from the Pacific, Asia, Middle East, Africa and Latin America. As a publication articulated by scholars who are connected primarily through Brazil, a number of chapters address this setting, even as they draw attention to the shifting territorial and linguistic boundaries of this country. For example, Chapter 1 not only points out the relatively recent inclusion of Amazonian regions into Brazil, but the arbitrary violence of the establishment of colonial boundaries, evident in the fate of the speakers of Amazonian *língua geral*, an indigenous-based língua franca, almost half of whom were killed in the Paraguayan War (1864-1870). Impoverished conscripts from the Amazon region were sent to their deaths in Paraguay by Portuguese-speaking officers they little understood:

> many soldiers from the 5th Infantry Battalion, who could not even understand the orders of their commander [in Portuguese], died on the battlefields of Paraguay as 'volunteers of the homeland', speaking a language understood by the enemy but unknown in their own trenches. (Freire, 2011: 102)

The annihilation of speakers of Indigenous languages and imposition of European languages also takes more subtle forms, through the authorising of exclusive linguistic frameworks for schooling, scholarship, business and government. The hegemony of English is evident in publishing practices in the global south (see Chapter 7), and in more positive portrayals of English as a *lingua franca* capable of reducing boundaries. For example, the opening lines of Brazil's national curriculum for English read:

> To learn the English language allows for the creation of new forms of student engagement and participation in an increasingly globalized and plural social world, in which the *borders* between countries and personal, local, regional, national, and transnational interests are continually more diffuse and contradictory.[1] (Ministério da Educação, 2018: 239, our emphasis)

In such a declaration, the relationship between language and social inequality is implicitly about the social valuing of some speakers, and thus of some languages or features of languages. It is essential to recognize how this may vary by *context* and how bureaucratic institutions, such as schooling, may reinforce certain inequalities (for an overview, see Philips, 2006).

Inequality is also expressed and reinforced through quotidian linguistic practices. Bourdieu (1984, 1990) illuminates how some ways of expressing oneself are more socially valued than others, depending upon the context. As scholars in linguistic anthropology have shown, 'ideas can be inculcated through speech that is persuasive in part because of its prestigious nature' (Philips, 2006: 476). 'Authoritative speech' describes the concept that 'by speaking in a particular style which is highly valued and/or associated with authority, or by speaking from within a particular discourse genre that is authoritative or associated with authoritative people, a speaker is more persuasive, more convincing, and more attended to' (2006: 476). Authoritative speech can be mapped onto racialized social hierarchies, as Chapter 2 shows.

The boundaries defining linguistic and social inequality are thus inherently shaped by what has come to be termed language ideologies. Language ideology, as succinctly defined by Alan Rumsey (1990), entails 'shared bodies of commonsense notions about the nature of language in the world' (1990: 346). Language ideologies 'represent the perception of language and discourse that is constructed in the interest of a specific social or cultural group' (Kroskrity, 2006: 501). They work in powerful ways on a micro-political level through affect and the generation of emotions such as shame, as Chapters 4 and 5 show in relation to Senegal and Kiribati.

The boundaries identified in the chapters that follow are constituted by divergences in meaning which necessarily involve heterogeneity. As such, each chapter questions the ways in which heteronormativist, monolingualist or racist discourses are legitimized. Boundaries, as we understand them, are constructed through dichotomies that reinforce hegemonic positions and legitimize oppressive norms of conventional cultural ideas of gender/race/language/culture. Under conditions of conservatism, repression and censorship, teachers and researchers need to deal with the relational, negotiated, and fluid nature of knowledge alongside its boundedness within ideological categories – a task undertaken in the final section of the book. Following on from this idea, the notion that meaning becomes plural and is influenced by 'otherness' is an integral element of the perspectives we collectively support in this volume.

Structure of the Book

This volume interrogates questions of social power, affect, identity construction, and imperialism as manifest in the relationships between language and exclusion, marginalisation and isolation, and as structured institutionally and pedagogically by schooling. The opening section presents work that takes a historical approach to boundaries (Chapters 1 and 2), and which identifies important shifts in boundary maintenance with the advent of digital technologies (Chapter 3). Section 2 focuses on cases in which language ideologies play an important role in constructing and maintaining inequalities along national and transnational scales in schools, universities and communities. Section 3 strikes a more optimistic note, with examples of transgression and resistance that challenge oppressive linguistic and social boundaries.

Section 1: The Shifting Boundaries of Linguistic Inequality

All boundaries have histories that include both the rules of differenciation and exclusion that structure them, and of the populations subjected to these rules. These histories are embedded in wider social, political and economic contexts, which, when ignored, allow boundaries to gain universalizing and naturalizing qualities that often strengthen them. In Chapter 1, Dennys Silva-Reis and Marcos Bagno break apart a number of dehistoricized boundaries that structure contemporary Brazilian nationalism. The first of these is the myth of a territory equivalent to the Brazilian nation in colonial times, and the second of a unified process of colonization. In fact, colonization of the Amazon was undertaken long after that of other regions, through a separate colonial administration, and through a different language, Amazonian *língua geral*.

Chapter 2 provides a critical overview of theoretical models of language and educational inequality. The piece pointedly asks how well concepts developed in other times and places apply to educational and linguistic processes in Brazil, and what distortions or misunderstandings are generated from their misapplication. This chapter, then, questions the mobility and universality of theory about language and inequality. The chapter ends with discussion of a teacher education project in public schools, which points to how shifts in racial identification and (anti)-racism in Brazil demand new theoretical tools for both properly recognising racialized social relations and challenging racism in schools, while also affirming other marginalised identities.

In Chapter 3, Daariimaa Marav shows how a long-standing urban-rural divide is maintained and even consolidated in the context of a shift in the language of power (from Russian to English), and the arrival of digital technologies. Marav examines how Mongolian university students from urban and rural backgrounds majoring in English use digital literacies in their daily lives. She shows how prior advantages are magnified through the types of work required in university classes. In turn, the students' engagement with digital technologies in and out of university and their English language proficiency affect their status, prestige and knowledge, reinforcing a historic rural-urban divide through new forms of symbolic capital.

Section 2: Language, Ideology and Inequality

In Chapter 4, Teresa Speciale builds upon Bourdieu's understanding of linguistic capital and, using affect theory and a decoloniality lens, shows how shaming perpetuates language inequalities in a Senegalese French-English bilingual school. African languages come to be defined as the antithesis of 'global' practices that afford opportunities for future success. The chapter argues that a masking of linguistic shaming policies under the guise of globalising education, in combination with students' privileged backgrounds, leads to a cycle of shaming wherein dominant language ideologies, hierarchies, and inequalities continue to be framed as not only legitimate but also inevitable.

Drawing together themes introduced throughout the volume, in Chapter 5 Indika Liyanage and Suresh Canagarajah analyse how nationals and international development workers on the small Pacific island nation of Kiribati demonstrate conflicting orientations to shame relating to using and learning English. They find a striking tension in language ideologies and affect: While international experts denigrate shame, treat it as backwards and limiting, and seek strategies to move Kiribati people to desire English, the local people treat shame as a positive mechanism to affirm community cohesion, regulate cultural change, and manage multilingual repertoires. The authors argue that the unresolved tensions produce a challenge for local ELT pedagogies.

Chapter 6 takes up questions related to English language teaching in Brazil. Junia Zaidan shows how, despite declarations that Brazilians will appropriate and indigenize the English language, the ideology of native speakerism nevertheless persists. The author examines the intimate linkages between native speakerism and instrumentalist, economic justifications of foreign language instruction.

In Chapter 7, the empirical and theoricital focus broadens to analyse knowledge production and circulation on education within a globalizing academic field. The authors ask how the criteria for excellence in Brazilian publishing reflect global language inequalities. To do so, they consider the national and international positioning strategies of the journal *Educação em Revista* (Education in Review), produced by the Postgraduate Program in Education of Federal University of Minas Gerais (UFMG). The chapter asks how the Coordination for the Improvement of Higher Education Personnel (CAPES) evaluation policy shaped the strategies that journals use to consolidate a reputation for quality.

Section 3: Transgression and Agency

In Chapter 8, Carolyn McKinney draws on decoloniality theory to analyze the anglonormativity underpinning South Africa's language in education policy. The chapter shows the persistence of monolingual language ideologies, despite the revolutionary change in langauge policy. Furthermore, based on empirical data, it argues that transgressing socially constructed language boundaries and disrupting monolingual language ideologies is essential to the repositioning of language as a resource for learning in South African schooling.

In Chapter 9, Dánie Marcelo de Jesus introduces themes of the discursively constructed body into discussions of inequality. He describes an effort to counter the silences around gendered and sexual identities in language classes and the preparation of English language educators. The chapter shows how this work provided space for and stimulated debate on gender-related issues within language teacher education at a Brazilian university, in an attempt to foster resistance against gender inequality.

Osman Z. Barnawi and Phan Le Ha extend this concern with gendered inequality and language. In Chapter 10, they first discuss how the English language has been positioned as key to the unfolding transformations of gender roles in Saudi Arabia, where national reforms position English as a language of new economy and social transformations. The authors contrast this broad-scale context with the dilemmas expressed by Saudi, female, Western-trained TESOL teachers as they contemplate their own new freedoms and the role English might play in women's empowerment.

Note

(1) 'Aprender a língua inglesa propicia a criação de novas formas de engajamento e participação dos alunos em um mundo social cada vez mais globalizado e plural, em que as fronteiras entre países e interesses pessoais, locais, regionais, nacionais e transnacionais estão cada vez mais difusas e contraditórias.'

References

Anzaldúa, G. (1987) *Borderlands: La frontera*. San Francisco: Aunt Lute Books.
Block, D. (2012) Economising globalisation and identity in applied linguistics in neoliberal times. In D. Block, J. Gray and M. Holborow (eds) *Neoliberalism and Applied Linguistics* (pp. 56–85). New York: Routledge.
Bourdieu, P. (1984) *Distinction: A Social Critique of the Judgement of Taste*. Cambridge, MA: Harvard University Press.
Bourdieu, P. and Passeron, J.C. (eds) (1990) *Reproduction in Education, Society, and Culture*. London: Sage.
Feltran, G. (2011) *Fronteiras de tensão: política e violência nas periferias de São Paulo*. São Paulo: Editora Unesp.
Gerrard, J. and Sriprakash, A. (2018) Migration and the borders of education. *International Studies in Sociology of Education* 27 (2–3), 107–110.
Heller, M. and McElhinny, B. (2017) *Language, Capitalism, Colonialism: Toward a Critical History*. Toronto: Toronto University Press.
Kroskrity, P. (2006) Language ideologies. In A. Duranti (ed.) *A Companion to Linguistic Anthropology* (pp. 496–517). London: Wiley-Blackwell.
Ministério da Educação Brazil (2018) *Base Nacional Commum Curricular*. Brasília: MEC.
Oommen, T.K. (1995) Contested boundaries and emerging pluralism. *International Sociology* 10 (3), 251–268.
Philips, S. (2006) Language and social inequality. In A. Duranti (ed.) *A Companion to Linguistic Anthropology* (pp. 474–495). London: Wiley-Blackwell.
Rumsey, A. (1990) Wording, meaning, and linguistic ideology. *American Anthropologist* 92, 346–361.
Stroud, C. and Prinsloo, M. (2015) *Language, Literacy and Diversity: Moving Words* (Vol. 7). New York: Routledge.

Section 1: The Shifting Boundaries of Linguistic Inequality

1 Across Linguistic Boundaries: Language as a Dimension of Power in the Colonization of the Brazilian Amazon

Dennys Silva-Reis and Marcos Bagno

In this chapter we seek to present a concise account (among many possible) of the linguistic policies that constituted one of the tools of colonization and exploitation of the Amazon by the Portuguese, including through the religious instruction imposed by Catholic missionaries. These linguistic policies – explicit or implicit – were based, initially, on the training and use of interpreters and, subsequently, on the systematization of a Tupi-based *língua geral* (*lingua franca*), which became the most important instrument for interaction between colonizers (especially Catholic missionaries) and the indigenous population. The widespread use of this *lingua franca* (known as *nheengatu*) did not eliminate the need for translators and interpreters: as will be seen, *nheengatu* was imposed on different ethnic groups who spoke languages from different language families, in a process marked by the physical and symbolic violence that characterizes a history of colonization over more than four centuries, beginning at the end of the 15th century.

Defining the territorial boundaries of the Amazon, implies several difficulties. The principle works of historiography of translation in Brazil present panoramic views that do not rigorously identify what is distinctive to particular spaces within the colonial territories. In publications by authors such as Milton (2001), Wyler (2003), Metcalf (2005), Barbosa and Wyler (2011), for example, the term *Brasil/Brazil* encapsulates a single historical-geographical entity, despite the profound ecological, demographic, ethnic, cultural, linguistic, etc. differences among the many geographical (and historical) subdivisions that it is possible to identify in such a vast territorial expanse and period of time. As we shall argue in the first section below, Portuguese possessions in South America did not constitute a homogeneous whole or a political-administrative unit: for a long time, the name *Brazil* was applied to a portion of those colonial possessions that did not include the Amazon. In addition, the colonization of the Amazon under Portuguese rule began than the rest of 'Portuguese' America, almost a century later.

In the period and space discussed in this chapter, *translation* and *teaching* are terms intrinsically linked to one another. The main objective of the missionaries, especially the Jesuits (considered in the history of Brazil as the country's first educators and teachers), was the evangelization of indigenous populations. This could only be done by means of a linguistic policy that would hasten integration of indigenous people into religious missions, by, instead of teaching the language of the colonizer, focusing on constructing a *lingua franca*, based on Tupi, in which conversion to Catholicism could be performed. The schools created by the Jesuits were based on the knowledge of this *lingua franca*, into which the rudiments of the Catholic faith were translated. From a certain phase, around the second half of the 18th century, a dispute began between those who undertook conversion and teaching through the *língua geral* and those who supported the implantation of the Portuguese language:

> During this tumultuous phase, questionnaires were sent to all sections of the local hierarchies in order to collect the necessary data for the adoption of new solutions. They deal with matters related to the sharing of missions and their territory amongst the various [teaching] institutions, their competence, and the curriculum for indigenous peoples (including the Portuguese language or more advanced studies, with the Order of Mercedarians even proposing Latin). The pedagogical, political and ecclesiastical arguments typical of each segment were reflected in their answers. Likewise, in addition to the different perspectives on the configuration of civil and ecclesiastical powers, different positions emerged concerning the capacities of the indigenous peoples, the learning of the catechism, and an elementary, technical or even more advanced pedagogy. In all domains, *language appeared as an important dimension of power.* Underlying intentions skillfully crafted speeches that lead, in numerous sectors, to a true tug of war, each side striving to shape the jurisdictional boundaries to suit its own ends. These boundaries change perpetually, depending on the influence of each group at a given moment. (Larcher, 2012: 78–79; our emphasis)

The result of these confrontations, as we know, was to be the expulsion of the Jesuits from the Portuguese colonies and the attempt to impose Portuguese as the only language for conversion and teaching in general. These attempts were frustrated because, as we shall see, *língua geral* remained in use in the Amazon until the first half of the 19th century.

Teaching could only exist during the long colonial phase because there was, firstly, *translation and interpretation*, and subsequently the *creation and imposition of a língua geral* that would serve as an instrument of catechism – that is, education was deeply linked to a colonial *language policy*. The use of an indigenous language for the process of *conversion* – spiritual and cultural in the broadest sense – mirrored the profound mixing of influences that would lead to the emergence of a new culture in the Amazonian territory. As we will argue throughout this chapter, the indigenous peoples were not passive recipients of a doctrine and a culture - the interactions were intense and radical on both sides:

> Although the priests insisted on the public conversion of the chiefs and on the immediate marginalization of the shamans, all of the customs and knowledge necessary for day-to-day survival were tolerated, and even transmitted within the villages. These related to food, methods of hunting, fishing and harvesting, canoeing, therapeutic knowledge, ritual dances and, above all, the use of a common indigenous language, the *língua geral* or *nheengatu*. (Arenz, 2012: 162)

Teaching and *translation*, thus, existed in a double movement of transfer, resignification and recomposition of culture by the indigenous population for the colonizers and by the colonizers for the indigenous population. This whole process 'profoundly influenced the imagination and way of life of the Amazonians, even beyond the colonial period' (Arenz, 2010: 161):

> Despite the mutual misunderstandings between Indians and missionaries, the new way of living and believing that emerged in those missionary communities, from the 17th century onwards, proved to be relatively long lasting, since it was the origin of the popular cultures practiced up until the present day in the Amazon. The amalgam of Iberian and Amerindian elements that characterize these cultures results mainly from the 'gaps' left open by both the superficiality of conversion and the tenacious attachment of the indigenous peoples to their ancestral traditions. (Arenz, 2012: 171)

Dealing with the history of oral interpretation is a task that involves a number of theoretical and practical issues. Alonso (2015) notes that interpretation has constituted, throughout history, an activity capable of organizing/structuring those events and situations in which the actors, principal or secondary, do not share the same cultural and linguistic identity. Moreover, 'the activity of the interpreter, as much as that of the translator, has contributed consciously or unconsciously to forging a common identity, particularly in those political and ideological projects that have imperialistic ambitions' (2015: 173). We also take into account the fact that the history of translation and interpretation in colonial times that began its construction in the West in recent decades, and is thus presented with almost exclusively colonial criteria regarding its periodization, ignoring or relegating – as cultural and postcolonial studies highlight – cultural and political periods of great importance to other societies, as if there had never been a translation or interpretation before the colony (Alonso, 2015: 178).

The Shifting Political Boundaries of the Amazon

The title of this article contains, in a historical perspective, an anachronism: the designation of 'Brazilian' for the Amazon of the colonial period. In fact, so-called Portuguese America was composed of two distinct administrative entities: the State of Brazil, and the State of Grão-Pará and Maranhão. The notion of a 'Brazil' along the lines of the current sovereign state emerged only in 1823, after the state of Grã-Pará and Maranhão merged with the State of Brazil, which had proclaimed independence from Portugal a year earlier. Official historiography, however, constructed within a typical nationalist ideology, has concealed this division of the colonial territory to create the myth of a territorial unit that has supposedly existed since the origins of 'Brazil'. The vast majority of Brazilians do not know that, for more than three centuries, the term 'Brazil' applied exclusively to the central-southern part of Portuguese America. The victory of this ideology is revealed even in the extreme difficulty of finding a reliable cartographic representation of that territorial division.

The same ideological rewriting of the past has sought to erase the sociolinguistic complexity of the historical conjuncture that gave birth to modern Brazil. In this rewriting of the past, the Portuguese language appears to have begun its triumphant expansion and its absolute dominion over 'Brazil' from the very moment the first Portuguese navigator stepped onto American soil. This was held to be due to the 'axiological and pragmatic superiority of Western culture that led to the victory of the Portuguese language in Brazil over its indigenous and African competitors' (Elia, 1979: 18), words that echo those of Serafim da Silva Neto, according to whom:

> the victory of the Portuguese language was not due to its violent imposition by the ruling class. It is explained by its superior prestige, which forced individuals to use the language that expressed the best form of civilization. (Silva Neto, 1950: 61)

For both authors, the process that led to the hegemony of Portuguese in Brazil is described as self-explanatory and even peaceful ('it was not due to imposition by the ruling class'), but reliance on the notion of 'victory' presupposes conflicts and disputes – there must have been losers to winners – and the use of 'competitors' by Elia shows that, in fact, Brazil's sociolinguistic history is a history of struggles and battles and, above all, of systematic genocides and, with them, of linguicides. Thus, even though he resorts to the idea of 'victory', José Honório Rodrigues (1985: 42) emphasizes that 'the cultural process that imposed one victorious language over the others was not so peaceful or easy. It cost unprecedented effort, the blood of the rebels, suicides, lives', because 'there was, indeed, a permanent state of war'.

Thus, what we call here the 'Brazilian Amazon' roughly equates, in the colonial period, to the State of Grão-Pará and Maranhão, an autonomous political-administrative entity, which only shared with the State of Brazil the status of colony of the Portuguese empire. The only reason for the anachronistic use of the adjective 'Brazilian' is to make clear to the reader that we are not dealing here with a wider Amazon, but only the portion of this vast territory that was occupied and colonized by the Portuguese and that, much later, was joined to Brazil, a term which has come to refer to the entire extent of the former Portuguese possessions in South America. Ultimately, the term Amazon covers a vast territorial extension that basically equates to the Amazon basin, the largest on the planet. This basin lies within the political boundaries of eight countries (Bolivia, Brazil, Colombia, Ecuador, Guyana, Peru, Suriname and Venezuela) and an overseas possession (French Guyana) covering more than 7 million square kilometers. As an administrative designation, there exist, in Peru and Colombia, 'departments' called *Amazonas*, in Venezuela an *Amazonas* state; and in Ecuador a region called *Oriente* ('the East') or *Amazonas*. In Brazil there is the state of Amazonas, the largest in the federation, but the term Amazon (*Amazônia* in Portuguese) applies to a much wider area of the national territory. To define the extent of governmental action in the region, Law 1,806, dated 6 January 1953, established the concept of 'Legal Amazon' (*Amazônia Legal*), which occupies a total of more than five million square kilometers, equivalent to 59% of the Brazilian national territory, but home to just 12% of the total population.[1]

From Linguistic Diversity to Forced Learning of *Línguas Gerais* (General Languages)

The linguistic diversity of the future Portuguese colonies in South America was indeed great. According to Aryon Rodrigues (2006: 24–25), there would have been 1,273 indigenous languages present in the territory of the future Brazil at the time of the Portuguese arrival, more than half of these (about 700) in the Amazon region alone. The large quantity of languages constituted a large obstacle for religious instruction aimed at the conversion to Catholicism of the indigenous peoples, and also for the occupation of the territory by the Portuguese Crown, which was also interested in the enslavement of indigenous labor. This impasse was resolved by the adoption of a language – Tupinambá – spoken on a stretch of the coast of the present state of Pará, near the mouth of the Amazon River, which become what was to be called *língua geral* (general language), a sort of *lingua franca*. The same process took place in the southern part of Portuguese America, where a *língua geral* also emerged. During the colonial period, therefore, there were two 'general languages': the *língua geral* of the Amazon and the *língua geral* of São Paulo. Both belonged to the group of languages known as Tupi, languages that were used in an extensive section of the Brazilian coast, from the current state of São Paulo to the mouth of the Amazon river, in Pará. Speakers of other languages that were not in the group were called *Tapuias* by the Tupi language speakers, a designation that was also used by the Portuguese and their descendants.

According to Barros (2003: 88–89):

> The emergence of the opposition between Tupi and Tapuia – which mirrored the opposition between Christianized and 'barbarian' indigenous peoples – proved to be a product of colonial Indian policy. The *Tapuia* category – a term of Tupi origin meaning 'enemy' – was used in Brazil to refer to non-Tupi indigenous groups, considered barbarians, as opposed to the Tupinambá group or other 'general language' nations. In linguistic terms, this took the form of an opposition between *língua geral* and *tapuia* or 'locked' languages ('*línguas travadas*'). [...] The Tupi vs. Tapuia dichotomy was related to the colonial ideology of a common language in a continuous territory. The *Tapuia* languages – seen as 'locked' and 'barbaric' – were considered a hindrance to colonization. The expansion of the Tupi – as 'general' – over the Tapuia languages reflected the idea that a territory should have only one language.

This preponderance of Tupi on the coast, where colonial occupation was concentrated over a long period (until the discovery of gold in Minas Gerais, at the end of the 17th century), enabled the formation of those 'general languages'. Both the general Amazonian language (*língua geral amazônica*, LGA) and the general São Paulo language (*língua geral paulista*, LGP) were based on varieties of Tupinambá spoken, respectively, on the northern coast (Pará) and on the southern coast (Rio de Janeiro, Espírito Santo). As a result, the two 'general languages' were very similar.

The adoption of these languages in the process of religious instruction, conversion (and enslavement) of indigenous peoples followed positions advocated by the Catholic Church, which preached the learning of native languages by missionaries so that conversion could take place in those languages. It was considered more efficient and faster to do this than first to teach the colonizers' language in order to subsequently preach Christianity in that language. It was thus up to the missionaries, especially the Jesuits, to learn and codify indigenous languages.

Father Vieira explains this language policy by attributing it to the founder of the Jesuit order, Ignatius of Loyola:

> And to help these souls [non-Christian peoples], what means or instruments have been given to us and taught to us by the saint and the most learned Patriarch [Loyola]? His Rule states thus. For greater help from the natives of the land in which they reside, *all [of us] shall learn their language.* (in Hackerott, 2012: 92, our emphasis)

It is for this very reason that the first description of Old Tupi was the work of a Jesuit, José de Anchieta, who in 1595 published one of the earliest descriptions of a non-European language at the outset of the colonial era.

This was the sole language policy followed by the Portuguese Crown until the first half of the 18th century:

> The policy of Portugal until the end of the 1720s was a frank incentive for the expansion of the 'general [Amazonian] language', because of what this represented in terms of the profitability of the colony. At various times, the King of Portugal rebuked the Carmelites, the Mercedarians, and the Franciscans of the Amazon, whose missionaries were not as fluent in *língua geral* as the Jesuits. Through the Royal Charter of November 30, 1689, Portugal recognized LGA [*língua geral amazônica*] as the official language of the State of Maranhão and Grão-Pará, determining that the missionaries should teach it to the Indians and even the Portuguese children concentrated in the embryonic urban centers that were forming in the region. (Freire, 2011: 63)

This language policy was carried out through acts of great violence, since it sought to impose a single language on populations who were forced to learn it in order to be instructed in Christian doctrine and, primarily, in communication with their 'masters', since, in the initial period of colonization, enslavement of indigenous peoples was official practice. Father João Daniel, a Jesuit, author of an extensive book on the Amazon, where he lived for decades during the 18th century, relates some of these violent practices. Among some non-Tupi indigenous tribes, only men could learn the *língua geral*, which prevented women from accessing the language of the Catholic priests. These women, however, were obliged to confess and, if they did not speak the *língua geral*, they had to use interpreters, which was frowned upon by the religious congregations:

> However, as the confessions of the Tapuias [indigenous people who do not speak Tupi] through interpreters bring many inconveniences, many missionaries have already endeavored to end this problem, sometimes with speeches and sometimes with punishments. Though the problem

is already much diminished, yet there are still some women who are not able to give up this abuse under any circumstances, so that some were beaten by the missionaries with clappers until they at least said 'enough!' in *língua geral*. Many resisted and took this punishment to the point where their hands were swollen and they bled, before finally deciding to do what they obliged to, which is to speak *língua geral*. (Daniel, 1976: I, 272)

The forced spread of the Amazonian *língua geral* created the paradoxical situation in which it was considered an 'Indian language' by the White settlers and the 'language of Whites' by indigenous speakers of other languages (Freire, 2011: 17).

The Fate of the *Línguas Gerais*

The two 'general languages' had rather different fates across colonial history. The southeastern *língua geral* was widely used, especially in São Paulo, and was carried to the inland by the so-called *bandeirantes*, explorers who ventured into the hinterlands in search of precious stones and indigenous people to enslave. These *bandeirantes* were almost all speakers of the *língua geral* of São Paulo, since they were *mamelucos*, that is to say, children of Portuguese men with indigenous women, from whom they learned the language. It is on their account that there are countless toponyms of Tupi origin in the Southeastern and Central-West regions of Brazil, where no Tupi language was ever spoken. As late as the end of the 17th century, Father Antônio Vieira wrote:

It is true that the families of the Portuguese and the Indians in São Paulo are so closely linked to each other that [...] the language spoken in these families is that of the Indians; as for the Portuguese language, the boys have to go to school to learn it. (in Hackerott, 2012: 99)

However, in this same period, the discovery of gold in the region of Minas Gerais caused an important linguistic shift. Attracted by the possibility of fast wealth, more than half a million Portuguese moved from Europe to the gold region in just over 50 years, which exponentially increased the number of Portuguese speakers, a language that was previously used by a small minority in the colony. Black slaves used in other regions (mainly in the Northeast, where they worked on sugar plantations) were reallocated to gold mining. With this, a melting pot emerged in the mining zone that brought together black slaves (speakers of diverse African languages, but also of rudimentary forms of Portuguese), new Portuguese colonists and other people born in Brazil. As the language of administration and the ruling classes, Portuguese began the process of ascension that led to it becoming the hegemonic language it is today.

This, and other factors, caused the total disappearance of the *língua geral paulista*. The fate of Amazonian *língua geral* was different:

> The language of internal communication in Amazonia throughout the colonial period and even into the first decades of the nineteenth century was, undoubtedly, the *língua geral amazônica* (LGA), which performed those basic functions traditionally carried out by any and all languages in a community, which ended up slowing down the process of Portuguese hegemony. (Freire, 2011: 46)

In the mid-18th century, the Portuguese Crown attempted to institute a new language policy in the region. Through a document that went down in history as the Directory of the Indians (1757), the Portuguese prime minister, Marquis de Pombal, decreed that only the Portuguese language should be used as a vehicle for teaching and learning in Grão-Pará and Maranhão, with the consequent prohibition of the use of the *língua geral* (or any other indigenous language) in education. This policy came alongside the expulsion of the Jesuits, considered too influential and representing an ideology that opposed the Enlightenment philosophy prevailing in Europe at the time, from both Portugal and its colonies. The same Father João Daniel quoted previously wrote his encyclopedic work on the Amazon during the period in which he was imprisoned, after being deported to Portugal. This new language policy, however, was unsuccessful:

> The concrete effect of this new ban was, however [...] little to nothing: the 'general Amazonian language' continued to be widely used, Portuguese only slowly gained space (and for reasons unrelated to its legal imposition) and indigenous languages continued to be spoken throughout the Amazonian world. (Faraco, 2016: 112)

This is because

> the detribalized Tupinambá language, differentiated from the tribal Tupinambá, had already acquired the status of *língua geral* and, although banned, continued in full expansion throughout the colony, because the system, agents and social practices that supported this expansion – the Regiment of the missions, the Jesuits and the organization of indigenous labor – remained alive and active. (Freire, 2011: 122–123)

One of the measures, of a strong symbolic nature, in the attempt to 'Portugalize' the Amazon was the replacement of several toponyms of indigenous origin with the names of places existing in Portugal. In this way, the names Santarém (formerly Tapajós), *Óbidos* (Pauxis), Borba (Trocano), Barcelos (Mariuá), Moura (Itarendaua), Vila Nova da Rainha (Parintins), Faro (Jamundás) etc., were instituted and remain to this day.

What actually led to the drastic reduction of the use of the general Amazonian language were other historical and political factors, the most important of which, undoubtedly, is linked to the rebel movement known as Cabanagem (1835–1840). Unhappy with Pará's marginalization after its adherence to Brazil in 1823, and with the extreme poverty of the region's inhabitants, several local leaders united to lead a revolt against the central power (a monarchical regime that conferred to Brazil the title of Empire). The empire's repression of the 'cabanos' (so called because the majority of the population lived precariously in mud and straw cabins) was relentless: once the revolt had been suppressed, about 40% of the population of Pará was exterminated, bringing the total casualties close to 40,000. These victims of repression were, in their vast majority, indigenous people and mestizos who spoke the 'general Amazonian language', which, thus, lost a significant contingent of its users.

Another factor that reduced the number of LGA speakers was the Paraguayan War (1865–1870), in which Argentina, Brazil and Uruguay (manipulated by powerful English capital) united against Paraguay, which was trying to establish a nationalist economic policy at the margins of British imperialism. Torn away from their Amazonian lands, enlisted by force (despite the name 'volunteers of the homeland', by which they are known in official history), many speakers of LGA (who were monolingual), indigenous people and indigenous-White mestizos, lost their lives in Paraguay. This created an unusual situation, since

> many soldiers from the 5th Infantry Battalion, who could not even understand the orders of their commander [in Portuguese], died on the battlefields of Paraguay as 'volunteers of the homeland', speaking a language understood by the enemy but unknown in their own trenches. On the other side, there was a similar situation with Paraguayan soldiers who were monolingual speakers of Guarani, some of whom were made prisoners of war and could only be subjected to interrogation with the help of Amazonian soldiers, bilingual in *língua geral* and Portuguese, who worked as interpreters and translators. (Freire, 2011: 102)

In fact, Guarani, even now spoken by the great majority of the Paraguayan population, is descended from another *língua geral*, also used in that country during the colonial period as a language of religious instruction and conversion. Despite the huge distance between the Amazon and Paraguay, the 'general Amazonian language' (called *nheengatu*, 'good language') and Paraguayan Guarani (called *abanheenga*, 'language of the people') belong to the great Tupi-Guarani family and are therefore fairly similar to each other, allowing for communication between Brazilian indigenous or mestizos soldiers and Paraguayan soldiers.

The decline of the *língua geral amazônica* was also due to other important factors, this time of an economic nature, such as the introduction of steam navigation, which impacted on linguistic issues in two ways. On the one hand, it destructured the traditional navigation and commerce system that 'favored the reproduction of the *língua geral* insofar as it limited the contacts of its users, spread throughout the towns and villages of the region, with Portuguese speakers' (Freire, 2011: 246). Modernized transportation allowed for more intense and rapid exchanges and, consequently, the expansion of the Portuguese language along the countless rivers of the Amazon basin. On the other hand, steam navigation also enabled the great influx of Northeasterners (almost half a million) who migrated to the Amazon during the so-called 'rubber boom' (1872–1910): 'spread among the rubber plantations, villages and settlements, all of them beared the Portuguese language, which caused the modification of the sociolinguistic landscape of Amazonia and removed any possibility of *língua geral* continuing its expansion' (Freire, 2011: 247).

Another important difference between the fates of the *língua geral* of São Paulo and the Amazonian version is that while the former is completely extinct, the latter remains spoken, under the name *nheengatu*, by the riverine population of *caboclos* (mestizos of White and indigenous descent), in the upper Rio Negro, in the extreme western part of the state of Amazonas, near the border with Colombia and Venezuela (countries where it is also spoken by small minorities), with an estimated 19,000 speakers.

The Role of Interpreters: Boundary Crossing and Building Realities

The sociolinguistic history of the Amazon, insofar as it can be summarized, is complex and unfolds in different stages. This history was periodized by Freire (2011: 112) as follows:

(1) the practice of interpreters (16th and early 17th centuries);
(2) the choice of Tupinambá and its expansion (1616–1686);
(3) the formalisation of the *língua geral* and its reproduction (1686–1757);
(4) the proposals for 'Portugalization' (1757–1850);
(5) the hegemony of the Portuguese language (from 1850 onwards).

We have already mentioned some aspects of phases 2 to 5, which concern the expansion and later decline of the *língua geral* in favor of Portuguese. From here onwards we will attend to the initial phase, which included the notable presence of interpreters.

An important aspect is that translation/interpretation in colonial time-space cannot be seen only from an instrumentalist perspective, in which translation practices would serve the purposes of communication between cultures. Translation is not a simple shuttling of 'messages', of given and fixed contents, so it is important to definine it from the outset,

> as an activity that does not reproduce something given (for example, an original), but which foremost produces cultural realities. [...] The bridge does not simply connect two existing banks. These appear as such only when a bridge crosses the river, not before. Just as the bridge does not appear as an *a posteriori* union of two preexisting borders, neither is translation an *a posteriori* mediation of different cultural situations. Rather, it produces them. (Scharlau, 2003: 106)

As such, translation is not a mere mediator in the colonial situation: it creates this situation, it profoundly changes the languages that thus come into contact and 'becomes the place where something new, hybrid, emerges, and where, ultimately, colonial power relations in all their contradictory tensions are articulated' (Scharlau, 2003: 104).

Thus, on the one hand, translated texts conveyed the logic of the European-Christian order, but, on the other hand, they provoked a reaction amongst the indigenous peoples insofar as they interpreted what they heard or read within the distinctive framework of the meaning of their own languages and cultures.

When, for example, missionaries chose to translate the concept of God with the name *Tupã*, or that of Devil with *Jurupari*, new metaphysical entities arose, which were neither the Christian god nor the devil nor the traditional deities of Tupi-speaking peoples: *Tupã* and *Jurupari* entered the Portuguese language with defining traits that they did not have in Tupi culture, just as God and the Devil acquired in Tupi (or, better, in the *língua geral* constituted from the Tupinambá) distinctive elements of the cosmogony and the mythology of their speakers. This process became even more complex when, because of the imposition of the Tupinambá on populations speaking other languages, the missionaries introduced *God-Tupã* and *Devil-Jurupari* into cultures that did not know any of these four previous entities. The creation of new syncretic supernatural entities through translation – a creation that clearly shows the inoperability of the concept of 'equivalence', so used in translation theories and above all in common sense – is demonstrated, for example, in the following statements by Couto de Magalhães, a military explorer very familiar with Tupi language and the religious beliefs of its speakers. In the already-independent Brazil of the late 19th century, he wrote:

> What I never encountered among the savages was the conception of a supernatural spirit whose mission was exclusively for evil, as the conception of Satan is among us. Jurupari himself is not in this category: the traditions I have gathered on this, which are only found today in the north of the Empire [i.e. the Amazon], are not complete, but the word Jurupari is equivalent to what our wetnurses describe us as a nightmare.

He is, according to the Indians, an entity that in the night covers the throats of children or even of men, to bring them afflictions and bad dreams. (Magalhães, 1876: 126)

Jurupari's equation to the Christian devil, therefore, was not a simple 'translation' of a term from the Portuguese to the Tupi language, but the very production of a new metaphysical entity. That is because, as Icíar Alonso (2015: 182) writes 'cultural identities have been constructed also through translation, in such a way that its function doesn't limit itself to purely linguistic matters, but communicates, above all, different world visions'.

Those responsible for the religious instruction and conversion of the indigenous populations left valuable testimony about these complexities of conversion-translation, often revealing the interpretation they made based on their language-culture-ideology, of what they considered to be their spiritual achievements with the 'natives'. Father José de Anchieta (1933), for example, wrote (in a letter dated 16 April 1563) about the (supposed) conversion of an old man in Itanhaém (São Paulo state coast):

After I gave him the first lesson, that there exists a single all-powerful God who created all things, etc., it was soon imprinted on his memory, and he said that he often prayed that God would produce food for the livelihood of all, but he thought that thunder was this God, even though he now knew that there was another true God, and that he ought to pray to him by calling him God the Father and God the Son. Because, of the names of the Holy Trinity, only these two I could translate, because it is possible to say them in his language, but we never found an adequate word or circumlocution for the Holy Spirit. Though he was not able to name the Holy Ghost, he knew how to believe.

The missionary attributes a 'memory' to the Indian man, that of having already made supplications to the 'one God', as if this entity existed in the culture of the 'convert'. But he records that the Indian 'thought that thunder was this God' (and, in fact, the name *Tupã* referred in Tupi to a deity responsible for thunder), but that from now on he would appeal to this same entity, but with another name: 'God the Father and God the Son'. In the missionary's view, the mere renaming (or translation) of the deity was sufficient assurance that the Indian had acquired a new faith. Even more symptomatic of this attitude is the recognition that it was not possible to find, in the indigenous language, 'a proper word or sufficient circumlocution' to deal with the Holy Spirit, but this did not prevent the Indian, even without knowing how to 'name' it, from 'believing'. The catechist's discourse reveals a belief in the power of translation as renaming, and renaming as the inescapable proof of conversion. This episode (and the discursive form it takes) shows, on a small scale, the complexities of the interactions that occurred in the colonial period (and even after it), in which translation, as we have said, was not a means, but the place where something was new, hybrid, and where ultimately the colonial power relations were articulated in all their contradictory tensions, to take up Scharlau's words quoted above.

In colonial space-time, therefore, translation did not focus only on languages, but became an operation that was the very genesis of new cultural forms, new orders (juridical, religious, epistemological, social, political, etc.) that went on to establish themselves and take root in the territories subject to the colonial enterprise and to establish them for posterity.

The colonization of the Amazon by the Portuguese began more than a century after the arrival of the first navigators in 1500. In contrast to older settlements – São Vicente (the first colonial village in Brazil, founded in 1534), Olinda (1537), Salvador (1549), Rio de Janeiro (1565) – it was only in the year 1616 that the Forte do Presépio was built, a fortified nucleus around which grew the city of Santa Maria de Belém do Grão-Pará, now known as Belém, capital of the state of Pará, at the mouth of the Amazon River in the Atlantic Ocean. Before then, the region was in the sights of several colonial powers: between 1500 and 1570, 22 incursions were organized by Spaniards, some descending along the Andes towards the Atlantic, others in the opposite direction. The French sent at least seven expeditions; the English, eight; the Dutch, five, going so far as to build some forts at the mouth of the Amazon (Freire, 2011: 113). With the foundation of what was to become Belém, the official and systematic occupation of the region by the Portuguese colonial government began.

In these expeditions, European explorers interacted with the indigenous people using gestures and signs or, depending on the availability, using interpreters. The documents preserved from that period relate, for example, that the Cocamas, a people living along the Napo River, a tributary of the Amazon (on the border between Brazil, Peru and Colombia), assisted the Spaniard Francisco de Orellana when he went down the great river in 1541–1542, from present-day Ecuador to the Atlantic, thus being considered the 'discoverer of the Amazon', who gave this name to the river because of a supposed tribe of warrior women he allegedly encountered (and with whom he is supposed to have fought a battle). According to the Dominican friar Gaspar de Carvajal, who participated in the expedition and produced an account of it, the Cocamas helped the navigators to write down a small glossary of their language, belonging to the Tupi family, which would have been useful for later contacts with other populations. Indigenous interpreters also worked on the expedition of the Spaniards Pedro Ursúa and Lope de Aguirre (1560–1561).

In general, European explorers used a practice developed by the Portuguese in their explorations of Africa some time previously: the capture of some local inhabitants, and transportation to Portugal, where they were taught Portuguese so that they could be used as interpreters (or *línguas* ['tongues'], as they were called during the colonial period).

In the mid 16th century, *feitorias* appeared in Brazil, places where the goods of the colony were stored for later shipment to the metropolis. The accumulation of these goods, for the most part, was due to barter, which was to some extent possible thanks to the *língua*, the interpreter who spoke the indigenous languages. The *língua* learned the language of the indigenous people by force, since, for the most part, those who held such an office in 16th-century Brazil were the exiled or the shipwrecked, that is, Portuguese criminals who were thrown among the indigenous people in order to learn their language and later to serve as interpreters for the Portuguese colonial authorities. According to Faraco (2016: 63),

> The *línguas* worked not only as linguistic interpreters, but also (and mainly) as mediators who acted both in the processes of revealing, for the European, the geography, the society and the culture of the territories visited or occupied; and in the imposition on local populations of the colonial logic in economic, political and socio-cultural relations. In this sense, *línguas*, by their linguistic knowledge, had a kind of power that made them crucial agents in societies created or recreated by European colonialism. In the *feitorias* they were effective officials of the colonial administration and were very well paid.

The figure of the *língua* was also important as a collaborating agent during the 16th century wars between the Portuguese and indigenous people, and also between the Portuguese and pirates, privateers and other colonizers (especially French, Dutch and Spanish) who also tried to occupy differents portions of Brazil (Hemming, 2007). At times, some indigenous people were kidnapped and taken to European countries to learn the language and customs of the colonizer and help in the conquest of the desired lands. It was a common practice at the time, and these Indians were called *filhados* as opposed to the *lançados* – colonists who were left in the conquered lands in order to learn the language of the Indians and then rescued to aid in colonization (Mariani, 2007).

Outside of the Amazon, on the Brazilian coast, amongst the initial measures to facilitate interactions between indigenous people and the Portuguese, those concerned with the explicit formation of *línguas* (interpreters) stand out. Some colleges founded by the Jesuits acted as specialized centers for the translation of religious discourse into *língua geral*: the focus was on members of the Society of Jesus who, although they could not administer the sacraments, assisted the priests in this task (Freire, 2011: 114). There are testimonies in letters written by Jesuits of the use of the so-called *mamelucos* (children of Portuguese men with indigenous women) in the mediation of relations between missionaries and indigenous people. These Portuguese practices from other parts of the colony were, to a certain extent, reproduced in the Amazon:

> From early on, missionaries, Portuguese residents and Indians of different linguistic affiliations acquired discursive capacity in the Tupinambá language, limiting the use of interpreters to non-Tupi affiliated languages, generally called *Tapuias*, considered by the Jesuits *línguas travadas* ('locked languages'). In this case, their function was to act in the first contact, as ambassadors, sent to groups speaking these languages, whom they had to persuade to resettle in the missions. (Freire, 2011: 115)

In this phase of Amazonian colonization, interpreters played a fundamental role in the process of converting the indigenous peoples. As long as the priests did not learn and spread the *língua geral*, and especially when they had to deal with speakers of *línguas travadas* (non-Tupi), interpreters were constantly used for worship and ceremonies, administration of the sacraments, and on other occasions such as the translation of the the Sunday sermon.

A number of historians of the colonial period emphasize the complex circumstances in which the important sacrament of confession was performed through interpreters. It was an extremely problematic situation because confession implies only two people: the 'sinner' and the 'confessor'. Everything that is revealed in the act of confessing must remain confidential, known in the Catholic tradition as the 'inviolability of confession'. Faced with language barriers and the obligation to perform the sacrament of confession on the 'converts', it became common practice to use an interpreter. In addition to the problem caused by the presence of a third person in the act of confession, there was also a strong distrust on the part of the Europeans towards the interpreters they used, as was often the case in the relations between the colonizers and the subjugated indigenous populations. According to Faraco (2016: 66),

> The *línguas* were indispensable (in view of the linguistic diversity with which the Portuguese were in contact); were rare (they generally had to be imprisoned and learn by immersion in the language of their captors, which is always a time-consuming process in adults) and therefore highly valued, *although not always entirely reliable* (our emphasis).

Although mistrust was widespread, it is worth noting a case that seems to contradict it. The story of the Indian woman Nathalia, which Father João Felipe Bettendorff, a catechist present in the Amazon in the 17th century, tells in one of his acts of conversion/condemnation of the 'natives', is interesting for two reasons: it involves an indigenous woman who does not serve only as a biological go-between (i.e. to produce *mestizos*: Metcalf, 2005), but as a linguistic go-between; and the fact that this female interpreter was more reliable than the male Indian interpreter, reliable to the point that her linguistic mediations served for the enactment of death sentences. In the words of the priest,

> (...) and so that the truth and sincerity of the interpreter named Nathalia not be doubted, let it be known that she was the daughter of one of the important chiefs of the Maraunizes nation and the uterine sister of chief Guacaziri, of the Chipiri village. An old woman, discreet amongst her own and the Whites, whose language she knew very well as a domestic in the house of captain-major Manuel Guedes, who had made her available for the service of God and of the King Our Lord, so that, through her, captain-major Antonio de Albuquerque and other ministers could undertake business in the North Cape, and they even passed the death sentence, based on the loyalty with which she acted as *língua* for all things. (Bettendorff, 1990: 434)

Nathalia was an indigenous woman related to important leaders and who was enslaved and forced to learn the language of the Whites, becoming a linguistic intermediary in delicate negotiations, which certainly enabled her trustworthiness in the eyes of the Catholic priests. She is one of the very rare Amazonian interpreters to have her name recorded. However, her case is the exception that confirms the rule, for suspicion always haunted the European settlers who needed interpreters to exercise their dominion over conquered lands and peoples.

One way of solving these problems was to intensify the learning of *língua geral* by the priests along with the so-called forced *Tupinization* of the indigenous speakers of so-called *nheengaíba* ('bad language', i.e. non-Tupi languages, also termed 'locked'). It was, of course, a violent process which entailed, as we have seen above, physical punishment along with the systematic annihilation of countless languages, often accompanied by the elimination of their speakers.

This process of Tupinization of the Tapuias occurred, according to Barros (2012), in two phases. The first was the establishment of a cadre of Tapuian interpreters, called 'ambassadors'. These were to act to convince Tapuian Indians to 'come down' to the Jesuit missions. 'One of the habits of the Jesuits was to leave Tapuia Indians from recently-contacted groups in the missions, so that they would learn the *língua geral* and as a way of consolidating political agreements' (Barros, 2012: 90). The following phase was the production of brief catechisms in the non-Tupi languages, using the translation of religious texts already produced in Tupi: 'The translation of the Tupi catechism into Tapuia languages was done through bilingual interpreters in Tupi and in the languages of Tapuia. In general, they were non-Tupi Indians, Christianized in *língua geral*' (Barros, 2012: 91). The author points out that

> known Tapuia catechisms, such as those in the Manaos and Kiriri languages (the latter spoken in the Northeast), use the word *Tupã* – of Tupi

origin – to translate *God*. The use of this Tupi word in the Christian texts in Manaos and Kiriri suggests the later shift of these groups to the Tupi language. The maintenance of a common word for the Christian God in all languages indicates a missionary strategy of seeking to maintain a single identity for God. (2012: 92)

The aim was to mix indigenous speakers of other languages with the indigenous speakers of *língua geral* in the so-called *aldeias de descimento* (resettlements), where the indigenous were 'contacted' in order to receive Christian doctrine and integrate into the colonial economy. The production of these catechisms should not be understood as a means of accommodating the languages of other families, or doing away with the homogenizing character inherent in the *língua geral* language policy: 'The use of the Tapuia languages in catechisms was intended only for the earliest contact with the non-Tupi groups, prior to their transfer to the resettlements, where they began to use *língua geral*' (Barros, 2012: 92). It was therefore a temporary strategy, since the final goal was always the imposition of *língua geral* on the 'converted' indigenous people who spoke other languages.

Conclusion

Translation, as we can see, was of fundamental importance in the initial phase of conquest and occupation of the Amazon by the Portuguese (and, further, by the other colonial powers), being central to both economic exploitation and religious instruction. However, it presented a series of difficulties and involved the training of translators capable of working with many languages and with the language of the colonizer, the expenditure of time and intellectual work for the production of material for religious instruction both in *língua geral* and in 'locked' languages (*línguas travadas*), the inconvenience of using interpreters in delicate situations (such as confession) and the ever-present mistrust. The policy designed to eliminate linguistic boundaries by making a single language, the Tupinambá, the largest vehicle of the colonial enterprise, was thus drawn up. This language was 'detribalized' and impregnated into the social life of the Amazon, used by indigenous speakers of Tupi and non-speakers alike, by their mestizo descendants and by much of the White population.

This colonial language policy was to have a profound influence on Brazilian culture: in addition to the myth of the immediate expansion of the Portuguese language from the early stages of colonization, the idea that there was only 'one indigenous language', usually incorrectly referred to as Tupi-Guarani became entrenched. This has obscured the great linguistic diversity of the colonial period (from which remain, even today, over 180 languages spoken across the country) and the processes of selection, normalization and imposition of the *línguas gerais* along with the consequent prevention of preservation and maintenance of the languages spoken by the many different populations that were initially forced to adopt an indigenous language different from their own and then to use exclusively Portuguese, without being provided effective and efficient conditions to learn the colonizer's language. Thus, in the Brazilian context, there are today many indigenous groups who do not have their own language anymore but use varieties of Portuguese that are considered 'deficient' and 'damaged', and that receive the derogatory and discriminatory label of 'Indian language' – a label often applied to any supposed 'error' detected in the speech of people who do not strictly follow the precepts of a rigid and obsolete linguistic norm.

The conquest and occupation of the Amazon occurred through various interconnected forms of symbolic, cultural and physical violence, and translation enters this network as one of the various means used to establish dominion over the region by the Portuguese. However, in line with the multiple contradictions that constitute colonial enterprises, translation also contributed to the formation of constitutive traits of Brazilian society and culture, thanks to ethnic miscegenation. This, alongside other forms of miscegenation, including linguistic mixing, resulted in the emergence of a unique Brazilian Portuguese, in which the European, indigenous and African confluences are manifold, profound and inseparable at all levels of the linguistic system, from phonetics to lexicon, through syntax and morphology. This confirms the words of Scharlau (2003: 108) for whom,

> To the extent that the colony is reformulated as a hybrid configuration, as a contact zone, and as a structure in which there is constant negotiation of intercultural relations, translation is placed in the center of observation. It is no longer an external happening, following these relations. Rather, it founds them and emerges among practices that create cultural interstices and contribute to the shaping of the colonial subject and, more generally, colonial difference.

Thus, in the harsh relations imposed by colonialism, *translation* is also transformation and, perhaps even more, *transfiguration*: a total and profound *reshaping* not only of the immediate physical environment in which translation takes place – translating in order to cut down forests, dig mines, divert rivers, erect cities, enslave or exterminate entire populations – but also of the subjectivities involved in the process and, of course, the transformation-transfiguration of all the elements involved in this process and present in this environment: languages, beliefs, world views, ethnicities, cultures and – to use a single word – the ceaseless transformation-transfiguration of a *society*.

(Translated by Joel Windle. An earlier version of this chapter first appeared in Portuguese as A tradução como política linguística na colonização da Amazônia brasileira. Letras Raras – A Tradução e suas linguagens, 2018, vol. 7, n. 2, pp. 8–28.)

Note

(1) https://ww2.ibge.gov.br/home/geociencias/geografia/amazonialegal.shtm?c=2, Accessed March 14, 2018.

References

Alonso, I. (2015) Historia, historiografía e interpretación. Propuestas para una historia de la mediación lingüística oral. In P. Ordóñez and J.A. Sabio Pinilla (eds) *Historiografía de la traducción en el espacio ibérico*. Cuenca: Ediciones de la Universidad de Castilla-La Mancha, 171–187.
Anchieta, J. de (1933) *Cartas, informações, fragmentos históricos e sermões do padre José de Anchieta (1554–1594)*. Rio de Janeiro: Academia Brasileira de Letras/Civilização Brasileira.
Arenz, K-H. (2012) 'Fils de Dieu et Fils des Pères' – l'évangelisation dans les missions jésuites en Amazonie portugaise au XVIIe siècle. In H. Didier and M. Larcher (eds) *Pédagogies missionnaires: Traduire, transmettre, transculturer*. Paris: Karthala.
Baigorri-Jalón, J. (2006) Perspectives on the history of interpretation: Research proposals. In G.L. Bastin and P.F. Bandia (eds) *Charting the Future of Translation History*. Ottawa: University of Ottawa Press, 101–110.
Barbosa, H.G. and Wyler, L. (2011) Brazilian tradition. In M. Baker and G. Saldanha (eds) *Routledge Encyclopedia of Translation Studies* (2nd edn, pp. 338–344). London/New York: Routledge.
Barros, Maria Cândida D.M. (2003) Notas sobre a política jesuítica da língua geral na Amazônia. In J.R.B. Freire and M.C. Rosa (eds) *Línguas gerais: Política linguística e catequese na América do Sul no período colonial*. Rio de Janeiro: EdUERJ.
Bettendorff, J.F. (1990) Crônica da missão dos padres da Companhia de Jesus no Estado do Maranhão. 2a. ed., Belém: Fundação Cultural do Pará Tancredo Neves/ Secretaria de Estado da Cultura, [1694–1698], 1990.
Daniel, J. (1976) *Tesouro descoberto no rio Amazonas*. Rio de Janeiro: Anais da Biblioteca Nacional.
Elia, S. (1979) *A unidade linguística do Brasil*. Rio de Janeiro: Padrão.
Faraco, C.A. (2016) *História sociopolítica da língua portuguesa*. São Paulo: Parábola.
Freire, J.R.B. (2011) *Rio Babel. A história das línguas na Amazônia*. 2nd. ed. Rio de Janeiro: EdUERJ.
Hackerott, M.M.S. (2012) Reflexões sobre a linguagem em sermões e cartas do padre Antônio Vieira. In C.A. Lagorio, M.C. Rosa and J.R.B. Freire (eds) *Políticas de língua no Novo Mundo* (pp. 87–125). Rio de Janeiro: EdUERJ.
Hemming, J. (2007) *Ouro vermelho: A conquista dos índios brasileiros*. São Paulo: EDUSP.
Kenny, D. (2011) Equivalence. In M. Baker and G. Saldanha (eds) *Routledge Encyclopedia of Translation Studies* (2nd edn, pp. 96–99). London/New York: Routledge.
Larcher, M. (2012) Les polémiques linguistiques aux missions du Maranhão et Pará. In H. Didier and M. Larcher (eds) *Pédagogies missionnaires: Traduire, transmettre, transculturer*. Paris: Karthala.
Mariani, B. (2007) Quando as línguas eram corpos – sobre a colonização linguística portuguesa na África e no Brasil. In E.P. Orlandi (ed.) *Política linguística no Brasil* (pp. 83–112). Campinas: Pontes Editora.
Metcalf, A.C. (2005) *Go-betweens and the Colonization of Brazil (1500–1600)*. Austin: Universtiy of Texas Press.

Milton, J. (ed.) (2001) *Emerging Views on Translation History in Brazil*. São Paulo: Humanitas.
Rodrigues, A.D. (2006) As outras línguas de colonização do Brasil. In S.A.M. Cardoso, J.A. Mota and R.V. Matos e Silva (eds) *Quinhentos anos de história linguística do Brasil* (pp. 143–161). Salvador: Funcultura.
Rodrigues, J.H. (1985) *História viva*. São Paulo: Global.
Scharlau, B. (2003) Repensar la Colonia, las relaciones interculturales y la traducción. *Iberoamericana* III, 12, 97–110.
Silva Neto, S. (1950) *Introdução ao estudo da língua portugesa no Brasil*. Rio de Janeiro: INL.
Wyler, L. (2003) *Línguas, poetas e bacharéis. Uma crônica da tradução no Brasil*. Rio de Janeiro: Rocco.

2 Navigating Soft and Hard Boundaries: Race and Educational Inequality at the Borderlands

Joel Windle and Kassandra Muniz

Introduction

In this chapter we are concerned with how different types of linguistic ideology contribute to the boundaries contributing to educational inequalities, and particularly the experiences and identities produced at the meetings of such boundaries, which we theorise in terms of borderlands (Anzaldúa, 1987). Recognising that some boundaries are more rigid, durable or 'hard', and others are more permeable and ephemeral, or 'soft' (Oommenn, 1995), we are also concerned with showing how theoretical conceptions of social and linguistic divisions as 'hard' or 'soft' have shifted over time. The setting we discuss is Brazilian education, and specifically language teacher education in provincial Minas Gerais – which Chapter 1 of this volume identified as the meeting-point at which Portuguese gained hegemonic status through the gold-rush induced influx of enslaved indigenous and African peoples, along with newly-arrived Europeans and existing colonists.

We write as teacher educators at the geographical epicentre of 300 years of mining operations that are everywhere in evidence in the scarred landscapes, red dust, and Baroque churches that hide the pain, exploitation and death of populations long considered disposable, the majority of whom are Afro-Brazilian. Our main focus is on the conditions and consequences of a massive expansion of Brazilian education over the past decade, which brought large numbers of students from previously excluded groups into the senior years of secondary education and into university. For example, the university from which we write grew from a student population of around 5,000 to over 15,000 over the decade to 2016, through the policies of the progressive federal government led by the Workers' Party (*Partido do Trabalho*, PT).

From a situation of few or no Black students in many courses, through affirmative action policies that accompanied this expansion, 48.5% of new students in 2019 were Black (including so-called 'brown' or 'mixed race' census categories). Nationally, the proportion of Black youth attending university doubled in the decade from 2005 to 2015 (Vieira, 2016).

This expansion, and specifically the Support Program for Federal University Restructuring and Expansion (REUNI), was also responsible for bringing the authors of the present chapter into contact through the opening of new teaching positions, and we are thus part of a wave of academic appointments who have challenged the elitism and conservatism of Brazilian higher education. However, we also write from distinctive positions and trajectories across multiple boundaries that are relevant to our analysis of our work as situated at the borderlands.

As Aznaldúa observes:

> The Borderlands are physically present wherever two or more cultures edge each other, where people of different races occupy the same territory, where under, lower, middle and upper classes touch, where the space between two individuals shrinks with intimacy. (1987: 18)

Through reflection on our work in a Brazilian provincial university and our own personal trajectories, we examine the extent to which successive theorisations of educational inequality relate to the pressures of system-wide expansion. Although Brazil has 'exported' theory on educational inequality through the work of Paulo Freire and examples of school reform taken up by influential US authors (Gandin & Apple, 2003), Brazilian scholarship most often 'imported' theory. Nevertheless, critical sociolinguistic work has recently emerged which relates inequalities to national linguistic ideologies (Muniz, 2016; Plaza Pinto, 2018).

Our main concern is with the relationship between language and race, a connection only partially addressed in the theoretical traditions we consider, as well as being ignored in much Brazilian research. As Plaza Pinto (2018) notes 'the linguistic economy is also a racial economy' (2018: 712). Three dimensions of racializing linguistic ideology, identified by Plaza Pinto, are used to structure our discussion:

(1) The homogeneity and stability of the connection between social position and speech, where social position is commonly defined by class and geography, masking how race is read from sociolinguistic performances.
(2) The definition of clarity of expression in terms of the speech and written genres used by White, 'educated' males, against which 'Black' speech is read as irrational and lacking argumentative structure.

(3) The identification of competence with the cultural, linguistic and academic performances of the 'educated', implicitly White, 'educated norm', demonstrated by achievement gaps between White and Black students in schools.

Plaza Pinto gives a prototypical example from Brazilian children's author Monteiro Lobato of Madam Benta (the White grandmother with refined speech who is knowledgeable of astronomy, history and Greek mythology) and Aunty Nastácia (the Black servant with rough speech who is knowledgeable of superstitions). The interconnected ideologies of linguistic variation based on homogeneity, clarity and competence reinforce boundaries of racialized social exclusion through a process in which those who travel across boundaries become 'foreigners in their own linguistic landscape' (Muniz, 2016: 771). Such journeys are unsettling both for individuals and institutions, provoking anxiety and a sense of being out of place, which has the potential to be turned into appropriation and resignification of place, specifically of educational spaces.

The Identification of 'Hard' Linguistic Boundaries

Plaza Pinto (2018) suggests that the ideology of 'homogeneous variation' (2018: 711) is based on a dichotomy between a 'prestige' norm of Portuguese spoken by an educated urban elite, and a non-prestige variety spoken by Black, working-class and rural populations. As long as prestige is aligned with White speakers, even projects to grant recognition to non-prestige varieties tend to reinforce a 'hard' association between a speaker's social status and a particular linguistic variety. The 'uncultured' variety of Portuguese has its place in the national linguistic space, just as its Black speakers have a legitimate (subordinate) place, but they must not, and indeed cannot, step outside of this ascribed place.

US variationist sociolinguistics, and Labov (1972) in particular, was at pains to show that the poor educational performance of Black students in America (Coleman, 1966) was not a result of linguistic deficiencies, but of group-level distinctions in interactional styles and speech. To the extent that the relationship between individuals and sociolinguistic variation was relatively unquestioned, group boundaries in this tradition can be thought of as fixed or 'hard', 'trapping' both African American Vernacular English and its Black speakers in subordinate, racialized social positions. The demonstration of equal linguistic complexity and sophistication across varieties placed only limited scrutiny on institutional judgements that marginalised Black students in schools. Nevertheless, the unsettling, threatening and 'foreign' nature of the situations faced by Black children in research settings and schools was identified as one of the reasons for responses that were truncated or even silence as a response.

Bourdieu's (Bourdieu & Passeron, 1979, 1990) account of class-based linguistic distinctions, while maintaining a view of relatively 'hard' between-group boundaries, offered an explanation of why and how such boundaries were energetically maintained. Bourdieu argued that the investment of privileged groups in both cultivating their distinctive interactional styles and making sure they were the only ones granted legitimacy gained ever greater intensity as educational credentials grew in economic importance across the 20th century. Bernstein's (1971) work on distinctive class-based oral cultures and distinctive interactional patterns in pedagogical relations strengthened the case for 'hard' and potentially hardening boundaries as language became more important to social stratification in both work and education. Bernstein argued that the eliciting contexts of schooling resulted in different types of linguistic performance depending on social class, with middle-class interaction styles more closely aligned with those expected and rewarded in schools (Bernstein, 1971). He used the notion of codes to distinguish between linguistic styles produced by class-based living conditions, lifestyles, and forms of sociability. By the same token, the specific social roles and relations in formal schooling were held by Bernstein to be responsible for the linguistic codes that predominate in classrooms, textbooks and examinations.

These models of hard linguistic boundaries bear traces of both national and historical peculiarities, as well as a methodological horizon of society as bounded by the nation-state. Such peculiarities include the central place of literary style and high culture in French education (Bourdieu & Passeron, 1979, 1990) and long-standing class-based cultures in England (Bernstein, 1971). Importantly for the Brazilian case, the relativism of Bourdieu, in particular, draws attention to how linguistic notions of 'clarity' and 'competence' are not socially neutral, but based on the practices of the most socially powerful – thereby undermining two of the linguistic ideologies identified by Plaza Pinto (2018).

There are also important distinctions amongst theories of hard social and linguistic boundaries. Where Bernstein saw a functional relationship between linguistic codes and institutional or community structures, Bourdieu saw the use of arbitrary cultural and symbolic goods as a tool for social domination. In the latter analysis, the linguistic styles of the dominant group become accepted as the neutral standard of competence against which all are judged, and against which all measure themselves, with schooling a central mechanism for enforcing and legitimising such judgements (Bourdieu & Passeron, 1990). Acquisition of linguistic and cultural competence appeared to be the work of schooling, but in fact schools acted to certify and reward those habits, outlooks and practices (what Bourdieu terms *habitus*) that can only be cultivated in the early years of childhood in bourgeois homes. This theoretical perspective, importantly, shifted the focus from disadvantaged groups and onto the ways in which elite groups dominate and control schooling.

It is worth noting that the work of both Bernstein and Bourdieu (as well as that of Labov) emerged in response to the educational tensions and even chaos caused by social and economic changes. In particular, they sought to explain what happens when new groups enter classrooms set up to function exclusively for those who share a high-status linguistic and cultural repertoire. With much more recent expansion of public education, these tensions are evident in contemporary Brazilian schooling, as in many other settings in which student retention has risen dramatically. Absolute exclusion is being replaced by 'exclusion from within', in which the physical presence of students is accompanied by alienation (Bourdieu & Champagne, 1992).

Brazilian examination systems help to reinforce this exclusion from within, promoting the cultural and linguistic attributes that are produced 'naturally' (i.e. fluently, confidently, with style) by a socially restricted group (Almeida, 2007). Grades also reflect this exclusion, with just one in 600 socioeconomically disadvantaged students receiving top grades in the school leaving certificate,[1] compared to a quarter of wealthy students (Toledo *et al.*, 2019). Another example of how education reinforces social exclusion linguistically is the value given to fluency in a foreign language, particularly in English, with a 'native-like' accent being a distinctive mark of social status only available to those who can invest in many years of private language courses and international travel (Windle & Nogueira, 2015; Zaidan, this volume).

This broad theoretical tradition, thus, strategically emphasises the strength of one boundary (sociolinguistic variation between groups), while undermining two others (clarity and competence as exclusive properties of the speech of privileged social and racial groups). Similar work relativising and 'validating' different sociolinguistic varieties can be identified in some Brazilian linguistic and educational research. To date, Afro-Brazilian Portuguese does not have the same prominence as a marker of identity as African American Vernacular English (Telles, 2014). As such, within the national imaginary it is more likely to be viewed as 'incorrect' and 'uneducated' rather than the distinctive product of historical circumstances and community interaction. The recent identification of an Afro-Brazilian Portuguese grammar as a product of linguistic contact involving Indigenous and African peoples (Lucchesi *et al.*, 2009) is a radical step away from the dominant linguistic ideology that views such forms in terms of degeneration and 'drift'. Even as some Afro-Brazilian, working-class and rural linguistic features slowly gain acceptance amongst more socially powerful speakers, others remain clearly excluded and markers of social and racial status. For example, the verb 'work' in the expression 'we work' is not inflected for first person plural in the speech of 80% of Afro-Brazilian Portuguse speakers (*nós trabalha*), but is universally inflected as *nós trabalhamos* in the speech of 'educated' urban elites (Lucchesi *et al.*, 2009). The type of work undertaken by Lucchesi has the potential to undermine the ideologies of clarity and competence as exclusive properties of 'educated' Portuguese and its racially 'prestigious speakers'.

Another line of Brazilian scholarship focuses on identifying and unmasking the latter two linguistic ideologies, and their propagation through schooling. High levels of stigma and shame are attached to the linguistic production of Black and poor segments of society – including north-easterners, and those who live in rural areas and urban peripheries (Bagno, 1999; Bartlett, 2007). Being poor and uneducated is demonstrated by an 'incapacity' to competently produce the urban middle-class norm (Lucchesi, 2015). Many current anxieties about dropping 'standards' are centred around the access of poor and Black students to university, including teaching courses, through affirmative action programs, potentially threatening the unity of the dominant linguistic norm that new teachers will no longer share.

When students from poor and rural regions, particularly the northeast, enter schools in major cities, they encounter ridicule from both teachers and classmates, as Damergian (2009) showed in a study of São Paulo public schools. One such internal migrant reported:

> The teacher would tell me to shut up and I would get annoyed. When I spoke incorrectly she made me stand behind the door as punishment ... I got anxious when the teacher punished me and when I returned to my chair, everybody teased me and I would cry. (Damergian, 2009: 261)

Teachers further believe that northeastern students 'write incorrectly because they speak incorrectly', marking down even technically 'correct' written work:

> I would not give 10 to a northeastern student if they wrote a composition with no mistakes but with the jargon of their state. I simply wouldn't punish them. I would give a regular grade, but not 10 ... They speak in an aggressive way. We are used to students from here, who are poor but well-brought-up. (Damergian, 2009: 258)

'Soft' Linguistic and Social Boundaries in the Age of Globalisation?

From the 1980s onwards, a second wave of theorising, often adopting ethnographic methods, saw subaltern linguistic and cultural practices as both more dynamic and variable, and as having the potential to gain acceptance in schooling through new understandings of literacy and language (Street, 1984; The New London Group, 1996). This line of theorising sought to confront educational inequalities by making explicit the hidden codes of the language(s) of power while opening up space for marginalised and new cultural formations, sometimes involving digital technologies and transnational circulation (Heath, 1983; Janks, 2009). A focus on micro-social relations and local practices, in homes, communities and classrooms, sought positive examples, some of which, such as hip-hop (Pennycook, 2007), were theorised as global phenomena. As with the first wave of theorising, this work has been criticised for exporting (or 'up-scaling') models that reflect the peculiarities and histories of the developed nations in which they were conceived (Connell, 2007).

Foundational work, such as that by Street, identified literate practices amongst 'illiterate' communities, showing how definitions of the concept of literacy are shifting and ideological (Street, 1984). Concrete proposals for more accessible curricula also arose from this movement, seeking explicit recognition of linguistic structures demanded by schools through frameworks such as systemic functional linguistics (Christie, 2004), incorporated into critical models of literacy (Luke, 2000). These models further sought to mobilise marginalised cultural and linguistic practices, as well as the new practices of digital literacy and the global circulation of cultural goods, through notions such as hip-hop literacy (Hill, 2008; Richardson, 2006). The rigid between-group boundaries that populated older theories appeared to be weakening in the face of evidence of linguistic mixing and hybridity (Hull & Schultz, 2001; Lam & Warriner, 2012). Nevertheless, some authors such as Hill (2008) pointed to the feelings of unease and loss of control felt by teachers who allowed hip-hop into their classrooms.

As with the first wave, the second wave of theorising was driven by apparently new and dramatic developments – the death of the welfare state and rise of neoliberalism, new digital technologies and media, and increased cultural and linguistic diversity worldwide (The New London Group, 1996). The New London Group declared that 'effective citizenship and productive work now require that we interact effectively using multiple languages, multiple Englishes, and communication patterns that more frequently cross cultural, community, and national boundaries' (The New London Group, 1996: 64). They characterised traditional schooling as exclusionary as a result of an out-dated, authoritarian pedagogy divorced from the social purposes that could empower students. There are traces of Bernstein in the tight functional relationship established between institutional and social organisation and the linguistic forms that are most 'adequate' to fulfil the needs of such organisation. In the multiliteracies model, language figures as a set of mobile resources or discourses, which marginalised groups must be taught to draw upon and reconfigure in ways that are more functional (Cope & Kalantzis, 2009).

The key boundary in this line of thinking is less between clearly defined social groups and more between 'in school' linguistic practices and 'out of school' practices (Hill, 2008; Hull & Schultz, 2002). As globalisation brought cultural and linguistic pluralism to society at large, schools lagged behind with fossilised models of language and literacy – a function more of the weight of history (monocultural nationalist state projects) than of the institutionalised strategies of socially powerful groups, as earlier theories suggested. The creativity of marginalised linguistic and cultural practices and their educational potential has been taken up in Brazilian work through notions such as 'literacies of re-existance' (Souza, 2009) and critical race literacy (de Jesus Ferreira, 2014). These reworkings emphasise the ways in which language is used not merely in symbolic struggles, but in response power exercised through direct state violence, as in the case of 'literacies of survival' in slums (Maia, 2017).

As a society, Brazil diverges in important ways from the narratives of globalisation that sustain understandings of educational inequalities in new literacy studies. For example, much of Brazil's welfare state was constructed after the 2003 election of President Lula, and formal employment grew over the 13 years of his Worker's Party government. Transnational migrants, a driving force of diversity in the settings described by the New London Group, comprise less than 1% of the Brazilian population, whose diversity owes far more to the history of slavery (see Windle, 2017). Race, and particularly skin colour, constitutes a powerful social boundary that is difficult to cross through discursive dexterity. Black Brazilians continue to experience worse educational and occupational outcomes than White Brazilians, in addition to direct racial discrimination (do Valle Silva & Hasenbalg, 2000; Hasenbalg *et al.*, 1999). Although racial mixing is a defining feature of Brazilian society, the economic elite is almost exclusively White and maintains a high level of social closure that makes Black social mobility rare (Telles, 2014). The presence of Black Brazilians in spaces such as airports, shopping centres and even universities, except in service roles, raises suspicion. This sits at odds with the interpretation the New London Group gives to social categories, including ethnicity (race is not part of their vocabulary), which they interpret largely as affinity groups (termed 'lifeworlds'):

> As lifeworlds become more divergent in the new public spaces of civic pluralism, their boundaries become more evidently complex and overlapping. The increasing divergence of lifeworlds and the growing importances of differences is the blurring of their boundaries. The more autonomous lifeworlds become, the more movement there can be: people entering and leaving, whole lifeworlds going through major transitions, more open and productive negotiation of internal differences, freer external linkage and alliances. (The New London Group, 1996: 71)

In short, this wave of theorising effectively challenges the ideology of 'hard' boundaries separating language varieties and their speakers, but in so doing risks underestimating both the ongoing salience of this boundary, and the workings of the ideologies of clarity and competence – which appear to be easily overcome through innovative curriculum designs. With a reliance on systemic functional linguistics, a 'racially neutral' school of communicative genres, some work also risks over-valuing traditional 'rational' genres that are deeply racialized. For example, even when assessment regimes incorporate themes related to youth and marginalized cultures, this is often done through texts in traditional academic genres, and responses are also expected to be in the form of traditional textual analysis (see Windle, 2014). Similarly, when linguistic variation is itself a theme in examinations, it is presented through extremely conventional academic forms that dissolve any personal connection to the actual speech that must be analysed. The academically prepared, White, urban student will be more likely to do well on examination items dealing with these marginalized cultures and linguistic forms than those who actually live them – as what is under examination is the ability to sit written examinations based primarily on the speed and accuracy of textual analysis.

Journeys through the Borderlands of Higher Education in a Time of Change

Brazil is passing through a number of important changes that challenge both the boundaries of between-group linguistic distinctions, as well as the boundaries characterised by discursive identity markers and collective mobilisation. These two divides, emphasised respectively by theories of reproduction and new literacy studies, come into focus in teacher education programs that are receiving large numbers of poor and Black students for the first time. The notion of borderlands offers a useful way of thinking through this movement. In *Borderlands*, Gloria Aznaldúa (1987) connects the physical border separating the US and Mexico with the psychological, cultural and linguistic borderlands in which she locates herself:

> A border is a dividing line, a narrow strip along a steep edge. A borderland is a vague and undetermined place created by the emotional residue of an unnatural boundary. It is in a constant state of transition. The prohibited and forbidden are its inhabitants. *Los atravesados* live here: the squint-eyed, the perverse, the queer, the troublesome, the mongrel, the mulato, the half-breed, the half dead; in short those who cross over, pass over, or go through the confines of the 'normal'. (Aznaldúa 1987: 25)

The rise of Afro-Brazilian identity movements and visibility in socially restricted institutional spaces confronts popular and academic discourses that deny the existence of racial boundaries in Brazil. This confrontation can be viewed as an example of how seemingly 'hard' social boundaries are at least partly open to resignification and appropriation as part of social struggles. One of the most visible signs of racial resignification is shifts in racial self-identification in the national census. Official figures distinguish dark black (*preto*) (8.2%), 'brown' (*pardo*) (46.7%) and white (44.2%), with Indigenous and 'yellow' (Asian) Brazilians making up less than one percent of the population (Silveira, 2017). A Black majority has only emerged since the 2010 census, and the proportion self-identifying as '*preto*' ('dark' black) and 'brown' grew respectively 15% and 7% in the years 2012–2016 alone (Silveira, 2017).

Tensions from both the occupation of formerly restricted spaces by Black students and the discursive affirmation of Afro-Brazilian identities are frequently deflected onto the terrain of ideologies of linguistic clarity and competence. As educators of language teachers in Brazilian public universities, we are used to hearing colleagues complaining that Black students lack basic literacy, making simple spelling errors in their written work and failing to conjugate verbs correctly in their speech. Many professors long for a return to the days when students came to university well-prepared to face a curriculum of formal grammar and canonical literature, fluent in English and without financial concerns or the necessity to work. As Bagno astutely observes, echoing Bourdieu, all evaluations of linguistic competence are in fact social judgements of the value of the speaker (Bagno & Bezerra, 2009). Students internalise some of these negative judgements, questioning their own capacity and feeling anxious about being exposed as 'frauds'.

We seek to reverse this anxiety, authorising and supporting trainee teachers to transgress and to teach to transgress (hooks, 2014). This objective is central to our work in a teacher-education project known as PIBID, over the period 2014–2016, in which student-teachers spent time working in schools across a range of curriculum areas. Kassandra led a project developing Afro-Brazilian curriculum and teaching (PIBID-Afro) and Joel led a project developing English language curriculum (PIBID-English). The projects had some common points of focus, including African and Caribbean literature and music, and also held some joint meetings, particularly relating to the theme of migration (described in the accounts below). We have previously argued that the project had an impact on how participating student teachers repositioned their own 'place' as educators and Afro-Brazilians, as expressed by Marti:

> Looking at African culture in the Caribbean, has made us move our bodies and minds from places that are already tired and superficial in relation to Black culture. Therefore, leaving the previous perspective on Black culture and broadening our horizons with the examples and trajectories observable in the African diaspora of the Americas, especially in Haiti, where we have taken note of the first Black anti-slavery

revolution in the Afro-Caribbean lands, was an act promoting Black Consciousness for us trainees, helping us to understand the Black agency in the history of the African people and their descendants, in a process of resistance in favor of life and freedom. ... I understand myself in this process as an heir and propagator of Black agency, be it in schools, media, quilombola communities, candomblé terreiros or university. (Windle & Muniz, 2018: 315)

In the remainder of the paper we consider how we are positioned within Brazilian higher education, and how our perceptions of our work in teacher education result from a journey across a number of boundaries, from a 'powerful periphery', Australia, and from a radically more subjugated one, northeastern Brazil. This journey has shaped the ways that we see others, and are read, as a White, Black, female, male, anti-racist and outsider/insider of distinctive kinds. We have adopted the narrative strategy of duo-ethnography, which can be defined as 'a method of qualitative research in which two researchers juxtapose their personal life histories in order to explore different perspectives on a given or agreed topic' (Lowe, 2018).

Kassandra: The gulfs that exist between university and school in Brazil remain immense. The abysses that lie in the way of Black female professors entering the university are similarly vast. As a consequence, when we try to reduce these abysses, recognizing the limits placed on our ability to do so, it produces a mixture of estrangement, surprise, enchantment and adversity.

The presence of a Black professor created a stir (*causou*[2]) 'caused' and still creates one every time that I need to be in schools for our projects. On one such occasion, in a school that caters mostly to Black students, the first reactions were of surprise and self-identification. When they got over their astonishment at learning that I was the supervisor of the PIBID-Afro student-teachers, a series of questions immediately followed. All broadly related to the 'Black world': 'Do you like Black music?' 'Who are your favorite singers?' 'Have you always worn braids (boxbraids)?' 'Do you like Afro hair as well?' 'What is it like at UFOP?' And a series of questions that sought to establish bridges between me, them, and my presence as a professor at UFOP.

Revisiting these moments, which were repeated in other schools, it is interesting to note that even for the teenage school students, the idea of frontiers was present. They understood that my Black and northeastern body must challenge the place that universities still occupy in the Brazilian social imaginary, although UFOP has this year, thanks to the recent achievements of the Black movements, had a Black majority intake of new students in 2019. It is a victory that illustrates well the functioning of borderlands that are displaced, rethought, questioned, but not broken, because my entry and that of so many other Black intellectuals in post-Lula universities does not yet mean fairness or elimination of institutional racism within the academy. It seems to me that even without the academic tools that would later come to them throughout the PIBID project, the PIBID trainee teachers knew very well that to live that intellectuality within the University is to live constantly on a tightrope.

PIBID-Afro provided me with many things that impacted my teaching, among them the possibility of establishing a better and greater connection between the contents that I taught at the university and school demands. Some of these demands were not necessarily even at the center of the concerns of school leadership, but in the body and speech of the students who were somehow 'reached' by the project. In Brazil, despite almost half of the population being identified and self-declared as Black, it was necessary to create a law in 2003 that aimed at introducing curriculum content on African History and Culture and that of the African diaspora into school curricula. It was in this opening that it was possible to create a teacher-education project on the subject of interdisciplinary approaches to African identities.

The racial question is still a delicate and painful point in the educational practices of Brazil. The absences are many, as are the silencings. In this sense, even occasional activities had a great impact among the university and school students. The idea of meeting as Black people through the interactions and exchanges promoted by the project, and of establishing a common diasporic thread for our pedagogical and interpersonal relationships has always been a strong and beautiful point joining me, the student-teachers and the school students.

The meeting between a Black, Brazilian female researcher and a White, English-speaking researcher from a small Australian town was most unusual, thinking about the context of tense racial relations in Brazil, and a most fruitful one. It provided, and still yields, academic production and affections. We shared not only an office, but also many ideas about the possibility of encounters amid conflicts and tensions that a meeting of such disparate cultures is apt to provide. In a duoethnography perspective, not only this text was born, but also others that have contributed to the possibility of academic-pedagogical work in the space of the borderlands, as Anzaldúa terms it, that is, not only in what dichotomized us in relation to our social identities; nor in the perspective of a total and naive conception of a homogeneous and tension-free multiculturalism.

In relation to this line of thinking, one of the most important activities, which generated other productive encounters, was hosting an event discussing immigration, Blackness, language and borders, to which school students were invited. We set up discussions between PIBID student–teachers from both projects and invited a Haitian immigrant,

Phanel Georges, who was a teacher in his country and discussed his linguistic and racial experiences in Haiti and Brazil, in which the issue of borders interposed constantly. Despite having a linguistic performance far ahead of most people in the university setting, for example, the fact that Phanel Georges was a Black Haitian man set him a place of inequality and discrimination in Brazil. His accounts of how his own Blackness was read in Haiti compared to Brazil had a strong impact on university and school students listening to his experiences. The fact that they met a Black man who spoke four languages already caused a surprise that only racism can explain. This activity, and the presence of Phanel himself, showed us how a transnational perspective entails a concept of borderlands that promotes the encounter between cultures in a political way in which subjects have the opportunity to (re-)know and establish bridges, drawing-out conflicts as a possibility for developing practices of re-existence (Souza, 2009). Practices of re-existence are anchored in an educational perspective that aims to re-create and recognize creativity, invention, culture, and transformation where there existed only mistrust and seemingly insurmountable barriers.

Joel: My experience of entering a Brazilian university, as one of a handful of foreign professors, was one of anxiety mainly about the bureaucratic uncertainties faced by many migrants – visas, work permits, recognition of qualifications, unfamiliar workplace structures. However it also proved to be a radicalizing experience, particularly through my close personal and professional relationship with Kassandra and through a number of unsettling experiences in which racial boundaries took on a sharper and more immediate form than they had in my prior experiences in Australia.

In contrast to Kassandra, my professional capacity and right to be in the university as a professor were unquestioned, despite a shaky grasp on academic Portuguese. My professional standing benefited from my status as a 'native speaker' of English, vouched for by a whiteness that indexes 'gringo' status (that of an outsider, but one often viewed through a lens of superiority in relation to local culture and peoples). In schools, this sometimes resulted in intense curiosity, often coupled with shyness, from both students and teachers, to the extent that they ignored others who were with me. When I accompanied a student seeking to enrol in an adult education course to a number of schools, I was always the person spoken to first and sometimes exclusively, requiring great effort to redirect attention to the student.

This deferential attention had a strong racial dimension. Counting on my Brazilian partner's superior knowledge of both Portuguese and local procedures, I sometimes brought him with me to resolve visa problems with the Federal Police. However, I soon learnt that I was treated with greater respect and patience as a White foreigner with inadequate

Portuguese than he was as a Black Brazilian, and that the linguistic and pragmatic experience he brought to such situations was that shared by the majority of the population in interactions with the state, of being ignored and disrespected. At a social event with professors from UFOP, I recall the relief of a colleague from dentistry when my partner confirmed he was not a professor at the institution: 'thank God, I couldn't for the life of me imagine what you could be a professor of'. Overall, working in schools located in peripheral locations, with Black students and a Black colleague, was viewed by some university professors and school teachers as a waste of time, a shame, a curiosity, inexplicable, or a fetish ('gringos love favelas' complained one teacher who described her students as 'animals').

Working in PIBID to challenge and subvert direct racism and racist linguistic ideologies involved a delicate navigation of authority invested in institutions and persons. Some teachers and school administrators resented the project, particularly when race and sexuality became 'too' visible as themes and when they were presented by trainee-teachers whose own legitimacy in the space of the school was fragile. My own institutional standing and Whiteness buttressed and gave legitimacy to the PIBID project, particularly when I was personally present, but was also subject to 'contamination' and a loss of credibility through association with 'outside' elements, 'outsiders', and positions seen as institutionally disloyal and 'political'. As the political is viewed as outside of the bounds of legitimate institutional knowledge (defined as linguistic and pedagogical), it is fair to say that we attracted a large amount of attention within the university, for activities viewed as 'scandalous', perhaps more so than in the schools, where many students and teachers were allies. As an openly gay professor, I became a visible object of both 'scandal' and unease at a perceived stepping outside of professional roles and expected silences. However, I also became a positive visible point of support for gay, lesbian and transgender university students, many of whom participated in the PIBID projects. PIBID thus became, institutionally, something of a borderlands associated with two unsettling and scandalous professors, and supportive of queer and Black cultural and linguistic performances (for examples, see Windle & Bravo, 2019).

As with Kassandra, students in schools attempted to make connections with me on project visits, but from a far narrower repertoire of mutual identification: they did so using the cultural 'universal' of football. Students often asked me which football teams I knew and which one I supported. This resonance led me to do some work with student teachers on Australian Rules Football, and some of the common issues addressed (and hidden) across codes, including racism and homophobia. One point of connection was Heritier Lumamba, an Afro-Brazilian who played Australian Rules Football and was sacked when he confronted racism in his team. Interestingly, many Australians assume that Heritier is an Indigenous Australian, and as such he is subject to the prototypical Australian model of racism, based on the genocide of Aboriginal nations.

Perhaps the most striking experience of visiting schools was changing my idea of what constituted a school. Many were shut-off from the city by high walls and all but invisible to the passer-by. I walked straight passed the first school I was meant to visit three times before I realised that a narrow gate in a high wall was the main entrance. At another school, I was shut-in along with all of the students when the doorman padlocked the only entrance and left his post. Students advised me to scale the wall if I wanted to get out. This unsettling experience raises questions about what kind of spaces students are placed in, how these spaces are closed off from other social spaces, and how access is regulated and subverted (by scaling the walls). The physical space of the walled school seems to be an apt metaphor for the racial and linguistic boundaries that are tied up with this space – sometimes hiding, sometimes containing, but never totally impermeable.

***

The effects of the movement into exclusive academic spaces and resignification of the legitimate uses of such spaces, and of legitimate occupants are clear in both duo-ethnographic narratives, as accounts of researchers and teachers who have transgressed the 'allocated' spaces in the racialized social hierarchy and become 'unsettling' or 'disturbing' as presences in university and in school. A number of our experiences reflect the linguistic ideologies identified by Plaza Pinto (2018). Black body and Black speech are seen as out of place in the academy, even as a White body is accepted, with linguistic divergence from the 'educated' and 'prestige' norm being acceptable. The super-linguistic competence of Phanel, fluent in Portuguese, French, English and Creole, is discounted by his status as a Black man and as a migrant. The racial hierarchy is reinforced in the differentiated linguistic reception of the university. Clarity can be seen situationally here – Kassandra is instantly legible as an ally for Black school students whereas Joel is read as an outsider who is difficult to situate socially (hence the reliance on football questions initially). In administrative interactions, Joel is read as having more to say and being more suited to speaking than others who are racialized as irrational or incompetent (which can further be understood as irrelevant and inconsequential), but this position is subject to 'contamination' by being excessively political or institutionally 'disloyal'.

Our experiences together were important for the opening up of new possibilities for teaching practice and the production of knowledge in ways that value and recognise the borderlands as a distinctive and productive space. This is a heretical space, where English is thought about with reference to Africa, and English and Afro-Brazilian Portuguese lose some of their taboos (as a forbidden and forboding 'boogie man' for English and as incompetence for Afro-Brazilian Portuguese). Thinking about English as more than an ally of imperialism helped to break-down barriers between Afro-centric curriculum development and foreign language curriculum development and those involved in this work (ourselves and our student teachers).

The two narratives presented above point to multiple and complex global hierarchies affecting and structuring our work as teachers – including capitalism, racism, patriarchy, militarism, and Christianity – the latter three gaining political force following the election of far-right military officer Jair Bolsonaro to the Brazilian presidency. They serve to locate our thinking as coming from, and together with, raced, sexed and gendered bodies, an epistemological stance that seeks dialogue and plurality amongst diverse political and ethical perspectives.

If we take all boundaries to be 'hard', it would be impossible to imagine our meeting and working together. There is a margin for cultivating what Sousa Santos (2014) calls an 'ecology of knowledge' that is based on intercultural recognition and exchange. Sousa Santos (2018) argues that we should prioritize knowledge that emerges as part of, and as the product of, struggles of resistance against oppression and against the knowledge that legitimises oppression. Many of these ways of knowing are not merely ways of thinking, but 'lived' knowledge. This involves the incorporation of so-called 'non-existent' knowledge, so-called because it is not produced in accordance with accepted methodologies and is produced by 'absent subjects' (subjects understood as incapable of producing valid knowledge due to their excluded status).

Thinking about our experiences in terms of the borderland implies thinking about the periphery as a kind of centre of the motor of the colonial system, and the central location for the production of resistance – if Minas Gerais is a borderland, it is also a heartland – the heartland of the struggles over the meaning and purposes of higher education. It is the heartlands of the contradictions of capitalism, of the collapse of the racialized system of slavery and its refraction into other forms of inequality. Our narratives help us to see boundaries as relatively permeable, particularly under conditions of rapid social and political change, and as interrelational. Boundaries are mobile, defined by the possibility of transgression. Border-crossing therefore becomes a definitional part of our work, even coming up against 'hard' boundaries is also a constitutional aspect – being accused of being 'out of place', of being irrational (outside of the genres that grant clarity to language and speakers), and of being incompetent (teaching culturally and linguistically useless rubbish). At worst, this work is illegible, unrecognisable as part of the world of school and university – not English or Portuguese or History or Geography, something beyond the role of the teacher, something that unsettles.

Conclusion

This chapter has sought to contrast theoretical traditions that emphasise, on the one hand, the 'hard' social boundaries set in place by broad social structures, and on the other hand the 'soft' social boundaries negotiated and acted upon by individuals in increasingly plural societies. The first tradition suggests that linguistic diversity is misrecognised by schools and society, a fact which benefits the most socially powerful groups that hold a monopoly on definitions of competence. The second tradition extends this critique to suggest that it is possible to make linguistic and cultural diversity visible, and for individuals and institutions to consciously enact more pluralist and egalitarian practices.

In the 'hard boundaries' school of theorising, linguistic inequalities are understood as markers of relatively fixed social categories, manifest in unreflexive speech and interactional patterns that betray social standing and origins before institutions such as schooling. The 'soft boundaries' approach sees linguistic inequalities in the discursive construction of identities, as much as in individual or group forms of speech, and as such focuses on the meta-pragmatic dimension of boundary construction. Language thus moves from a definition based on variation in speech to one based on differentiation in discourse.

Both theoretical traditions, emerging from developed nations, are challenged by the shape of contemporary Brazilian society and educational inequalities. Despite, this, they share in common an attention to the dynamic relationship between social change, schooling as an institution, and language that is valuable in assessing current shifts in Brazil, and particularly the partial democratisation of higher education generally, and teacher training in particular. Although encountering the 'hard' boundaries of centralised curriculum and testing regimes to a greater extent than ever before, an influx of politicised teachers from marginalised groups has the potential to force progressive change in public education settings that regularly fail their students, and fail to recognise their culture and language. This is the hope that drives our own work in teacher education and as researchers.

Using duoethnography, we have presented narratives of the generative contexts of our scholarship, seeking to highlight how our experiences are materially and socially specific. These point to the centrality of unsettling, disturbing, and even scandalous effects resulting from the movement of bodies, languages and ideas across the borderlands of legitimate knowledge, speech, institutions and racialized social hierarchies. We believe that such accounts can contribute to the construction of self-reflective, emancipatory scholarship in which subjects located in the global periphery become more active and creative producers of the theories we ourselves use and teach.

Notes

(1) Defined as the top 5% of grades.
(2) The expression *causar* is used in the hip-hop movement refer to creating a noticeable presence in spaces where black bodies remain unwelcome and unrecognised.

References

Almeida, A.M.F. (2007) A noção de capital cultural é útil para se pensar o Brasil. *Sociologia da educação: Pesquisa e realidade. Petrópolis, RJ: Vozes*, 44.
Anzaldúa, G. (1987) *Borderlands: La frontera*, San Francisco: Aunt Lute.
Bagno, M. (1999) *Preconceito lingüístico: O que é, como se faz*. Sao Paulo: Edições Loyola.
Bagno, M. and Bezerra, M. (2009) *Não é errado falar assim!: Em defesa do português brasileiro*: Parábola.
Barros, C. (2012) Notas sobre um catecismo manuscrito na língua geral 'vulgar' da Amazônia (século XVIII). In C. Alfaro, M.C. Rosa and J.B. Freire (eds) *Políticas de Línguas no novo mundo* (pp. 1–275). Rio de Janeiro: Editora da UERJ.
Bartlett, L. (2007) Literacy, speech and shame: The cultural politics of literacy and language in Brazil. *International Journal of Qualitative Studies in Education* 20 (5), 547–563.
Beck, U. (2007) Beyond class and nation: Reframing social inequalities in a globalizing world. *The British journal of sociology* 58 (4), 679–705.
Bernstein, B. (1971) *Class, Codes and Control*. London: Routledge and K. Paul.
Bourdieu, P. (1973) Cultural reproduction and social reproduction. In R.K. Brown (ed.) *Knowledge, Education, and Cultural Change: Papers in the Sociology of Education* (pp. xii, 410). London: Tavistock [distributed in the USA by Harper & Row Publishers Barnes & Noble Import Division.]
Bourdieu, P. (1984) *Distinction: A Social Critique of the Judgement of Taste*. Cambridge, MA: Harvard University Press.
Bourdieu, P. and Champagne, P. (1992) Les exclus de l'intérieur. *Actes de la recherche en sciences sociales* 91–92, 71–75.
Bourdieu, P. and Passeron, J.-C. (1979) *The Inheritors: French Students and their Relation to Culture*. Chicago: University of Chicago Press.
Bourdieu, P. and Passeron, J.-C. (1990) *Reproduction in Education, Society, and Culture* (1990/ed.) London; Newbury Park, CA: Sage.
Bourdieu, P. and Wacquant, L. (1999) On the cunning of imperialist reason. *Theory, Culture & Society* 16 (1), 41–58.
Brice Heath, S. (1982) What no bedtime story means: Narrative skills at home and school. *Language in society* 2, 49–76.
Campbell, C. and Sherington, G. (2006) *The Comprehensive Public High School: Historical Perspectives* (1st edn.) New York: Palgrave Macmillan.
Christie, F. (2004) Systemic functional linguistics and a theory of language in education. *Ilha do Desterro A Journal of English language, literatures in English and cultural studies* (46), 013–040.
Coleman, J.S. (1966) *Equality of Educational Opportunity*. Washington: U.S. Dept. of Health, Education, and Welfare, Office of Education.
Connell, R.W. (2007) *Southern Theory: The Global Dynamics of Knowledge in Social Science*. Cambridge: Polity.

Connell, R.W., White, V. and Johnston, K. (1992) An experiment in justice: The Disadvantaged Schools Program and the question of poverty, 1974–1990. *British Journal of Sociology of Education* 13 (4), 447–464.

Cope, B. and Kalantzis, M. (2009) 'Multiliteracies': New literacies, new learning. *Pedagogies: An International Journal* 4 (3), 164–195.

Damergian, S. (2009) Migração e referenciais identificatórios: Linguagem e preconceito. *Psicologia USP* 20 (2), 251–268.

de Jesus Ferreira, A. (2014) Teoria racial crítica e letramento racial crítico: Narrativas e contranarrativas de identidade racial de professores de Línguas. *Revista da ABPN• v* 6 (14), 236–263.

do Valle Silva, N. and Hasenbalg, C. (2000) Tendências da desigualdade educacional no Brasil. *DADOS-Revista de ciências sociais* 43 (3), 423–445.

Freire, P. (1970) *Pedagogy of the Oppressed*. New York: Herder and Herder.

Gandin, L.A. and Apple, M.W. (2003) Educating the state, democratizing knowledge: The citizen school project in Porto Alegre, Brazil. In M.W. Apple (ed.) *The State and the Politics of Knowledge* (pp. 193–219). New York: Routledge.

Girard, A. and Bastide, H. (1963) La Stratification Sociale et la Démocratisation de L'enseignement. *Population (french edition)* 435–472.

Hasenbalg, C.A., do Valle Silva, N. and Lima, M. (1999) *Cor e Estratificação Social* Rio de Janeiro: Contra Capa Livraria

Heath, S.B. (1983) *Ways with Words: Language, life, and work in communities and classrooms*. Cambridge: Cambridge University Press.

Hill, M.L. (2008) Toward a pedagogy of the popular: Bourdieu, hip-hop, and out-of-school literacies. *Bourdieu and Literacy Education* (pp. 136–161). Mahwah, NJ: Erlbaum.

Hooks, B. (2014) *Teaching to Transgress*. New York: Routledge.

Hull, G. and Schultz, K. (2001) Literacy and learning out of school: A review of theory and research. *Review of Educational Research* 71 (4), 575–611.

Hull, G. and Schultz, K. (2002) *School's out: Bridging out-of-school literacies with classroom practice* (Vol. 60): New York: Teacher's College Press

Janks, H. (2009) *Literacy and Power*: Routledge.

Labov, W. (1972) *The Logic of Nonstandard English*. Harmondsworth: Penguin.

Lam, W.S.E. and Warriner, D.S. (2012) Transnationalism and literacy: Investigating the mobility of people, languages, texts, and practices in contexts of migration. *Reading Research Quarterly* 47 (2), 191–215.

Lareau, A. (2002) Invisible inequality: Social class and childbearing in black families and white families. *American Sociological Review* 67 (5), 747–777.

Loveman, M. (1999) Is 'race' essential? *American Sociological Review* 64 (6), 891–898.

Lowe, R. (2018) Duoethnographic projects in the language class. *Modern English Teacher*. 21 (1), 74–77.

Lucchesi, D. (2015) *Língua e Sociedade Partidas: A polarização sociolinguística do Brasil*. São Paulo: Contexto.

Lucchesi, D., Baxter, A.N. and Ribeiro, I. (2009) *O Português Afro-Brasileiro* Salvador: EDUFBA..

Luke, A. (2000) Critical literacy in Australia: A matter of context and standpoint. *Journal of Adolescent and Adult Literacy* 43 (5), 448–461.

Muniz, K. (2016) Ainda sobre a possibilidade de uma linguística 'crítica': performatividade, política e identificação racial no Brasil. *D.E.L.T.A.* 32 (3), 796–786.

Maia, J.d.O. (2017) Fogos digitais: Letramentos de sobrevivência no Complexo do Alemão/RJ.

Oommen, T.K. (1995) Contested boundaries and emerging pluralism. *International Sociology* 10 (3), 251–268.

Pennycook, A. (2007) Language, localization, and the real: Hip-hop and the global spread of authenticity. *Journal of Language, Identity, and Education* 6 (2), 101–115.

Plaza Pinto, J. (2018) Ideologias Linguísticas e a Instituição de Hierarquias Raciais, *Revista ABPN* 10, 704–720.

Plowden, B.H.P. (1967) *Children and Their Primary Schools: A Report. Research and Surveys*: HM Stationery Office.

Richardson, E. (2006) *Hiphop Literacies*. New York: Routledge.

Silveira, D. (24 November 2017) População que se declara preta cresce 14,9% no Brasil em 4 anos, aponta IBGE. *O Globo*. Retrieved from https://g1.globo.com/economia/noticia/populacao-que-se-declara-preta-cresce-149-no-brasil-em-4-anos-aponta-ibge.ghtml Accessed: 16 May 2018

Sousa Santos, B. (2014) *Epistemologies of the South: Justice Against Epistemicide*. London: Paradigm Publishers.

Sousa Santos, B. (2018) *The End of the Cognitive Empire: The Coming of Age of Epistemologies of the South*. Durham: Duke University Press.

Souza, A.L.S. (2009) Letramentos de reexistencia = culturas e identidades no movimento hip hop. Brazil: Parabola.

Street, B. (1984) *Literacy in Theory and Practice*. Cambridge: Cambridge University Press.

Telles, E.E. (2014) *Race in Another America: The Significance of Skin Color in Brazil*: Princeton University Press.

The New London Group. (1996) A pedagogy of multiliteracies: Designing social futures. *Harvard Educational Review* 66 (1), 60–93.

Thomson, P. and Holdsworth, R. (2003) Theorizing change in the educational 'field': (Re)readings of 'student participation' projects. *Int. J. Leadership in Education* 6 (4), 371–391.

Toledo, L.F., Arruda, M. and Prata, P. No Enem, 1 a cada 4 alunos de classe média triunfa. Pobres são 1 a cada 600. *Estadão*, January 18, 2019. Accessed: 10 April 2019 www.estadao.com.br/infograficos/educacao,no-enem-1-a-cada-4-alunos-de-classe-media-triunfa-pobres-sao-1-a-cada-600,953041.

Vieira, I. (2 December 2016) Percentual de negros em universidades dobra, mas é inferior ao de brancos. *Agência Brasil*. Retrieved from http://agenciabrasil.ebc.com.br/educacao/noticia/2016-12/percentual-de-negros-em-universidades-dobra-mas-e-inferior-ao-de-brancos. Accessed 10 April 2019.

Windle, J.A. and Bravo, B. (2019) Plurilingual social networks and the creation of hybrid cultural spaces. *Papers in Applied Linguistics* 58 (1), 139–157.

Windle, J.A. (2017) Hidden features in global knowledge production: (Re)positioning theory and practice in academic writing. *Revista Brasileira de Linguística Aplicada* 17 (2), 355–378.

Windle, J.A. (2014) Digital literacy, cosmopolitanism, and the subaltern. *Polifonia* 21–29.

Windle, J.A. and Muniz, K. (2018) Constructions of race in Brazil: resistance and resignification in teacher education. *International Studies in Sociology of Education*.

Windle, J.A. and Nogueira, M.A. (2015) The role of internationalisation in the schooling of Brazilian elites: Distinctions between two class fractions. *British Journal of Sociology of Education* 36 (1), 174–192.

3 Rural-Urban Divides and Digital Literacy in Mongolian Higher Education

Daariimaa Marav

Introduction

This chapter investigates how a long-standing social boundary in Mongolian society is affected by a shifting linguistic landscape. It seeks to show how the rural-urban divide is enacted or reinforced through unequal access to new technologies and linguistic resources, as digital literacies and the English language gain importance relative to the previously hegemonic regional language, Russian and traditional academic literacies. I argue that geographically-defined histories of access to and participation in online and English-oriented literacies have implications for participation in higher education and the accumulation of types of cultural, linguistic and social capital that will influence future life chances.

Urbanisation in Mongolia has intensified since the country moved from socialism to a market-oriented economy in 1990. Particularly, as the political, educational, cultural, economic and financial hub of the country, Ulaanbaatar has been facing rapid urbanization mainly due to internal – rural to urban – migration. The migration is mostly caused by the uneven economic and social development in urban and rural areas in Mongolia (International Organisation for Migration, 2018). The rural people have flocked to Ulaanbaatar in search of employment-related economic and educational opportunities, better living conditions and health services or to reunite with family members (International Organisation for Migration, 2018). As a result, nearly half (47%) of the total population (3.1 million) in Mongolia are living in the capital city and nearly 20% are living in two other cities, Darkhan and Erdenet (National Statistical Office of Mongolia, 2018). These cities are much more developed in terms of infrastructure, and economic and educational resources than the rural areas, which include 21 *aimags* and 329 *sums*, where a third of the population lives, most of whom practise agriculture. In Mongolia, an *aimag* is like a province. It is subdivided into smaller administrative units, *sums* and *bags*.

This 'old' boundary between urban and rural areas takes on a new shape in the form of a digital divide, which has important consequences for how educational opportunities are made use of and produced. This digital divide is evident in differential rates of internet use between the urban and rural areas in Mongolia, even though the number of internet users in the country increased dramatically from 709,625 to nearly 2.2 million between 2010 and 2018, according to the statistics on internet use in Mongolia produced by the National Statistical Office of Mongolia. For instance, while over 80% of the residents in urban areas used the internet, the percentage of internet users in the other 19 *aimags* did not reach the national average of 70%.

The social boundary between rural and urban is sharply experienced even by those who move to the capital city, and is visible in patterns of access not merely to technology, but to the linguistic forms and literacies embedded in online platforms and communities. Hence, virtual spaces continue to map onto long-standing territorial divisions in Mongolia, despite shifts in both the proportion of the population living in urban centres and the supra-national linguistic market. In light of globalisation and a changing social and economic environment in Mongolia, young people are now required to be literate in English, and to know how to use computers and the internet to access information, education and employment for their future. However, because of the differences in infrastructure development as previously mentioned and the educational resources gap in urban and rural areas in Mongolia, there is deep inequity amongst Mongolian young people in their access to and uses of the internet and English language. Even among urban people, depending on whether they live in apartments or in *ger*[1] districts, there is a digital divide because the *ger* districts are poorly serviced areas, located on the outskirts of the cities.

In addition to the digital divide at a macro-level, depending on the geographical locations where people live and the unequal distribution of resources and opportunities, there is also a divide at a micro-level, depending on people's age, personal networks, income and education levels, and access to computers and digital literacies. For example, according to Johnson (2003), who surveyed 313 residents in Ulaanbaatar and interviewed 18 of them, the educated young people from a higher SES (socioeconomic status) started using the internet earlier. The people with more diverse social networks tended to use the internet more because of peer pressure and also because of the support they received from their friends and workmates in gaining expertise in the use of the technologies (Johnson, 2003). It seems likely that such a digital divide would also be evident amongst students in higher education. Thus, this chapter attempts to investigate what factors affect Mongolian university students' digital literacy practices and what opportunities arise from the students' English and digital literacies drawing on perspectives offered by Pierre Bourdieu's theory of social practice and the field of Literacy Studies, which analyses literacy practices within the social and cultural contexts in which they occur.

In the remainder of the chapter, first, I will provide some background information on the status of English language in Mongolia and its relationship to technology and globalization. Then, I will introduce and discuss the study and finally analyse the findings, focusing on the relationship between inequalities and boundaries in a context of linguistic and technological flux.

Linguistic Capital in Mongolia

Historically, Mongolians were under the political, economic and even linguistic influence of Russia for about 70 years, from the 1920s to 1990. The strong influence of the Russian language is evident in the fact that Mongol Bichig (traditional Mongolian script) was replaced by the Russian Cyrillic alphabet in 1941 (Billé, 2010). The Soviet and Mongolian cadres reasoned that the Cyrillic alphabet would allow Mongolians to study and read in Russian more easily and foster cooperation between Russia and Mongolia (Cohen, 2005). To this day, the Mongolian language continues to be written in the Cyrillic alphabet. Russian was the only mandatory foreign language taught in schools, with obligatory Russian language instruction starting in fourth grade, facilitating Mongolian intellectuals' education in Russia and being a requirement for higher education and employment in the socialist period (Cohen, 2005). In fact, fluency in Russian was a marker of educated Mongolians (Cohen, 2005). In other words, Russian was desirable linguistic capital, the embodied cultural capital that comprises various language practices valued within a field – linguistic market and provides advantages in achieving a higher social status (Bourdieu, 1991).

Russian evidently symbolised modernity and cosmopolitanism until 1990 (Billé, 2010; Cohen, 2005; Marzluf, 2012) when Mongolia started its transition from a socialist system to a democracy. From that time on, English language took the place of Russian language. This linguistic shift was triggered by the policies that have positioned English favourably in Mongolia and made English language education compulsory and very popular, such as the Nationwide Programme on English Language Education: 2009–2020 (Government of Mongolia, 2008b) and the Millennium Development Goals-based Comprehensive National Development Strategy of Mongolia: 2007–2021 (Government of Mongolia, 2008a), the forces of globalisation and the increasing use of the internet (Marav, 2016). The policies have definitely been influenced by globalisation: the relationship between globalisation and policy development is complex and reciprocal.

Today, English language has become a dominant foreign language in Mongolia through which individuals can gain access to a number of opportunities such as ensuring their future employment, fully participating in the global information society and studying abroad. This is not unique to Mongolia as globalisation necessitates access to English as the global or international language in today's world (Pennycook, 2007). English is established in Mongolia 'as a prestige international language bearer of modernity' (Billé, 2010: 243). Especially, within the context of contemporary globalisation, young Mongolians access popular culture and music through English (Dovchin, 2011, 2015). Another factor contributing to the current status of English in Mongolia is the rise in the use of the internet in people's everyday lives as English still dominates the internet (Internet World Statistics, 2017), not only in terms of the content but also in terms of intercultural communication.

Though English, an agent of globalisation, confers power and access as linguistic capital in Mongolia, this is also associated with constraints as evidenced in Marav's study (2014, 2016). For instance, there is an urban-rural divide in accessing good quality English language education in Mongolia. This educational inequality is attributed to many factors including differences in educational infrastructure and resources, and a lack of high-quality English teachers not only in rural schools but also in some urban public schools. Furthermore, depending on their financial situation, Mongolian families invest in their children's English language education hoping this will facilitate their children's access to higher education, global knowledge economy and social mobility. While some parents send their children to private international schools, adopting English as a medium of instruction, or bi-lingual private schools in Ulaanbaatar, some still enrol them in public schools. Mostly, the graduates who attended private schools continue their post-secondary education abroad. In general, children from less privileged families or social groups are excluded from good quality English education in Mongolia.

Overall, Mongolia has experienced enormous social, economic and political change since 1990. Of particular note is a shift from a Soviet-style to a Western-style system in the political sphere and ever-increasing access to the internet in the technological sphere. These shifts have contributed to the growing cultural status of English mediated in particular through globalisation and the digital literacy practices of Mongolians. English has become linguistic capital, a form of cultural capital, which enables many Mongolians to access other types of capital.

Research Outline

This chapter is based on the data collected for my doctoral study, extending the analysis to place educational inequality at the centre of the theoretical and empirical contribution. The study used a mix of methods but with the qualitative predominating: a survey completed by 98 students to obtain general information about the students' uses of digital technologies and English, and to provide a broad context for the in-depth case studies, and detailed case studies of six students (Marav, 2016). Although not 'ethnographic' in the strictest sense, the study drew on methods of ethnographic research. Green and Bloome (1997) distinguish usefully between three different approaches to ethnography: doing ethnography, adopting an ethnographic perspective, and using ethnographic tools. This study employed elements of two of these approaches: an ethnographic perspective and ethnographic tools. By being present in the university setting, I could see the reality of the students' uses of digital technologies. As Bourdieu (1993) argues, 'one cannot grasp the most profound logic of the social world unless one becomes immersed in the specificity of an empirical reality' (1993: 271). To illuminate the students' digital literacy practices across different contexts and circumstances, and the different values or meanings attached to the practices, I also employed a multiple case study approach (Swanborn, 2010; Yin, 2012).

I conducted a survey with 98 students in their 3rd and 4th year of undergraduate study, majoring in English language in a public university in Ulaanbaatar, the capital city of Mongolia. Anonymous and voluntary responses were required in the hope of gaining more honest responses. The students were asked about their background or demographics, the reasons they were learning English, how they used the language and the internet in their everyday lives, the language choices they made in particular online activities and the roles they thought English and digital literacy practices would play in their future lives and careers. SPSS (version 20) software was used to analyse the quantitative data.

To complement the survey data, I conducted case studies with six students who completed the survey. The survey provided general but valuable information about the students' perceptions of English and digital literacies and their uses of those literacies, while the case studies produced more textured perspectives on their digital literacy practices. The case study participants included five females and one male student from diverse family and educational backgrounds. They were all in their final year of university when the data were collected. Pseudonyms were used to protect their identity in this study because of ethical concerns. I investigated many aspects of the university setting and interviewed the case study participants twice to gain deeper understanding of their digital literacy practices. An observation was conducted during the second individual interview with participants for about an hour asking them to use a laptop computer connected to the internet in a way that they described as typical uses for them. I also invited them to write their techno-biographies as narratives.

Here, in order to identify cultural and linguistic boundaries and their effects, qualitative data from the survey and case studies are analysed drawing on Bourdieu's theory of practice. It is noteworthy that Bourdieu's theoretical framework, especially his concepts of capital, habitus and field, help to foreground the operation of social power in distinctions in students' trajectories, across economic, social, cultural and symbolic domains. The practices researched are connected here to underlying factors that constitute social boundaries, such as the inequalities that the participants had in relation to their English proficiency and access to digital technologies.

English and Digital Inequality

Forty-three of the survey respondents were from urban areas including the capital city, Ulaanbaatar, and two other cities, Darkhan and Erdenet. The rest of the participants, 55 students, were from rural areas. Their mean age was 21 (SD = 2.16). They used the internet to be informed, to entertain themselves, to communicate with their friends and online communities, and to practise or improve their English skills. However, there was an urban-rural divide in accessing the internet. The study revealed that over 80% of the students from urban areas accessed the internet often whereas 50% of the students from rural areas accessed the internet with the same frequency. Furthermore, the students from urban areas mostly used English in their online activities, while students from rural areas mostly used Mongolian or they mixed English and Mongolian (see Marav, 2016 for detailed information about the survey results). This language and digital divide is delineated further in case studies below.

The six case study participants were 21–23 year olds in their final year of the university. Only Alimaa was from Ulaanbaatar and because of her parents' influence and educational background (father – pianist, Head of an NGO; mother – IT engineer, journalist), she exposed herself to English in kindergarten and the internet in her secondary school – earlier than the other case study participants. She spent most of her free time on the internet at home. Nomin and Ariun were from rural areas and they had not studied English before they became students. They learnt some basic computer programmes, but not in depth, in grades 9 and 10. Bat was the only male case study participant whose English was fluent. He grew up in a rural area in southwestern Mongolia and when he was a child, his mother was an English teacher in a rural school. Bat's mother was unemployed at the time the data were collected. Because of his mother's influence Bat began to study English when he was in the 5th grade in secondary school. He did not have much access to computers during his schooling. He learnt how to use computers and the internet after he became a university student, which was typical for many students from rural areas.

Another two participants, Saraa and Naraa, lived in suburban areas of Ulaanbaatar. They both started studying English in their 6th grade. However, neither of them were happy with their English proficiency when they entered university. Saraa used a computer to do her homework for the first time when she was in her first year of university. For Naraa, she learnt more and more about computers when her parents bought a desktop computer in her first year of university. In fact, Naraa was ashamed of living in a *ger* district and did not tell the other students. In her final year at university she decided to live in a dormitory as it was hard for her to take a bus every day and she needed more time for her work and study. However, some people were surprised about her decision as only the students from the rural areas stayed in dormitories. All the case study participants, though they were from different families with different educational backgrounds and SES, had different histories of access to technologies and English learning, and believed that both English and digital literacies would enable them to get jobs after their graduation, study abroad, get information easily and quickly, learn more and entertain themselves.

However, depending on their English proficiency and the volume of their different types of capital, some of the case study participants were privileged, while some were disadvantaged in their everyday digital literacy practices. This inequality was mostly related to their previous educational backgrounds and the social contexts in which they lived. The disadvantaged ones had to struggle to gain a positional good through their digital literacy practices, to fit within the field of higher education, not only academically but also socially. For example, as previously mentioned, Ariun and Nomin had not been able to access English language education in their secondary schools in the rural areas where they lived and they both had limited networks in Ulaanbaatar where they studied. The fact that Nomin did not use Facebook was a manifestation of her limited social capital, though this was also part of her strategy to control her online activities in terms of their usefulness. Notwithstanding, she had less opportunity to practise her English because of her limited social capital:

> Int: What are the benefits of communicating in English with other people?
> Nomin: It is hard to say that it is beneficial for me because I hardly communicate with others in English. I use English to write emails occasionally and to translate some basic materials for other people. My use of English is quite limited. Extract 1 (Nomin – interview 1)

This helps to explain why her digital literacy practices on the whole were directed towards improving her English. She even wanted to engage with blogging in English to practise her English and to extend her social networks to English speakers. Nomin described an incident where she 'excluded' herself because of her English proficiency:

> Last year a person suggested to me to present a paper at a conference in South Korea. He may have thought my English was good. But I did

not participate in that conference because my English was not good enough to present at a conference. When I think back now, I might have excluded myself. Generally, I do not undervalue myself, but at that time my English was not as good as now. Extract 2 (Nomin – interview 1)

Nomin's dissatisfaction with her English proficiency was the reason she had not wanted to participate in a conference which would have provided an opportunity to learn and establish networks. There was a mismatch between this opportunity and her disposition to take it. Her decision not to participate in the conference provides evidence of the fact that the already disadvantaged are further disadvantaged or that prior exclusions lead to further exclusions (Bourdieu, 1984).

Furthermore, Ariun said that she did not have networks in Ulaanbaatar except for her classmates (interview 2). She was concerned about her 'social fit' (Reay *et al.*, 2009: 1111). Her friends on Facebook were her university classmates with just a few from her rural secondary school. In fact, she was the only participant who was concerned about her future:

> After the group discussion I felt ashamed of myself. Those students all work and study at the same time. I do not work. I do not study well like some other rural students who had not studied English during their schooling. I am lazy with my study. Maybe I cannot learn English. My parents want me to study well. Especially, my mother wants me to learn English well and go to the US to study. I cannot take TOEFL. After the graduation, I may go back to my town and get a job there. For me, it is hard to get a job in the city. Extract 3 (Ariun – interview 2)

She blamed herself for not gaining enough cultural capital to be employed in the city and to study abroad. I think that this was caused by her limited cultural and social capital and her lack of agency, 'the strategic making and remaking of selves, identities, activities, relationships, cultural tools and resources and histories, as embedded within relations of power' (Moje & Lewis, 2007: 18). In addition, her feeling of shame because of her relatively poor English proficiency was a form of 'linguistic shame stemming from violation of social boundaries symbolised by language' (Liyanage & Canagarajah, this volume). Ariun's English proficiency level and her limited social capital may have also influenced her concern about her future and her self-doubt. As aspirations are never individual (Appadurai, 2004), if she had had more friends or networks in Ulaanbaatar, she may have been more optimistic about her future and enjoyed matching aspirations. Though Ariun wanted to improve her English she was not as 'agentive' as Nomin, another participant from a rural area who had not studied English at school. In fact, Ariun was the only participant who had internet access on her mobile but she used it just for Yahoo Messenger.

By contrast, Alimaa's ways with digital technologies were beneficial for promoting her English and digital literacies further and doing well in her studies, as English and digital literacies were privileged cultural capital in the field of higher education in Mongolia:

> Mostly, I got high scores for my assignments and coursework thanks to my English and the internet. Students said that this was because Alimaa was a good student. Actually, I could get information quickly using the internet and my English. Whoever gets the information first, he or she walks a step ahead of the others. But today everybody is using English and the internet. So now a person who uses them wisely can move ahead of the others. Searching for information online has become 'an art'. Choosing the right keywords, knowledge about the reliable websites and our English proficiency *are all necessary for the use of the internet*. Extract 4 (Alimaa – techno-biography)

In addition, her communication in English with her friends demonstrated her cultural capital, which in turn may have created opportunities for her to extend her networks to English-speaking peers and thus improve her English. In this case, her cultural capital was converted into social capital:

> It is easy to write in English when I communicate with my friends. Because of this some girls seem to be making themselves distant from me. Also, this was noticeable when we are engaged with the messenger conference. When we type quickly and in English, some people cannot catch up with us. Extract 5 (Alimaa – interview 1)

Who you know mattered in this case, as Alimaa could gain an advantage by promoting her English and digital literacies through her personal networks or social capital. She sometimes discussed and collaborated on her assignments with her friends. In fact, evidence of a trend emerged in the analysis, that some of the participants socialised with the people who knew English or were from the same background. Alimaa, Bat and Saraa mostly used English in their social networking on Facebook while the other participants did not.

Bat was critical about how some students who had internet access at home used it. In particular, he was against excessive chatting:

> Based on my observation of my classmates, I think that some students just use the internet for chatting while some students do not have internet access at home because of their financial circumstances. In this sense, I have been excluded. Sometimes I come home quite late after using the internet for a while. But there is no negative impact on me. Importantly, I use the internet in proper ways. Most students from the rural areas are excluded from internet use. They do not use the internet based on its usefulness for them; instead, they just check their email and chat. Extract 6 (Bat – interview 2)

He felt excluded sometimes for not being available on the internet as he could not afford a home internet connection. He suggested that students should use the internet appropriately whether they had abundant or limited internet access and that they needed to be more digitally literate. Because of his limited internet access, Bat had developed a task-oriented or goal-oriented digital habitus in which he enacted 'a taste for the necessary' (Robinson, 2009).

Clearly, the participants' offline inequalities such as social background, whether they were from urban, suburban or rural areas, significantly influenced their access to English and digital literacies. Some participants expressed their views on this:

> During my first and second year at university, I did not have internet access at home. At that time when I heard some students talk to each other about what they had learnt on the internet I understood how the internet was important. At that time I was excluded. I felt disappointed as I could not keep up with the current news or information. Now I feel different. Extract 7 (Saraa – interview 1)

> As a rural kid, computers were alien creatures to me until I was required to take a course in basic computer skills in my freshman year. I remember spending hours in an internet café (not accessing the net) trying to do the assignment which asked me to make an exact duplicate of a page that our teacher had prepared in Microsoft Word using many different formats. Just typing the text was hard enough for me. Extract 8 (Bat – techno-biography)

According to the participants, there was a divide in using computers and the internet amongst the university students, depending on their wealth, social background and, especially, their educational background. Their previous educational background, that is, their schooling, influenced their digital literacy practices, particularly their English language knowledge. For example, after finishing primary school, Naraa was transferred by her parents from a suburban school to one in the city centre. She had discovered that there were many differences in the quality of teaching between the suburban and city centre schools. Some students from rural areas were not able to study English because the language was not taught in their schools. I think these were taken-for-granted inequalities amongst the university students in the field of higher education resulting from the urban-suburban-rural discrepancies in Mongolia.

Discussion and Conclusion

Unequal internet access and resource gaps in urban, suburban and rural areas in contemporary Mongolia at first glance appear to be largely material divisions. However, the resources or capital to which students had access (including territorial location, social networks, and family and educational background) shaped their engagement with the internet, facilitating and facilitated by English proficiency, and contributing to distinctive digital literacy practices. In this study, as capital attracts capital: the participants who were already advantaged in terms of using English and digital literacies were more likely to develop themselves further, accumulate more capital and fitted in the field of higher education academically and socially. However, some students from suburban districts in Ulaanbaatar and rural areas with limited access to English and digital literacy practices experienced the deepening of existing inequality and further marginalisation. They may have had difficulties 'fitting in socially' (Reay *et al.*, 2009) and crossing 'language boundaries which can involve complex emotional states (such as shaming) which shape individual desires and decisions about language learning and use' (Liyanage & Canagarajah, this volume). This could also be seen as a form of symbolic violence, which 'may take the form of people being denied resources, treated as inferior or being limited in terms of realistic aspirations' (Webb *et al.*, 2002: xvi), and attributed to their social backgrounds. Nomin's decision not to participate in a conference because of her English and Ariun's self-blame regarding her English proficiency as well as her concern about her future are examples of symbolic violence that were exercised by these participants because of their perceptions of their English proficiency. In addition, as Johnson *et al.* (2008) argue, symbolic violence is reinforced through students unable to access the internet because they live in lower socioeconomic areas where the internet is not available, yet they need the internet to complete their assignments. In this case, Naraa was also subjected to symbolic violence as she could not have the internet at home because she lived in a *ger* district where a connection was not available. However, this marginalisation seemed to make some participants more strategic in their digital literacy practices. Nomin's endeavour to improve her English on the internet was evidence of this. Developing agency, thus, seems to be critical in both learning and in raising the aspirations of young people.

The internet was used in a number of ways by the participants; in particular, its use as a form of embodied cultural capital became routine in their everyday lives. Certainly, to engage with digital literacy practices on the internet the participants needed to be digitally literate and proficient in English. As a result, their English and digital literacies had symbolic value for the participants and helped them to access and accumulate all types of capital. It is noteworthy here that all case study participants, except Ariun, earned money during their university years using their English and digital literacies working as tourist guides, doing some translation work and teaching English. On the whole, the students appropriated their English and digital literacies to access different types of capital and accrue them for achieving their aspirations. They were exposed to a number of opportunities thanks to these literacies. Most importantly, they were able to develop themselves further by learning, by being tactical and by being resilient to some of the constraints associated with their background. These literacies were the gateways for accessing resources and social status, and transgressing social and language boundaries for the participants.

In addition, the study indicates that just having digital technologies does not determine real access to computers and the internet. Though Ariun had a personal laptop with free wireless connection, she did not engage with digital literacy practices as much as the other participants. The quality and nature of access to digital technologies (Snyder *et al.*, 2004) and relevant skills, knowledge, language and social support to use them meaningfully (Warschauer, 2003) are important to overcome the digital divide and lessen inequalities amongst students. Although the urban/rural and digital/non-digital divides in terms of physically accessing the internet have weakened in Mongolia, now it is gaining new dimensions, that is, inequalities of skills and meaningful usage, e.g. searching, evaluating, selecting, appropriating and adapting online information and benefitting from it.

Although the study highlights the important role of family income and students' prior education and experiences with digital technologies in their digital literacy practices, it is important to ensure that university students have equal opportunities to use the internet. Higher education in Mongolia needs to take measures for building an educational infrastructure that will support students' formal and informal learning. Some of the participants in this study were marginalised as they could not afford the technologies. At the very least, if such students could get access to the internet at university, it would minimise their marginalisation and eventually would contribute to addressing issues of social justice and equality. Marginalised and disadvantaged students are exposed to symbolic violence in Mongolian higher education as they are excluded from a variety of materials and resources on the internet for doing their assignments and supporting their learning. Of course, it is neither possible nor desirable to mandate that students use the internet in exactly the same way, yet they must at the very least be informed about how to use the internet critically and effectively for their academic studies and for their personal development.

The study also indicates a need to ameliorate inequalities in digital access among Mongolian schoolchildren in urban, suburban and rural settings. Studies at individual, classroom and institutional levels in these contexts are required to extend the discussion initiated in this study of how some students from rural backgrounds struggle more than their peers from other backgrounds in fitting into higher education both academically and socially. Importantly, such research will address issues of social justice. Clearly, higher education provision in Mongolia needs to be taken seriously by the relevant institutions and the government as higher education contributes to social mobility and equal opportunities for students. To do so requires recognising that even as territorial and social boundaries are being increasingly crossed and redefined by new digital practices, some long-standing divides, such as that between rural areas and the city, are in fact strengthened by the new dimensions of information technologic and linguistic globalisation.

Note

(1) Traditional dwelling in Mongolia, which is a portable round-shaped felt tent, used by the nomads for centuries. Many Mongolians still live in *ger* districts that have no plumbing and do not meet sanitary requirements, having to buy drinking water from local water stations.

References

Appadurai, A. (2004) The capacity to aspire: Culture and the terms of recognition. In V. Rao and M. Walton (eds) *Culture and Public Action* (pp. 59–84). California: Stanford University Press.
Barton, D., Ivanic, R., Appleby, Y., Hodge, R. and Tusting, K. (2007) *Literacy, Lives and Learning.* London & New York: Routledge.
Billé, F. (2010) Sounds and scripts of modernity: Language ideologies and practices in contemporary Mongolia. *Inner Asia* 12, 231–252.
Bourdieu, P. (1984) *Distinction: A Social Critique of the Judgement of Taste* (R. Nice, Trans.). Cambridge, MA: Harvard University Press.
Bourdieu, P. (1991) *Language and Symbolic Power* (G. Raymond and M. Adamson, Trans.). Cambridge, MA: Harvard University Press.
Bourdieu, P. (1993) Concluding remarks: For a sociogenetic understanding of intellectual works. In C. Calhoun, E. LiPuma and M. Postone (eds) *Bourdieu: Critical Perspectives* (pp. 263–275). Chicago: Polity Press.
Cohen, R. (2005) English in Mongolia. *World Englishes* 24 (2), 203–216.
Dovchin, S. (2011) Performing identity through language: The local practices of urban youth populations in post-socialist Mongolia. *Inner Asia* 13, 315–333.
Dovchin, S. (2015) Language, multiple authenticities and social media: The online language practices of university students in Mongolia. *Journal of Sociolinguistics* 19 (4), 437–459.
Government of Mongolia (2008a) *Millennium Development Goals-based Comprehensive National Development Strategy of Mongolia: 2007–2021.* Ulaanbaatar, Mongolia.
Government of Mongolia (2008b) *Nationwide Programme on English Language Education in 2009–2020.* Retrieved 1 March 2015, from http://www.mecs.gov.mn
Green, J. and Bloome, D. (1997) Ethnography and ethnographers of and in education: A situated perspective. In J. Flood, S.B. Heath and D. Lapp (eds) *Handbook of Research on Teaching Literacy through the Communicative and Visual Arts* (pp. 181–202). New York: Macmillan.
International Organisation for Migration (2018) *Mongolia: Internal Migration Study.* Ulaanbaatar, Mongolia.
Internet World Statistics (2017) *Internet World Users by Language.* Retrieved 15 December 2017, from http://www.internetworldstats.com/
Johnson, C.A. (2003) *Exploring the digital divide in Mongolia: Who uses the Internet and what factors affect its use?* Paper presented at the Bridging the digital divide:

Equalizing access to Information and Communication Technologies, Dalhousie University, Halifax, Nova Scotia.

Johnson, N.F., Macdonald, D.C. and Brabazon, T.M. (2008) Rage against the machine? Symbolic violence in E-learning supported tertiary education. *E-Learning* 5 (3), 275–283.

Marav, D. (2014) *We Can Do Anything in the Cyberworld Except Conceive: Mongolian University Students' Everyday Digital Literacy Practices*. (Unpublished doctoral dissertation). Monash University, Australia.

Marav, D. (2016) Mongolian students' digital literacy practices: The interface between English and the internet. *Papers in Applied Linguistics* 55 (2), 293–317.

Marzluf, P. (2012) Words, borders, herds: Post-socialist English and nationalist language identities in Mongolia. *International Journal of the Sociology of Language* 218, 195–216.

Moje, E. and Lewis, C. (2007) Examining opportunities to learn literacy: The role of critical sociocultural literacy research. In C. Lewis, P. Enciso and E. Moje (eds) *Reframing Sociocultural Research on Literacy: Identity, Agency, and Power* (pp. 15–48). Mahwah, NJ: Lawrence Erlbaum Associates.

National Statistical Office of Mongolia (2018) *The Statistics on Population of Mongolia*. Retrieved 01 March 2019, from http://www.en.nso.mn

Pennycook, A. (2007) *Global Englishes and Transcultural Flows*. London and New York: Routledge.

Reay, D., Crozier, G. and Clayton, J. (2009) 'Strangers in paradise'? Working-class students in elite universities. *Sociology* 43 (6), 1103–1121.

Robinson, L. (2009) A taste for the necessary: A Bourdieuian approach to digital inequality. *Information, Communication & Society* 12 (4), 488–507.

Snyder, I., Angus, L. and Sutherland-Smith, W. (2004) 'They're the future and they're going to take over everywhere': ICTs, literacy and disadvantage. In I. Snyder & C. Beavis (eds) *Doing Literacy Online: Teaching, Learning, and Playing in an Electronic World* (pp. 225–244). Cresskill, NJ: Hampton Press.

Swanborn, P.G. (2010) *Case Study Research: What, Why and How?* London: Sage.

Warschauer, M. (2003) *Technology and Social Inclusion: Rethinking the Digital Divide*. Cambridge, MA: The MIT Press.

Webb, J., Schirato, T. and Danaher, G. (2002) *Understanding Bourdieu*. Australia: Allen & Unwin.

Yin, R.K. (2012) *Applications of Case Study Research*. London: Sage.

Section 2: Language, Ideology and Inequality

4 A Cycle of Shame: How Shaming Perpetuates Language Inequalities in Dakar, Senegal

Teresa Speciale

Linguistic shaming has long been a crucial aspect of assimilation policies around the world. In colonial African schooling, linguistic shaming took the form of both physical and psychological punishments. If students were heard speaking a language other than the colonial language, they would be beaten and oftentimes made to wear or carry a 'symbol' that marked them as linguistic transgressors; the symbol ranged from a button to a bone to a sign that read 'I am stupid' or 'I am a donkey' (wa Thiong'o, 1994: 11). These methods continued widely in many African countries until the 1990s and can still be observed today in some schools (Alidou *et al.*, 2006).

This chapter examines the complex role shaming plays in the continuing construction and promotion of the belief that African languages are inferior to European languages and therefore not appropriate for educational settings. Drawing on data collected during a 16-month ethnographic study,[1] I focus on findings from the Bilingual Academy of Senegal (BAS), a private secondary French-English bilingual school in the capital of Dakar. I use a decoloniality lens (Mignolo, 2012; Ndlovu-Gatsheni, 2015) to contextualize and bring together Bourdieu's (1991) Euro-centric practice theory and affect theory (Lutz & White, 1986) with the complicated colonial histories and legacies that continue to affect how different languages (and by extension their speakers) are valued throughout Africa and in Senegal in particular. I argue that BAS's strict language policies, which included the explicit banning of African languages, in combination with students' rather privileged backgrounds, leads to a cycle of shaming wherein dominant language ideologies, hierarchies and inequalities continue to be reproduced and accepted as legitimate and inevitable.

The Senegalese Context

Senegal is a former French colony that gained its independence in 1960. Colonial language policies elevated French above local Senegalese languages and instilled an institutional and ideological system of linguistic-socioeconomic hierarchies. However, the acquisition of French was reserved for specific elite groups through formal schooling (Errington, 2001). Colonial linguistic-socioeconomic hierarchies continue to this day, with French designated as the official language and sole medium of instruction at all levels of the public education system and government administration. While the constitution states that national languages[2] can be used in schools, in practice they are rarely used in any official capacity.

Despite its status as the official language, French is only spoken by approximately 20% of the population and is mostly used in urban areas by a wealthy, well-educated minority (Leclerc, 2015). In contrast, Wolof is spoken by over 90% of the population, and Pulaar and Sereer are spoken by around 26% and 11% respectively (Leclerc, 2015). All of these languages have various dialects and forms depending on geographic region. For example, Wolof has a variety referred to as 'Urban Wolof' that is markedly different from that spoken in more rural areas because it integrates French vocabulary and grammar into Wolof speech (McLaughlin, 2008). In the capital of Dakar, Urban Wolof is used much more frequently than French. Even in public schools, where French is the sole official language of instruction, it is quite common to hear Wolof spoken in hallways, between classes, and oftentimes teachers will codeswitch between French and Wolof when teaching lessons.

Apart from the official and national languages, there is also a growing demand for English acquisition. However, only Senegal's wealthier families are able to afford English medium education. This demand coincides with a dramatic increase in recent years in the number of private schools in Senegal.[3] Although the majority of these private schools are French-only and follow the State's official language policy, bilingual schools are proliferating. Secular[4] private bilingual schools are predominantly French-English and are highly sought after. Students are drawn to these schools because speaking English is a marker of being fashionable and sophisticated (Ngom, 2006), while parents think of English and French as maximizing opportunities for social and economic mobility (Speciale, 2012). In the past, French-English private schools primarily catered to expatriates living and working in Senegal, whose employers covered most if not all of the high tuition fees. Today, while French-English private schools generally have higher fees than French-medium private schools, the increasing number of medium-fee French-English schools, such as the Bilingual Academy of Senegal, is providing access to students whose families previously could not afford this type of language education.

Theoretical Framework

To understand the role of linguistic shaming in the reproduction and acceptance of the belief that African languages are inferior to European languages, I apply a decoloniality lens to Bourdieu's practice theory and affect theory in order to place the practices of linguistic shaming within larger historical, cultural, and political-economic post-colonial systems.

Decoloniality theorists aim to disentangle and overcome the 'logic of coloniality underneath the rhetoric of modernity' that continues to dominate and oppress former colonies (Mignolo, 2005: 10). Arising out of colonialism, 'coloniality' encompasses 'long-standing patterns of power ... that define culture, labor, intersubjective relations, and knowledge production' (Maldonado-Torres, 2007: 243). Decoloniality reveals the larger historical, cultural, and political-economic systems that 'continue to produce alienated Africans that are socialized into hating Africa that produced them and liking Europe and America that reject them' (Ndlovu-Gatsheni, 2015: 489) and urges us to place the linguistic shaming practices at schools like BAS within that context.

Using the decoloniality lens I draw on Bourdieu's practice theory to understand how everyday school practices reproduce dominant hierarchies and ideologies. I draw specifically on Bourdieu's concept of capital, which is a 'set of actually usable resources and powers' (Bourdieu, 1984: 114) that are socially and interactionally determined; they are not fixed and may vary depending on the context (Lareau & Weininger, 2003). Bourdieu divides capital into four types: economic, cultural, social, and symbolic. Economic capital refers to any kind of monetary or economic resources. Social capital refers to a person's networks and connections that can be mobilized to acquire other forms of capital. Cultural capital encompasses different types of 'culturally specific "competence[s]"' (Weininger, 2005: 87), such as ways of speaking, behaving, and dressing. Lastly, symbolic capital is the recognition, or legitimation, that an individual or object receives from a group.

Language is an important source and index of cultural capital. Linguistic capital refers to both knowledge of the 'legitimate' language and the ability to use this language in the correct 'linguistic market' or context (Bourdieu, 1991). The education system is a key site where recognition of legitimate language competence is instilled in students because, as Bourdieu (1991) points out, schools have a 'monopoly ... in the reproduction of the [linguistic] market without which the social value of the linguistic competence, its capacity to function as linguistic capital, would cease to exist' (1991: 57).

I add to Bourdieu's practice theory literature on affect theory to understand how emotions – in particular negative emotions such as shame – are used to propagate and sustain inequalities. As anthropologists have demonstrated, emotions are cultural and social (Lutz & White,

1986). People learn feeling: what to feel; when and where it is appropriate to feel or to demonstrate emotions; what types of emotions are appropriate to what types of people; and how emotions should feel. Furthermore, negative emotions, like shame, can be used to reinforce social inequalities. Connecting this to Bourdieu's theory, Bartlett (2007) argues that 'shame feelings [are] intimately connected to [people's] sense of linguistic capital and, more broadly, cultural capital' (2007: 551) because more privileged patterns of language use (e.g. accent, dialect) are rewarded, while other patterns are seen as unacceptable or inappropriate.

This framework places BAS' language policies and shaming practices within the structures and histories particular to the postcolonial context of Senegal. It highlights how dominant forms of speaking, knowing, and being operate within the classroom and the school, and how these daily practices serve to sustain and reproduce larger structures of inequality.

The Bilingual Academy of Senegal and Research Methods

The Bilingual Academy of Senegal (BAS) is a private secondary (6th to 12th grades) French-English school located in the capital of Dakar. It is owned by a white European couple, the Joneses, who opened the school in the early 2000s.[5] Madame Cardoso, a Senegalese teacher who has been at the school since it opened, serves as acting director for the majority of the year when the owners are in Europe. Most of the teachers at the school are Senegalese. Despite most of them having decades of teaching experience and advanced degrees in their fields, all of them are hired only on a part-time basis. In contrast, a small group of three to four foreign teachers (mainly American) are hired on a full-time basis to teach English classes at all levels (from 6th to 12th grade), as well as math and science in 6th and 7th grades (in English). These foreign teachers are not required to have any teaching experience because the Joneses believe that native speakers are better teachers because they will model 'proper' accents, grammar and language usage for students.

At the time of fieldwork in 2016, there were approximately 250 students at the school, the majority of whom were Senegalese. A smaller number came from other African countries, and some had dual citizenship in France or the United States. Most of the students' parents worked in embassies or in international organizations; others had professions such as doctor or lawyer. All of the students spoke French fluently before entering the school in 6th grade, which was a prerequisite for acceptance to BAS. Most students spoke little to no prior English. However, due to BAS' strict language policies and intensive language study, as they advanced in the school students in higher grades developed almost complete English fluency.

Primary research methods for this study included observations across multiple school spaces such as classrooms, the cafeteria, school courtyards, and hallways; interviews with students, teachers, administrators, and parents; and a student questionnaire. At BAS, over 100 hours of classroom observations, 47 interviews, and 115 student questionnaires were conducted.

The Global Logic of BAS

The culture of the Bilingual Academy of Senegal was shaped extensively by a desire to make the students 'global' so that they could succeed academically, professionally, and socially. At BAS, success was largely defined as gaining English fluency and attending university in Europe or North America. The school's mission was described by Mrs Jones as trying to make the students 'citizens of the world who respect other people and can be comfortable anywhere in the world because they will be able to go and ask sensible questions and realize people are going to be different and not make faux pas.' Though framed in the benevolent language of helping the students, this 'global' logic masked an underlying ideology about what it does and does not mean to be global – namely to be European, not African.

Two key processes were at work in defining this global logic at BAS. First, there was consistent shaming and devaluing of students' use of African languages.[6] Students' language use was strictly policed. They were not allowed to speak African languages anywhere in the school. Additionally, specific days of the week were designated 'English days' or 'French days', where students had to speak the designated language or be punished. One student, who speaks Wolof, explained what happened if students were caught speaking African languages:

Teresa: I never hear the students speaking Wolof.
Student: Yeah, because we don't have the right to.
Teresa: What happens if the teachers hear you speaking Wolof?
Student: You get in trouble.
Teresa: What happens?
Student: I know that I got caught speaking Wolof a lot of times and all you have to do is you have to clean the tables at the cafeteria. And people are really gross when they eat at the cafeteria so it's not pleasant.

Cleaning the cafeteria tables was embarrassing for many of the students who were accustomed to having servants clean up after them. Additionally, the form of this punishment was especially noticeable because it was the only kind that consisted of physical labor; all other forms of punishment at the school were more passive, such as writing a paper or sitting in detention. Following in the colonial education tradition of having students carry a 'symbol', cleaning the cafeteria tables publicly marked students as linguistic transgressors because it was a punishment reserved only for language infractions. In this way, shaming was used to further legitimize European (i.e. colonial) languages within the school, as students were rewarded for mastering them and simultaneously punished for using African languages.

The second part of the process of becoming global was the transformation of cultural and linguistic 'Europeanisation into an aspiration' (Quijano, 2007: 169). At BAS there was a clear distinction between 'global languages' such as French and English, and 'non-global' African languages. When asked if the school made any effort to incorporate African languages, Mrs Jones responded,

> No ... because the parents don't really want it. The parents say we send our children here to learn English and speak French. We can speak in our Wolof or Sereer, whatever it is, at home. And they say we know these are not world languages, and they say we'd like them to keep up their culture but this is not a priority for us. The priority is that they learn good French and good English. And so, that's one of the reasons. But also because we would agree with them [the parents].

Indeed, parents' views of the school were that its purpose was to give their children the linguistic capital necessary to study and work outside of Senegal. One parent compared the linguistic capital her child was gaining from learning multiple languages to a piggy bank, where 'you just add value to your life'. At BAS, therefore, knowledge and mastery of French and English were framed as crucial if students were to succeed; but this success was defined and understood within unequal structures that devalued and shamed non-Western ways of speaking, knowing, and being (Maldonado-Torres, 2007; Quijano, 2007).

A Cycle of Shaming

The students at BAS all came from families with relatively high socioeconomic status. This provided them access to a school like BAS, which imparted them with linguistic capital unavailable to the majority of Senegalese students. However, while BAS students were near the top of the linguistic-socioeconomic hierarchy within Senegal, their positioning became muddied when extended to a more global context. As students attempted to make sense of where they fit in within more global hierarchies, they often utilized the global linguistic logic of BAS to differentiate themselves from others who they viewed as having less linguistic, economic, and cultural capital. In this way, a cycle of shaming was created as students attempted to 'assert or construct [their] superiority' (Bartlett, 2007: 554) in efforts to overcome the tension between trying to be global while African.

This shaming cycle was clearly evident in discussions about accent. At BAS it was not enough to be fluent in French or English; in order to truly be global and successful a person must also have a 'native-speaker' accent. This belief about the importance of accent informed school hiring policies, with only native-English speakers hired to teach English classes, even if they had no teaching experience. Students echoed this belief, with one student sharing, 'English-speaking Senegalese people, it's not that their English is bad, but it's not the same English than those that are in America ... So if you listen to the people speak in my class you would think they are native speakers because they have the accent, most of them.' This student is working to differentiate himself from others who have similar linguistic capital. He is mimicking the shaming techniques that have become normalized at BAS by critiquing the accents of others; in doing so, he is legitimating and reproducing the ideology that native-speaker (i.e. Western) ways of speaking are superior to African ways of speaking (Shohamy, 2006).

The shaming cycle was also evident when students talked about the use of African languages in education. Following BAS' global logic, students generally opposed the inclusion of these languages, citing the fact that they are not global. For example, one student said, 'I think that if you're teaching just Wolof as a language, I don't think that's really relevant because you need to admit the fact that Wolof is a language that's only spoken in Senegal'. These attitudes about African languages also extended to their speakers. For example, when asked what languages she speaks with her friends, one student said, 'When you're out with people we speak French mostly, because I think Wolof is more for people that are kind of not too into school.' When asked to explain what she meant by this, she expanded,

> It's like the people that didn't go to school, the workers, the boutiquiers [shop workers], people outside. And then people that also are in public schools. I realize that they speak much more Wolof than French. So mostly them. ... If you hear someone speaking Wolof, that either means that they're in the public school, or their family is really traditional or large or something.

This student is clearly linking language to behaviors and life circumstances that are antithetical to how success is understood at BAS, such as not working hard in school and being 'traditional'. She is also speaking to larger linguistic-socioeconomic hierarchies by associating Wolof speakers with workers and people in public school.

Interestingly, however, this student speaks both Wolof and French with her family. Because this student is learning in an environment where African languages are shamed and devalued, she worked to differentiate herself from others who speak African languages by shaming those who do not have access to the linguistic, cultural, and economic capital that she does. This cycle of shaming reinforces and reproduces dominant hierarchies and ideologies by both unquestionably praising European languages and ways of speaking as superior and reducing African languages to something that must be 'chase[ed] out of the mouth, ears and minds of African students born into these languages' (Nyamnjoh, 2012: 140).

Discussion and Conclusion

Linguistic shaming policies and practices help to sustain dominant hierarchies and, as illustrated in Liyanage and Canagarajah's chapter in this volume, help establish both membership and exclusion in social groups. Unlike the I-Kiribati Liyanage and Canagarajah worked with, who shamed others in order to protect local community solidarity, BAS students used linguistic shaming in order to announce their membership in a global community. Through shaming, ideologies about which languages are appropriate and beneficial come to be viewed as legitimate and inevitable, and inequalities are understood as the price of being global.

The students at BAS held precarious positions within linguistic hierarchies, both benefitting from and being hindered by larger post- and neo-colonial structures of inequality. By applying a decoloniality lens to Bourdieu's (1984) theory of capital and social reproduction, the precariousness and contextual specificity of their privileged status is foregrounded. The economic, cultural, and social capital of these Senegalese students' parents and families provided access to a bilingual education that equipped them with the linguistic capital necessary to engage in a more globalized world; in turn, reinforcing their elite status within local symbolic and material hierarchies. However, because Bourdieu's theory is based on class-ed European contexts, it does not take into account how ongoing coloniality of power (Quijano, 2007) positions students as they move across symbolic as well as geographic borders.

Students' precarious statuses are illustrated in the different ways acceptance to and attendance at universities in Europe and North America were perceived and understood by differently positioned participants. While the school, students, and their families read attending global universities as a great accomplishment (which it was, no doubt) and a marker of privilege in Senegal, the universities that students attended were largely non-elite in global perspectives and rankings. For example, one of the school's American English teachers described the universities as representing 'first world mediocrity'. Students' relative privilege did not persist beyond the geographic borders of Senegal, becoming uncertain and precarious in globalized university spaces.

Through its policies, BAS reified strict social and symbolic linguistic and cultural boundaries. Students straddled many linguistic and cultural borders, and therefore had the opportunity to draw on and create new and hybrid modes of thinking, knowing, and being (Anzaldúa, 1987). But by framing success as beyond their immediate borders, students saw little benefit in learning or engaging with their local languages. As a result, large portions of students' linguistic resources came to be reframed as handicaps to future success.

Shame was a central tool in the construction of the global logic of BAS. As shown in this chapter, shaming is a complex process whereby an individual may simultaneously feel shame and shame others. The culture of BAS was such that students' global identities were celebrated, while their African identities came to be associated primarily with shame. This split carried over to students' lives outside of school, where they would shame others who portrayed outward markers of being African, by claiming that they are traditional or not interested in schooling. Students passed the shame from themselves to others by attempting to distinguish themselves as modern and global. In this way, a cycle of shaming was created and linguistic-socioeconomic hierarchies and inequalities continue to be further legitimated and perpetuated.

Notes

(1) This chapter is based on a larger 16-month ethnographic research project focused on students at three private secondary schools in Dakar, Senegal with different languages of instruction (French-English, French-only and French-Arabic).
(2) In Article I of the 1971 Senegalese constitution, Jola, Malinka, Pulaar, Sereer, Soninké and Wolof were deemed national languages. In 2001, Article I was expanded to state that 'all codified languages are national languages.' For a language to be considered officially codified, it must have a defined writing system and an elementary grammar. To date, 21 languages have been codified.
(3) All but two of the fourteen regions of Senegal have seen a reduction in the number of public schools. In the capital of Dakar, over half of all registered schools are categorized as private (Sénégal Ministère de l'Education Nationale, 2013). Private school enrollments also continue to rise, with private secondary school enrollments increasing from 65,000 students in 2000 to 160,000 in 2012 (World Bank, 2016).
(4) In addition to secular (non-religious) French-English schools, there are also a large number of religious French-Arabic schools.
(5) Due to IRB restrictions, the name of the school and all participants have been changed. Additionally, some of the identifying characteristics of the school have been modified or omitted.
(6) Because not all of the students were Senegalese, I refer to their home languages as African languages.

References

Alidou, H., Aliou, B., Brock-Utne, B., Diallo, Y.S., Heugh, K. and Wolff, H.E. (2006) *Optimizing Learning and Education in Africa – The Language Factor: A Stock-Taking Research on Mother Tongue and Bilingual Education in Sub-Saharan Africa.* ADEA, Paris.
Anzaldúa, G. (1987) *Borderlands/La Frontera: The New Mestiza.* San Francisco, CA: Aunt Lute Book Company.

Bartlett, L. (2007) Literacy, speech and shame: The cultural politics of literacy and language in Brazil. *International Journal of Qualitative Studies in Education* 20 (5), 547–563.

Bourdieu, P. (1984) *Distinction: A Social Critique of the Judgement of Taste*. Cambridge, MA: Harvard University Press.

Bourdieu, P. (1991) *Language and Symbolic Power*. In J.B. Thompson (ed.) Oxford: Basil Blackwell Ltd.

Errington, J. (2001) Colonial linguistics. *Annual Review of Anthropology* 30, 19–39.

Lareau, A. and Weininger, E. (2003) Cultural capital in educational research: A critical assessment. *Theory and Society* 32, 567–606.

Leclerc, J. (2015) 'Senegal' in L'aménagement linguistique dans le monde, Quebec, TLFQ, Université Laval. Retrieved from http://www.tlfq.ulaval.ca/axl/afrique/senegal.htm. Accessed 16 October 2019.

Lutz, C. and White, G.M. (1986) The anthropology of emotions. *Annual Review of Anthropology* 15, 405–436.

Maldonado-Torres, N. (2007) On the coloniality of being: Contributions to the Development of a Concept. *Cultural Studies* 21 (2–3), 240–270.

McLaughlin, F. (2008) The ascent of Wolof as an urban vernacular and national lingua franca in Senegal. In Vigouroux, C.B. and Mufwene, S.S. (eds) *Globalization and Language Vitality: Perspectives from Africa* (pp. 142–170). London: Continuum International Publishing Group.

Mignolo, W.D. (2005) *The Idea of Latin America*. Malden, MA: Blackwell Publishing.

Mignolo, W.D. (2012) *Local Histories/Global Designs*. Princeton, NJ: Princeton University Press.

Ndlovu-Gatsheni, S.J. (2015) Decoloniality as the future of Africa. *History Compass* 13 (10), 485–496.

Ngom, F. (2006) Loanwords in the Senegalese speech community: Their linguistic features and sociolinguistic significance. In P. Nowak and P. Nowakowski (eds) *Language, Communication, Information* (pp. 103–113). Poznan, Poland: Sorus Publishers.

Nyamnjoh, F.B. (2012) 'Potted plants in greenhouses': A critical reflection on the resilience of colonial education in Africa. *Journal of Asian and African Studies* 47 (2), 129–154.

Quijano, A. (2007) Coloniality and modernity/rationality. *Cultural Studies* 21 (2–3), 168–178.

Seargeant, P. (2009) Language ideology, language theory, and the regulation of linguistic behavior. *Language Sciences* 31 (4), 345–359.

Sénégal Ministère de l'Education Nationale (2013) *Rapport nationale sur la situation de l'éducation*. Dakar, Senegal.

Shohamy, E. (2006) Imagined multilingual schools: How come we don't deliver? In O. García, T. Skutnabb-Kangas and M. Torres-Guzmán (eds) *Imagining Multilingual Schools: Languages in Education and Glocalization* (171–183). Tonawanda, NY: Multilingual Matters Ltd.

Speciale, T. (2012) *Considerations for mother tongue education in African urban contexts: The case of Dakar, Senegal* (Unpublished Master's thesis). The George Washington University.

wa Thiong'o, N. (1994) *Decolonising the Mind: The Politics of Language in African Literature*. Harare, Zimbabwe: Zimbabwe Publishing House Ltd.

Weininger, E.B. (2005) Foundations of Pierre Bourdieu's class analysis. In E.O. Wright (ed.) *Approaches to Class Analysis* (82–118). Cambridge, UK: Cambridge University Press.

World Bank (2016) Senegal: Engaging the private sector in education. SABER Country Report. Washington, DC. Retrieved from: https://openknowledge.worldbank.org/handle/10986/26523. Accessed 16 October 2019.

5 The Role of Shame in Drawing Social Boundaries for Empowerment: ELT in Kiribati

Indika Liyanage and Suresh Canagarajah

> *You don't want to be seen as you are trying to differentiate yourself from everyone else by the fact that you speak a different language. But things are changing you know, I speak openly to my kids in English in public. I have a message to deliver to everyone else ... but I know, behind my back I know the kind of things people are talking about, you know, I'm trying to be different, I'm trying to be a European, I'm trying to be a white. You know, which in an egalitarian context like Kiribati, those are insults. ... One of the most important things in Kiribati life is the avoidance of being shamed ... And one of the things that brings shame to you is when you try to be different from the rest. And I think that's what people are running away from and it's a pity that it's affecting the way they speak English and their confidence in speaking in English.*
> (Wanga: A local, Director of a tertiary education institute in Tarawa)

The experiences of Wanga, a Kiribati local, of social denigration and ridicule because of his attempts to use English sit uneasily with assumptions that English is a universally desirable commodity (Motha & Lin, 2014) in the context of global mobility and interconnectedness in a supposedly borderless world (Ohmae, 1995; Paasi, 2009). The desirability of English underpins much of the pedagogical orientation of English language teaching (ELT). Resistance to learning and use of the language in order to avoid shaming that follows violation of local community precepts, as is the case in Kiribati, is not just a challenge to ELT practitioners to negotiate more locally amenable pedagogies. It alerts the field more generally to the importance of ongoing interrogation of assumptions about language competence, motivation, and pedagogical practice, and to pursue understanding of the salience of symbolic and social boundaries in English language teaching and learning. In contexts of ethnic contact, language is of itself an important and powerful symbolic boundary delineating group membership (Beier & Kroneberg, 2013; Lamont & Molnár, 2002), but it can also be a point of differentiation that expresses social solidarity, emblematic of broader alignment with shared practices and core values that are recognised and widely agreed upon by group members as definitive of group membership. The significance of the liminal experiences of English language learners has not gone unremarked; theorization of identity and language learning (see Norton & Toohey, 2011; Peirce, 1995) has explored the social nature of identity as multiple and a site of struggle through which learners negotiate their relationship with language/s use across a spectrum of desire, ambivalence and resistance (Peirce, 1995).

In the case of the I- Kiribati (the people of Kiribati), attachment to the local language (*te taetae ni Kiribati*) as a social boundary exemplifies the nature of boundaries more generally, that is, as 'a dialectic interplay of processes of internal and external definition' (Lamont & Molnár, 2002: 170). For the I-Kiribati, the boundary between locals and outsiders in terms of language use is represented oppositionally, that is, the use of English is associated with the values and identity of a group of outsiders that are contrary to agreed social principles central to local community membership. Given the option of using English, use of the local language confirms allegiance to local values and differentiation from outsiders. Equally, outsiders recognise this differentiation on the basis of values, but contest the symbolism of language use as the basis for a social boundary that constrains the learning and use of English, and experience difficulty understanding rejection of the consequential opportunities for individual and national development they consider desirable. Because language choice has become symbolic of demarcation of an 'us' from a 'them', ELT and English language learning and use by locals has become a source of tension in Kiribati. To sustain local community values and cohesion, locals who, like Wanga, transgress the boundary by use or promotion of English are threatened with social exclusion through shaming, a practice acknowledged as a social mechanism for institution and maintenance of normative behaviours that construct social boundaries (Lamont *et al.*, 2015). This notion of language learning and use as a form of crossing or transgression of social boundaries poses a number of questions relevant for ELT practitioners.

In this chapter, we analyse how Kiribati nationals and international development workers demonstrate conflicting orientations to shame relating to using and learning English. We begin with a theoretical consideration of shaming as a form of social regulation, and then review some of the extant literature on shame in language learning and the concept of linguistic shame. We draw on interview data to discuss how, while international experts denigrate shame, treat it as backwards and limiting, and seek strategies to move Kiribati people to desire English, the local people treat it as a positive mechanism to affirm community cohesion, regulate cultural change, and manage multilingual repertoires. We argue that their practice of shaming has the potential to counter neoliberal ideologies that are individualistic and materialistic, as introduced by international development agencies on this island nation in the central Pacific Ocean. However, the unresolved tensions in the perspectives of the powerful outsiders and dependent locals lead to confusions in educational priorities and prove somewhat debilitating for the local ELT pedagogies.

Linguistic Shame and Language Teaching/Learning

Shame as an emotion constructed and experienced in and through social practices and participation in discourse communities, and as a powerful influence on language learning and use, aligns with recent more general thinking on the influence of emotions in language learning that argues the socioemotional dimension is central to the process. Researchers and practitioners have historically regarded emotions (or affect in SLA research) as individual variables facilitating or hindering the cognitive activity of language learning (e.g. Krashen theory). Considerable research has been undertaken from a cognitive perspective to attempt to identify or establish cause and effect between emotion (or affect) and learning outcomes, a product-oriented approach that concentrates on individuals in classrooms and that ignores the dynamic interactional, dialogic nature of language learning experiences (Aragão, 2011).

Motha and Lin (2014) explore emotions and language learning in theorizing the role of desire in TESOL, an idea that allows us to explore shame and shaming practices as a constraint potentially competing with or mitigating any desires to learn and use English experienced by I-Kiribati. Like shame, desire is seen as situated, intersubjectively co-constructed and emerging in lived experiences of social, historical, political, institutional, and economic contexts. Motha and Lin (2014) acknowledge that although the desire to experience what English represents or is associated with – identity, prosperity, success, happiness – is central to the endeavour of learning the language, 'it is simultaneously capable of arousing significant internal conflict, ambivalence, repression, and even animosity' (2014: 331) because desire is 'constructed within a complicated constellation of relationships among individuals, institutions, and states' (2014: 344).

We find examples of linguistic shame stemming from social exclusion because of membership of recognized groups, or from violation of social boundaries symbolized by language. That multilinguals can experience shame related to use of a mother tongue instead of a high-status dominant language has been observed in a variety of settings (e.g. Chatzidaki & Maligkoudi, 2012; Coronel-Molina, 1999; McCarty *et al.*, 2006).

More relevant to the situation in Kiribati are instances of shame involving boundary violation, experienced because of use of a powerful, ostensibly desirable language in preference to a local vernacular. In rural Indonesia, users of English outside the classroom are shamed by scorning them as *kebarat-baratan* ('pretending to be a like Westerner') (Lamb & Coleman, 2008), and in Singapore, where English is an official language, Malay-speaking students reported fearing the ridicule of their peers if they used English outside the classroom, accused of portraying themselves as 'one clever person, superior' (Stroud & Wee, 2007: 41). Use of English in some settings in Sri Lanka is stigmatized as *kaduwa* ('sword'), attempting to 'cut down' or diminish interlocutors with a more powerful language (Kandiah, 1979). When use of another, possibly more powerful or dominant language symbolizes not just crossing a boundary, but threatens the dissolution of the boundary and the group it identifies, shaming practices can intensify as they are used to defend ethnic or cultural group identity, as in the instances reported by Pavlenko (2005) in which those failing to transmit a minority language are accused of being 'language traitors' or 'language killers'. These examples of shaming for projecting an out-group identity in violation of local solidarity, or for abandoning the local language in favour of a powerful new language, illustrate how the social consequences of crossing language boundaries can involve complex emotional states which shape individual desires and decisions about language learning and use.

Data

Interview data were collected during a three-year collaborative development project between the Governments of Kiribati and Australia. The first author was a consultant and English language teacher educator throughout this project. Both authors had their own English education in the former British colony of Sri Lanka, are familiar with manifestations of shame in using English in classrooms and society in their own country, and are in a position to understand the postcolonial perspectives of the I-Kiribati community. A balanced representation of local and foreign professionals – three local teachers and three foreign experts – is used here to compare perspectives on shaming practices as a social mechanism for enforcing community cohesion within social boundaries. Local participants (referred to by pseudonyms) were Zameeta, female principal of a High School and English teacher, Wanga, director of a tertiary education institute in Tarawa, and Atang, English teacher at a high school. The foreign experts, all native speakers of English, were John, senior embassy official, and Jill and Elaine, employed as overseas consultants to improve English language and literacy skills. We use selected interview excerpts to present shaming practices in Kiribati and discuss how ELT pedagogy in such circumstances might accommodate the positive aspects of using shaming practices to sustain social boundaries, rather than dismissing shaming practices simply as negative influences on learning and use. Negotiation of how, when and where boundaries of language use can be crossed without abandoning local values and identities might demand reassessment of current conceptions of effective practice, of notions of motivation, and of competence.

Kiribati

One of the poorest nations in the Asia-pacific region (Burnett, 2013; Tisdell, 2000), the nation of Kiribati is a landmass of around 800 square kilometers, comprised of one island and 32 atolls, 12 of which have no permanent inhabitants due to their small size or lack of fresh water (Storey & Hunter, 2010). Kiribati shares the conditions of many other decolonized states; the English language retains status as an official language of administration by a local elite and, in pursuit of development, is promoted as a critical element of participation in global economic growth and activity. Foreign experts and local policymakers alike believe that 'it is realistic to accept that a globalizing society needs an elite workforce highly literate in English' (Lamb & Coleman, 2008: 201) as the means of reaping the promised benefits of free movement of goods and services in a global economy.

This ethic of private benefit and individualism is in sharp contrast to local traditional egalitarian values, but is in practice a continuation of a regime of 'linguistic apartheid' (Orelus, 2011: 15) that followed British colonization and has continued since independence. Development of English literacy in a select few locals for employment in colonial administrative activities (Fanon, 1967) commodified English as political and socioeconomic capital. This disrupted pre-colonial socio-political-economic relations, promoted foreign value systems and practices, and instituted a divisive boundary in relations between colonizer and colonized, and between I-Kiribati themselves. Regulation of access to English, and withholding the language from the majority of the population, established a complex sociolinguistic divide, marked by association of English proficiency and education with foreigners and an elite group of locals, which persists in contemporary Kiribati.

Social Boundaries, Shame and ELT in Kiribati

For foreign experts such as Jill and Elaine, charged with development of English language and literacy, and John, overseeing the expenditure of aid monies that fund their work, the reluctance of I-Kiribati to learn and use English is a frustrating obstacle to achievement of project objectives. Rather than interrogating their own objectives, assumptions or approaches, they attribute their difficulties to the I-Kiribati community value of egalitarianism. More directly, they identify shaming practices of disparagement or denigration of individuals who, by use of the language of outsiders, differentiate themselves and threaten community cohesion by failure to adhere to this value. While the foreign experts recognise these values and practices as constituting points of differentiation that mark a powerful social boundary for the people of Kiribati, they dismiss them as contradictory to what they understand from the perspective of development ideologies to be the best interests of the community. What informs the foreign experts' analyses of the situation is, understandably, their own values, beliefs, practices, and experiences that make it difficult for them to acknowledge or recognise shaming practices as positive behaviour. This is, of course, central to the differentiation between locals and outsiders that the I-Kiribati are determined to perpetuate, for reasons that are discussed in what follows.

The problem that confronts the foreign experts is firstly most visible in the learning and use of English by the I-Kiribati. Although they encounter evidence that many locals have the requisite English proficiency to 'operate in meetings, speak to each other in English, and things like that' (John: 19–20), 'people are reluctant to speak in English to each other' (John: 18–19). Jill observed, for example, that,

> ... some of them would not speak in English in a workshop situation ... because we did a lot of focus groups, when they get into the groups they would completely speak in Kiribati doing the work ... the actual focus group work and when it came to report back it was very difficult to get anyone to speak up ... It was just too confronting for them. They would do it if they could do it in I-Kiribati and a couple of them did ... but they really just didn't feel that they could do it in English. (Jill: 76–85)

Although it is clear that Jill is aware that 'there seems to be a real pressure to speak in I-Kiribati' (126–127), she analyses the behaviour of the local teachers from a conventional SLA perspective of individual variables; the characterisation of using English as 'very difficult' and 'confronting' suggests attribution of the behaviour to, for example, shyness, or to fear that self-perceived inadequacies might lead to embarrassment in the presence of the foreign 'native speaker' expert, a dismissal of local pressures to avoid using English. Given that the workshop participants are English teachers, reluctance to use the language suggests some explanation other than lack of proficiency is warranted.

Jill is cognisant of the fact that there is not only a reluctance to use English, but a corresponding 'real pressure to speak in I-Kiribati'. She acknowledges that the I-Kiribati 'pride themselves on being egalitarian ... and that's a part of their culture they are proud of, that no one is above anybody else. They are all equal' (Jill: 273–282). She is aware of the shaming that occurs when English is used, of 'the rejection of English in the common, you know, "What, do you want to be an imatang (foreigner/white person)?" ... how dare you speak English sort of thing' (Jill: 275–277). As John puts it, 'if you speak English you are trying to raise yourself up above everyone else. You think you are better than everyone else' (John: 149–151). Yet, curiously, Jill remains puzzled that even locals who are proficient in English choose to use their local language: 'Even the people I work with in the office, senior public servants, if they're speaking to each other, they don't speak in English.' (Jill: 506–508)

Elaine's view is that the I-Kiribati claims of egalitarianism are 'actually rubbish, you know, they're not egalitarian at all' (Elaine: 222–230), that there is an 'egalitarian myth' (Elaine: 244). It is clear that shaming practices, and the values they represent, are evident to foreign experts but regarded in ways very different to those of the local I-Kiribati. While they represent a sharp differentiation between two cultural positions, the foreign experts find it difficult to accept that these differences constitute a boundary that I-Kiribati are averse to violating. They are sceptical of the egalitarian ethic and the shaming practices that use ridicule to discourage use of the language of the out-group, preferring instead to dismiss this as 'an excuse for not actually moving ahead' (Elaine: 244–249). Their inclination to Western individualism makes it difficult for them to understand that 'in a traditional society, there is NOTHING more important than one's relationships' (Scheff & Retzinger, 2000: emphasis in the original).

For the I-Kiribati, the practices of shaming those who use English are in fact less about language than about community solidarity and identity. The dilemmas faced by the locals are complicated by the disruption of historical colonial domination and continued presence of expatriate English-speaking aid and development workers; English symbolizes values and a social class system antithetical to a determination to adhere to their own social organisation, which, as Wanga affirms, is 'an egalitarian culture ... we were taught through our socialisation and when we were small that everyone is equal and you cannot be above everyone else' (Wanga: 37–38). Using English violates the egalitarian ethic by appearing 'to make yourself different, not only different but also above everyone else ... (and) ... You don't want to be seen as you are trying to differentiate yourself from everyone else because you speak a different language' (Wanga: 41–42, 140). The difference that is invoked by use of English is potent because it is identified with white European outsiders who have historically asserted higher status and continue to be seen this way by locals. To use English is considered 'Okakanimatang. Mmmm ... like to be a ... European and, you know, the expats, they speak in ... the white people. Matang means white people, you know ... So when you try to speak in English, they will say you, okakanimatang' (Zameeta:

169–179). The shame of behaving like a European or expatriate also reflects a strong movement since independence to distance the country from the ways of the former colonizers, to reassert local character and identity. There was a realization that 'we don't have to be like the British any more. And there is that rush to localize things' (Wanga: 73–74) that is formalized in 'the revised development strategy, how to develop without losing their cultural identity. So obviously it is a high priority for the people and the government' (Jill: 162). Shaming from the I-Kiribati perspective is a positive practice that reflects commitment to community objectives of a shared future in which their distinctive identity is maintained. As part of that identity, egalitarianism is a value realized as not behaving differently to others, rather than as the individualistic focus on equality of opportunity or treatment that informs the views of the foreign experts.

There is evidence that many I-Kiribati are proficient in English, that teachers 'can speak English very well' (Zameeta: 56), that 'in the office it is used as an official language … when we write letters or when we do correspondence, we have to do it in English' (Atang: 62–64), and that qualifications can be obtained (Jill: 285–286). Atang recounts his experiences of I-Kiribati 'that I lived with, when they were here [i.e. in Kiribati] they cannot speak even a word in English but they're now in New Zealand they can express themselves in English' (Atang: 276–278). What is important is that to maintain the egalitarian ethic these things are not flaunted in the community as suggestive of higher status or difference from others. To do so, for example to use English with other locals, is to invite shaming for threatening community solidarity, and '… one of the most important things in Kiribati life is the avoidance of being shamed…' (Wanga: 161). Fear of social exclusion from the vernacular-speaking mainstream makes shaming practices powerful normative mechanisms to make individuals align with community expectations because 'the culture cannot be you know … be abandoned because it is very strong' (Zameeta: 198–213). In a relationally-oriented community, to ignore the social significance of practices such as shaming represents an abandonment of values central to I-Kiribati identity.

While we can identify the positive aspects of shaming practices for locals, there remains the issue of English language learning as a point of tension for locals and foreign experts alike. The Kiribati government – and the general population – acknowledges the value of English as linguistic capital but pursues the dual objectives of development and retention of cultural identity. I-Kiribati 'realise (on one hand) the importance of acquiring English and communicating English but on the other they try and they allow culture to … sort of to control the things and to affect the way they really communicate in English' (Wanga: 166–168). For those who do choose to learn and use English, it is not easy given an array of discouraging obstacles. For a start, shaming practices 'affect the way our students are learning English and their confidence in speaking it outside the classroom situation' (Wanga: 48–50). It affects teaching practice, with even experienced teachers quite proficient in English feeling ashamed to use the language in the English classroom 'because when they do, you see others giggling and laughing' (Zameeta: 132–135).

When everyone shares the local vernacular, communication is easier than using an additional language that evokes mocking or ridiculing responses, especially if some do not have the proficiency necessary for quick and effective communication. Wanga, who declares a strong commitment to improving ELT and English proficiency across the community, admits he resorts to using the vernacular when teaching to ensure effective communication with his students. Zameeta describes similar experiences, and the comments of teachers in her school who, 'Every time I ask them "Why don't you speak English, teach in English?", they say, "Most of them will ask me to speak Kiribati again, explain everything in Kiribati" or, "It is taking up my time to speak in English and then translating everything"' (Zameeta: 122–124). As for learners, despite encouragement by teachers to use English in the language classroom, 'laughing at others discourages them and they're afraid to speak out if, because they don't like to be laughed at' (Zameeta: 229–230). In addition to the practice of shaming for being different or *okakanimatang* by using English, learners are also ridiculed for shortcomings in their attempts to use the language: 'when you make mistakes in front of Kiribati people they will easily laugh. They will easily give you a laugh. They will laugh at you and that's a ... sort of a discouraging to learn to speak' (Atang: 161–163).

Negotiating Boundaries: Policy and Pedagogical Options

In contemporary Kiribati, learning and using English situates many I-Kiribati in negotiation of complicated and multilayered desires entangled within colonialism, subjugation, threats of disruption and unravelling of the bonds of a traditional egalitarian ethos, the promises of globalization, and national policy imperatives. The advocacy by foreign experts of English, and identities as an English user, as good and desirable compete with strongly defined I-Kiribati identities and the desirability of community solidarity. The potent practices of shaming those who violate the boundary between local and outsider devalues English and strengthens desires to avoid experiences of shaming associated with it, and appear to rule out the option of liminal multilingual hybridity that would allow porosity of the social boundaries between two clearly differentiated groups. The perception of English as an object of desire needs to be powerful when pursuit of it involves a corresponding lack, social exclusion from solidarity with the community. The desires of the state, institutions and teachers as reflected in policy have not convinced

I-Kiribati to 'constitute the learning of English as such a desirable pursuit and the absence of English, a language that is not a part of their history, their heritage, and often not even present in their everyday life, as a lack' (Motha & Lin, 2014: 334). ELT that ignores these contextual circumstances fails to account for the needs of learners. Despite a growing orientation in ELT towards contextual responsiveness (see, e.g. Huang, 2017; Littlewood, 2013; Liyanage & Bartlett, 2008; Liyanage *et al.*, 2016), the possibilities of social situations in which English itself is not considered desirable and of the complex ways in which this might constrain individual responses to learning have not received much attention. Dominant communicative pedagogies view reluctance to engage in language use as a matter for remediation in the classroom setting (Humphreys & Wyatt, 2014; Vongsila & Reinders, 2016); effective learning is seen to depend upon positive attitudes to the language and motivation to integrate (Carreira, 2011; Wu, 2003) and use the language in the target community. In Kiribati these responses are inadequate and inappropriate, and alternatives are needed if a place for English that does not threaten to disrupt social relationships is to be found.

The current practices of I-Kiribati in use of English offer some direction. Rather than a softening or weakening of boundaries between the values and practices of locals and outsiders, clear contextual boundaries are maintained that designate contextually appropriate sites of English use, keeping English and vernacular distinct for different purposes and relationships. This contrasts with many studies of post-colonial contexts in which cultural interfaces produce 'a range of multiplex and transnational identities' (Lamont & Molnár, 2002: 184). Our local interviewees identify some of these sites – official occasions, meetings with outsider/expatriate officials and development workers, official written correspondence, settings outside Kiribati where English is an appropriate lingua franca. Thus while shaming appears to be a rigid and indiscriminate practice, the I-Kiribati in fact demonstrate a 'cultural flexibility' (Borovnik, 2005: 132) that allows boundary violation without punitive consequences. This suggests a reassessment of the objectives and approaches of local ELT. The outdated curriculum that focuses on English literature, and the policy of using English as medium of instruction symbolize invasive colonial culture and outsider identity, and need to change. Communicative language teaching approaches that assume use and exposure outside the classroom are in fact expecting learners to engage in shameful communicative practices and are counterproductive, and a more instrumental approach is needed that targets specific contexts of English language use. Conventional models of proficiency that target 'native speaker proficiency' in all four macro-skills might not be appropriate for the needs of all learners, and teaching and learning might be more successful if tailored more closely to individual needs rather than a universal one-size-fits-all approach.

Questions of shame and shaming practices need to be foregrounded explicitly in the language classroom in order to clarify the boundaries of language use. In practical terms, activities such as roleplays, for example, in which learners adopt clearly defined fictional identities, can allow exploration of interactions with outsiders without the risks of shaming attached to expecting learners to use English in classrooms among their own in-group. If roles include pretentious locals or elitist outsiders, playing out shaming practices in fictional contexts creates opportunities for analysis of and reflection on these practices and how they impinge upon language use, both the vernacular and English. Awareness of language as a symbolic boundary in the context of local objectives to balance development with continuation of local cultural practices and identity could equip learners and users of English with explicit appreciation of the significance of the language practices of shaming, and the consequences.

The experience of ELT and shaming in Kiribati reminds us that 'boundaries are shaped by context, and particularly by the cultural repertoires, traditions, and narratives that individuals have access to' (Lamont & Molnár, 2002: 171) and that 'the notion of boundaries is crucial for analysing how social actors construct groups as similar and different and how it shapes their understanding of their responsibilities toward such groups' (Lamont & Molnár, 2002: 187). While foreign experts consider the shaming practices used by the I-Kiribati to sustain their differentiation of themselves from outsiders as limiting their capacity to learn and use English, locals are performing their responsibilities and affirming their shared belonging as more important to them. Assumptions of universal desires for English, for the purported advantages of globalisation, ignore the corresponding urge of individuals, groups and communities to differentiate themselves, to sustain cultural identities, to retain autonomy, to resist neo-liberal ideology that elevates the private benefit of individuals above the relationships that sustain community. The Kiribati experience alerts ELT practitioners and policymakers to the emotional dimension of language learning encompassing more than the individual, and more than the immediate classroom environment; local community norms must be accommodated if social boundaries are not to be an obstacle to learning and use of English. For the I-Kiribati, their preference for controlling the use of English in their community through shaming has allowed them to resist the external pressures of cultural appropriation and hybridity, to assert the primacy of local values and relationships over the demands of neoliberal development agendas, but not without implications for their future. Maintaining community interests and local ways of life, which shaming is supposed to enforce, doesn't have to conflict with contact and progress, but the lives and futures of the I-Kiribati are poised on one of the most fundamental physical boundaries, that between the land and the sea (Lange, 2010). While they pursue a development path that preserves cultural identity, events beyond their control mean that many may need to be relocated to contexts where they must navigate different social boundaries. ELT needs to be responsive to this suite of circumstances and accommodate the diverse motivations and functions for English learning and use with contextually appropriate pedagogies.

References

Aragão, R. (2011) Beliefs and emotions in foreign language learning. *System* 39 (3), 302–313. doi:10.1016/j.system.2011.07.003.

Beier, H. and Kroneberg, C. (2013) Language boundaries and the subjective well-being of immigrants in Europe. *Journal of Ethnic and Migration Studies* 39 (10), 1535–1553. doi:10.1080/1369183X.2013.833685.

Borovnik, M. (2005). Seafarers' 'maritime culture' and the 'i-kiribati way of life': The formation of flexible identities? *Singapore Journal of Tropical Geography* 26 (2), 132–150. doi:10.1111/j.0129-7619.2005.00210.x.

Burnett, G. (2013) Approaches to English literacy teaching in the Central Pacific Republic of Kiribati: Quality teaching, educational aid and curriculum reform. *Asia Pacific Journal of Education* 33 (3), 350–363. doi:10.1080/02188791.2013.787389.

Carreira, J.M. (2011) Relationship between motivation for learning EFL and intrinsic motivation for learning in general among Japanese elementary school students. *System* 39 (1), 90–102. doi:10.1016/j.system.2011.01.009.

Chatzidaki, A. and Maligkoudi, C. (2012) Family language policies among Albanian immigrants in Greece. *International Journal of Bilingual Education and Bilingualism* 16 (6), 675–689. doi:10.1080/13670050.2012.709817.

Coronel-Molina, S.M. (1999) Functional domains of the Quechua language in Peru: Issues of status planning. *International Journal of Bilingual Education and Bilingualism* 2 (3), 166–180. doi:10.1080/13670059908667687.

Fanon, F. (1967) *The wretched of the earth. (C. Farrington Trans.).* Harmondsworth: Penguin. (Original work published 1961).

Huang, L. (2017) *Western TESOL Programs and Contextually Responsive ELT in China.* (Unpublished M. Ed. thesis), Deakin University, Melbourne, Australia.

Humphreys, G. and Wyatt, M. (2014) Helping Vietnamese university learners to become more autonomous. *ELT Journal* 68 (1), 52–63. doi:10.1093/elt/cct056.

Kandiah, T. (1979) Disinherited Englishes: The case of Lankan English. *Navasilu* 3, 75–89.

Lamb, M. and Coleman, H. (2008) Literacy in English and the transformation of self and society in post-Soeharto Indonesia. *International Journal of Bilingual Education and Bilingualism* 11 (2), 189–205. doi:10.2167/beb493.0.

Lamont, M. and Molnár, V. (2002) The study of boundaries in the social sciences. *Annual Review of Sociology* 28 (1), 167–195. doi:10.1146/annurev.soc.28.110601.141107.

Lamont, M., Pendergrass, S. and Pachucki, M. (2015) Symbolic boundaries. In N.J. Smelser and P.B. Baltes (eds) *International Encyclopedia of the Social & Behavioral Sciences* (2nd edn, Vol. 23, pp. 850–855). Amsterdam: Elsevier.

Lange, H.D. (2010) Climate refugees require relocation assistance: Guaranteeing adequate land assets through treaties based on the National Adaptation Programmes of Action. *Pac. Rim L. & Pol'y J.* 19, 613–640.

Littlewood, W. (2013) Developing a context-sensitive pedagogy for communication-oriented language teaching. *English Teaching* 68 (3), 3–25.

Liyanage, I. and Bartlett, B.J. (2008) Contextually responsive transfer: Perceptions of NNES on an ESL/EFL teacher training programme. *Teaching and Teacher Education* 24 (7), 1827–1836. doi:10.1016/j.tate.2008.02.009.

Liyanage, I., Díaz, A. and Gurney, L. (2016) Re-envisioning teacher education programmes for international students: Towards an emancipatory and transformative educational stance. In C.M. Lam and J. Park (eds) *Sociological and philosophical perspectives on education in the Asia-Pacific region*. Singapore: Springer.

McCarty, T.L., Romero-Little, M.E. and Zepeda, O. (2006) Native American youth discourses on language shift and retention: Ideological cross-currents and their implications for language planning. *International Journal of Bilingual Education and Bilingualism* 9 (5), 659–677. doi:10.2167/beb386.0.

Motha, S. and Lin, A. (2014) 'Non-coercive rearrangements': Theorizing desire in TESOL. *TESOL Quarterly* 48 (2), 331–359. doi:10.1002/tesq.126.

Norton, B. and Toohey, K. (2011) Identity, language learning, and social change. *Language Teaching* 44 (4), 412–446. doi:10.1017/S0261444811000309.

Ohmae, K. (1995) *The end of the nation-state*. New York: Free Press.

Orelus, P.W. (2011) Linguistic apartheid and the English-only movement. *Encounter: Education for Meaning and Social Justice* 24 (3), 15–22.

Paasi, A. (2009) Bounded spaces in a 'borderless world': Border studies, power and the anatomy of territory. *Journal of Power* 2 (2), 213–234. doi:10.1080/17540290903064275.

Pavlenko, A. (2005) 'Ask each pupil about her methods of cleaning': Ideologies of language and gender in Americanisation instruction (1900–1924). *International Journal of Bilingual Education and Bilingualism* 8 (4), 275–297. doi:10.1080/13670050508668611.

Peirce, B.N. (1995) Social identity, investment, and language learning. *TESOL Quarterly* 29 (1), 9–31. doi:10.2307/3587803.

Scheff, T.J. and Retzinger, S.M. (2000) Shame as the master emotion of everyday life. *Journal of Mundane Behavior* 1 (3), 303–324.

Storey, D. and Hunter, S. (2010) Kiribati: An environmental perfect storm. *Australian Geographer* 41 (2), 167–181.

Stroud, C. and Wee, L. (2007) A pedagogical application of liminalities in social positioning: Identity and literacy in Singapore. *Tesol Quarterly* 41 (1), 33–54. doi:10.1002/j.1545-7249.2007.tb00039.x.

Tisdell, C. (2000) Poverty in the Pacific Islands. *The International Journal of Sociology and Social Policy* 20 (11/12), 74–102. doi:10.1108/01443330010789296.

Vongsila, V. and Reinders, H. (2016) Making Asian learners talk: Encouraging willingness to communicate. *RELC Journal* 47 (3), 331–347. doi:10.1177/0033688216645641.

Wu, X. (2003) Intrinsic motivation and young language learners: The impact of the classroom environment. *System* 31 (4), 501–517. doi:10.1016/j.system.2003.04.001.

6 Native-speakerism and Symbolic Violence in Constructions of Teacher Competence

Junia C.S. Mattos Zaidan

Imagine you are a novice teacher of English in a Latin American country. You are taking part in a local conference organized by the association of English teachers. You spend three days wondering why the sessions are conducted exclusively in English since everyone taking part speaks the same mother tongue, Portuguese. Although you speak English fluently, you avoid posing questions and making comments because you feel people will pay more attention to how you say things than to what you say.

Or perhaps you are a working-class undergraduate student of English in the same country, attending a state funded university. At the completion of your BA, you proudly invite your family to attend your end-of-course research presentation. Your mother, a woman of colour who barely finished elementary school, feels completely lost during the session in which the presentations, opening, closing remarks, and all comments and questions are made in a language she cannot understand – English.

Or you might be a high school student in the outskirts of a Brazilian city. One morning, the school inspector shows up in your class with what she says is 'great news'. Five students in your class have been selected to study English in a special course offered by the Government aimed to supplement and 'strengthen' regular curricular English classes, with teachers trained by the British Council. You are not among the selected students though. Neither is your high school English teacher part of the English teaching team working *inside* of your school.

Reported in the interviews, questionnaire and observations carried out during the research partially reported in this paper, these anecdotes set the scene for the present discussion by displaying some of the material effects of cultural reproduction (Bourdieu & Passeron, 1970/1990) pertaining to the field of English language teaching in the metropolitan area of Vitória, the capital city of the state of *Espírito Santo*, in Brazil. Though in different degrees and with particular nuances, the stories exhibit in broad strokes what constitutes professional and academic prestige, how positions are legitimized, what counts as 'real' English, and the implications of English-only institutional practices, as well as the (mis)representation people seem to have of a language that features in the national curriculum as a tool for international communication, but that ends up promoting particular national cultures instead.

The subjects experiencing the symbolic violence portrayed in the anecdotes are constituted through and help to perpetuate mechanisms that conceal the cultural asymmetries among social groups, thus arbitrarily naturalizing and imposing the practices, values and standards of hegemonic groups. The hegemony, in this case, is Anglo-American and manifests itself through enduring boundaries enforced by notions of 'authenticity' and 'native-likeness' despite widespread growing scholarly work on the myth of the 'native speaker' (Davies, 2003; Holliday, 2006; Rajagopalan, 2007) and on World Englishes (Kachru, 1997), English as a *Lingua Franca* (for e.g. Seidlhofer, 2011) and English as an International Language (for e.g. Sharifian, 2009), which, despite their slightly different perspectives on the spread of English, overlap in terms of their recognition of the sociolinguistic diversity of the contexts in which the language is used. Moreover, a number of policies, resistance tactics, anti-discrimination statements issued by several institutions and campaigns have also engaged in the deconstruction of native speakerist discourse around the world, which is nevertheless still dominant (cf. Modiano, 2009 and Petrić, 2009).

In this chapter, we draw on Pierre Bourdieu and Passeron's analytical framework of education *as* symbolic violence (Bourdieu & Passeron, 1990) in order to discuss cultural reproduction of boundaries as effected through native speakerism, the ideology within the field of English Language Teaching (ELT), 'characterized by the belief that "native-speaker" teachers represent a "Western culture" from which spring the ideals both of the English language and of ELT methodology' (Holliday, 2006). As an integral part of native speakerism, the myth of 'authenticity' – which here we sometimes term 'authenticism' – is also addressed as engendering notions such as 'purity', 'originality', 'genuinity' and 'quality' that constitute the tacit rules of this linguistic market where 'social agents share the *doxa* of the field, the assumptions that "go without saying", that determine the limits of the doable and the thinkable' (Grenfell, 2008: 59).

The material effects of the often-unquestioned supremacy of anglo-American references for ELT include both the negative evaluation Brazilian teachers tend to have of themselves – a conclusion Braine (2010) also gets to by researching ELT in Asia – and social inequality, as evidenced, for example, in job recruiting practices. This resonates with Speciale's analysis of the role of shaming in cultural reproduction in the Senegalese educational context (in this volume). Although shaming and the resulting punishment is enacted in different ways in the specific Brazilian context analyzed, they are nevertheless material effects of native-speakerism that, like in Speciale's analysis, further constitute tacit mechanisms to reinforce the alienation of post-colonial subjects. Like the Senegalese, Brazilians are all too often caught up in a cycle that socializes them into sacralizing the USA and Europe and hating their own cultural traits. While we acknowledge the advance in Brazilian research and initiatives that proposed discourses favouring 'non-native' speaker perspectives over the last decades (cf. Brazilian National Curriculum Parameters, 1998; Cox & Assis-Peterson, 1999; Rajagopalan, 2007, 2012), we contend that the competing discourse of native speakerism nevertheless prevails (cf. Holliday, 2015) thus disrupting efforts to appropriate and transform the English language, as proposed by the national parameters. Ultimately, we argue that native speakerism, embedded as it is in the capitalist logic of oppression and domination, requires that we take account of class stratification and poverty in order to understand its dynamics, a claim that also compels us not to turn a blind eye to the fact that even anti-native speakerist discourse may become highly commodifiable, hence, easily captured as a way to maintain unequal social structures.

Violence, Reproduction and the Usual Blind Spot

Pierre Bourdieu's work is centrally concerned with how domination is enacted, and with human suffering. His conceptual framework was influenced by lived experience and deep concern with the 'dispossessed' (Schubert, 2008) in the context of growing capitalist brutality in the former French colony of Algeria.

Bourdieu's commitment to denouncing class stratification and social inequality strengthens the often neglected situatedness of his work within a broader Marxist framework, despite the controversy such a claim fuels among several strands of Marxism. Class struggle is for the first time addressed in the cultural sphere, as opposed to the traditional conceptualization based on the primacy of economic factors that, up until the 1960s, oriented Marxian social critique. As a central concept in his oeuvre, violence is thus taken beyond the notion of physical force to *also* encompass the symbolic dimension.

So, if violence is not perpetrated exclusively through physical force, how can its analysis be carried out? One of the answers to this question lies in Bourdieu's engagement with language. To Schubert (2008: 183), 'the notion of symbolic violence follows on, and is a consequence of, his understanding of language'. It is because language is indexical of a number of components of a person's background that any examination of a given social field must not take it for granted. For example, when they interact orally, interlocutors immediately spot clues about one another, such as whether the person comes from an English-speaking country, whether the variety of English she speaks is prestigious or stigmatized, her location in the socioeconomic spectrum, her educational background, and so on. In other words, our perception of who we are talking to – as well as our interlocutor's perception of who we are – is not based only on the content spoken, but also on *how* we express ourselves, which is more often than not a source of concern for many speakers of English, students and teachers alike, as we can recall from one of the aforementioned anecdotes. Since *difference* (be it related to gender, ethnicity, age group, sexuality, language or any other) tends to be equated with *deficiency*, thus inscribing inequality, linguistic diversity is misrecognized and stigmatized, producing stratification. Social mobility and access to cultural and material resources are restricted or granted depending on how one is positioned in the socioeconomic spectrum in which one's *cultural capital* is either devalued or recognized.

The intrinsic relationship between language and violence is what Bourdieu and Passeron (1990) focused on in their examination of education as a system that promotes reproduces and maintains social inequality through the naturalization of boundaries framed by language and culture. Considering Bourdieu's work as a whole, nowhere else is the notion of violence more prevalent than in his study of education, in collaboration with Jean Claude Passeron (1990). By drawing on extensive empirical research on the French educational system – with a focus on secondary schools and transition to higher education – they conclude that the educational system reproduces social structures by concealing cultural asymmetries and arbitrarily imposing the culture of a dominant group. Disparity is made invisible, hence, accepted as 'natural' by society. Therefore, in their view, 'social origin predetermines educational destiny, i.e. both the chain of subsequent school-career choices and the resulting differential chances of success or failure' (Bourdieu & Passeron, 1990: 80). In their chapter on pedagogic authority as a regulator of the contents that 'merit transmission' (Bourdieu & Passeron, 1990: 109), the authors remind us that 'no one acquires a language without thereby acquiring a *relation to language*' (Bourdieu & Passeron, 1990: 116, emphasis in the original). It is this very relation to language as a totem of a supposedly 'higher culture' that is at stake in ELT. The symbolic capital of so-called 'native-like' English is not something people who possess it are necessarily willing to problematize, however engaged they may seem in fighting prejudice against 'non-native' teachers. The way language is produced reflects and maintains social affiliation, i.e. privileged classes use language as a 'means of excluding the vulgar and thereby affirming their distinction' (Bourdieu & Passeron, 1990: 117–118).

We can think of 'the vulgar' as the formal traits (i.e. lexical, phonological, prosodic, syntactic, etc) of varieties of English that do not enjoy the prestige of so-called Inner Circle Englishes (Kachru, 1997). The pedagogic authority 'non-native' teachers are invested with, i.e. the 'power of symbolic violence exerted within a relation of pedagogic communication' (Bourdieu & Passeron, 1990: 10) does not prevent them from simultaneously being subjected to symbolic violence.

What follows is a reproduction of western values and 'canonical' varieties of English by non-native teachers themselves, irrespective of whether they enjoy prestige in the way they speak the language. As the authors argue, reproduction does not depend on teachers' willingness to reproduce the social structure or being aware of the fact that they end up acting to serve the institution and its social function. Though apparently deterministic, the argument is actually stressing that, historically, no other mechanism of transmission of power and privileges has been as disguised as the educational system, which implies, as a corollary, that one must deal with its structuring nature in order to subvert it. In the specific case of ELT, the system is further affected by the pressure of a powerful industry that systematically invests in the interaction with academics and government agents to carry out research, publish papers, and design policies that will reflect their interests, respectively. Certification of proficiency in English, teacher training programs, materials design and internationalization policies are some of the mechanisms that tend to establish centripetal forces to enhance rather than challenge native speakerism in Brazil as we shall discuss ahead.

For Brazilian scholar Dermeval Saviani, whose *Historical Critical Pedagogy* (2008) was conceived out of dissatisfaction with the conceptual insufficiency of what he termed 'critical reproductivist theories' – including, among others, Bourdieu and Passeron's model – a truly critical theory of education needs to actually *engage* with social change and not only denounce the structures of oppression. The intriguing absence of Saviani's comprehensive critique in Brazilian Applied Linguistics research can be addressed both in terms of the disciplinary insulation of ELT towards related fields whose discussion topics do not revolve around the English language and of a colonized attitude leading to importing theories instead of acknowledging the relevance of locally produced knowledge. Still, despite the potential of Saviani's model by repositioning the critique of oppression privileging class struggle, as far as the need for reconfiguration of the conceptual matrix in ELT is concerned, no other theoretical framework has drawn so much attention to language in face of power asymmetries and oppression within a capitalist mode of production as Bourdieu and Passeron's.

Notwithstanding the steady substantial change in ELT research over the last decades with the shift of focus from cognition towards more socially embedded research topics (ethnicity, race, gender, sexuality, language rights, to mention a few), class related issues still tend to be consigned to oblivion. By remarking that in TESOL 'we seem uncomfortable acknowledging poverty in our communities', Ramanathan and Morgan pose two provocative questions:

> Is it because class issues get tied to Marxist concerns, and that many of us see ourselves as having moved into post-Marxist terrains? Or is it because West-based TESOL is by and large a middle-class endeavor oriented primarily towards middle-class learners? (Ramanathan & Morgan, 2009: 155)

The two explanations presented by the authors are not mutually exclusive. I would further argue that in this *field* (to use Bourdieu's term), class-blindness is both a concealed precondition for profitability and market expansion *and* a consequence of the mechanisms that sustain the ELT industry, in a dialectic and continuous relationship, which makes Bourdieu's notion of education *as* violence all the more relevant for the critique of native-speakerism and authenticism. After all, it is precisely by misrecognizing or ignoring the inequities in the socioeconomic order that social agents contribute to their naturalization. But the explanation for the erasure of discourses on class in several fields – or, in any case, for its neglect in ELT – cannot be circumscribed to people's attitudes towards their own class and ideological affiliation. Rather, factors range from the commodification of class starting in the 1970s to the ascendancy of neoliberal doctrine in the 1980s. As Rampton *et al.* (2006) argue, it also results from 'the retreat from class analysis in research in the 1990s, and ... failure to work the connections between class, gender and ethnicity' (Rampton *et al.*, 2006: 7). Or the reification of English as is the case with English as a Lingua Franca's hypostatization and fetishization leading to an historic-social myopia in relation to class struggle (O'Regan, 2014).

To what extent do Brazilian teachers of English reproduce native-speakerism and the myth of authenticity? Through which mechanisms does symbolic violence manifest itself? Do these social agents perceive themselves and their students as inscribed in a socially unequal field? In order to discuss cultural reproduction as effected through native speakerism and authenticism, we set out to answer these questions through the study described in the next section.

The Study – Design and Background

The study took place in the metropolitan region of Vitória, the capital of Espírito Santo, in the southeast of Brazil, in 2017. It included an online questionnaire answered by 52 teachers and student teachers of English about their educational background, teaching practice, professional development and their feelings and opinions about their work. Three semi-structured interviews were conducted face to face, on a one-to-one basis with one female teacher from a state public school, who holds an MA in Applied Linguistics; one male teacher from a private school, who has a BA in *Letras* and one female student-teacher in the last semester of her BA in *Letras* at the Federal University of Espírito Santo.

Observations were also carried out of three discussion forums and meetings about curriculum reform at the Federal University of Espírito Santo, in which professors and undergraduate students took part. We made the decision to include the university both because the author is part of staff and has access to a range of processes and also in view of the backwash effect that the university entrance mechanisms, as well as curriculum contents and other academic practices tend to have on local primary and secondary school teaching as well as on commercial language school practices.

A balance of varied teaching profiles was included with the number of teaching years ranging from 8 to 13. As for teaching qualification, 32% of respondents of the questionnaire were student-teachers taking their BA in *Letras* (English Language and Literature); 43% hold a BA in *Letras,* 19% have an MA and 6%, a PhD; 92% of the certified respondents have taken their BA over the last 15 years, at the Federal University of Espírito Santo, the only local state funded university.

Findings and Discussion: Questionnaire and Interview

Although the study was made up of a larger amount of data, the emerging categories which are relevant to the present analysis are discussed in the sub-sections below, namely, 'native speaker' and 'native-likeness' (constructs that point to models inherited from theoretical Linguistics and Applied Linguistics, as well as speech resembling Anglo-American speakers); and 'authenticity' (a notion of socially constructed legitimacy based on a supposed origin).

'Native Speaker' and Native-likeness

Owing to their open-endedness, several questionnaire questions provided some assessment of participants' attitude towards native-speakerism. In order to avoid social desirability bias, we did not ask them questions about these topics directly since we believe that most teachers in Espírito Santo nowadays have, one way or another, been exposed to some form of anti-native speakerist discourse due to its dissemination through conferences, publications, curriculum content, social media discussions, etc. To that end, we made a point of not giving them multiple choices for answering the question about their 'level of English'.

Many respondents used expressions such as 'native', 'native-like', 'almost like a native', 'very natural' referring to 'native'-likeness. These notions were also rather recurrent in teachers' comments about the Association of English Language Teachers in Espírito Santo. Out of the 29 teachers taking part in the study, 72% expressed in some way that 'being in touch with native speakers in the Association's events' was an advantage. Fragments of some extended responses show the strong presence of native speakerism.

> I may sound like a native to non-native speakers, it's a funny thing. And I kind of like it when they tell me I speak like an American. But I know my English is not native-like. I don't mind, I can communicate. (Questionnaire respondent A)

> I answered my English is 'Native-like' because I lived in the US for more than ten years and learned the language naturally. I think it's very important to speak without an accent if you wanna be a teacher. (Questionnaire respondent B)

When asked the same question in the interview, one of the teachers answered 'very good', and went on to explain her own assessment:

> Because that's what it is! Very good, but not 'perfect'. Worrying about speaking English like a native doesn't make sense nowadays. English is a global language, so, people communicate despite their accents and, more than that, despite the phrasal verbs they don't know. (Interview response – State public school teacher)

In fact, the figure of the 'native-speaker' seems to hover around as an unquestionable ontological given, even when teachers challenge it, as the state public school teacher above; or even when they show an affirmative attitude towards their English, as Questionnaire respondent A. This ingrained notion is reproduced through the educational system, (Bourdieu & Passeron, 1990) and establishes underlying rules on how cultural capital gets distributed.

To the attitudinal open-ended question asked about participants' feeling in relation to their English (cf. Table 6.1), as many as 52% of the teachers eventually evaluated themselves negatively, which is surprising, considering that only 15% had mentioned some dissatisfaction with their own language skills earlier in the Questionnaire. This suggests that they tend to exhibit a more positive de-centered view when considering the factual status of their proficiency, whereas, attitudinally, they devalue their English on grounds of distance in relation to American and British varieties, which is evidence of an ingrained native speakerist ethos (cf. similar findings in Zaidan, 2013). Speciale's (this volume) reference to the antropology of emotions to discuss shaming as a

Table 6.1 How do you feel about your English?

	'Not confident'/ lacking fluency	'Love it'	'Just functional'	I wish I had no accent	Advanced/ Proud of it
Number	27	18	18	10	21
%	52%	35%	35%	19%	40%

reproduction mechanism in the Senegalese context can be illuminating to our analysis in the sense that, as she argues, emotions are culturally socially constructed, in other words, they are learned. Negative feelings about one's own characteristics and capacities are, thus, part and parcel of the process of reproduction of inequalities. Based on responses to the Questionnaire, Table 6.1 displays feelings and perceptions which are often mutually inclusive. It is followed by an excerpt of a rather representative questionnaire response and a fragment of the interview.

> I think anyone will know I learned English at school as soon as I open my mouth. I just don't use much slang neither do I speak as fast as an American, though I communicate. This sometimes even prevents me from speaking English out of the classroom. With students, I don't feel so insecure, though some of them have almost 'native'-like. (Interview response – female student-teacher)

> I'm okay with my English. I think even this kind of question you are asking is a problem because it seems to assume that there <u>should</u> be something wrong, or that how I feel about my English in relation to other Englishes should matter. I feel as if I always had to prove my linguistic competence even though I've been doing this for almost 12 years! (Questionnaire respondent C, emphasis by the respondent)

There is a lot to unpack from the excerpts above. As a particularly insidious form of symbolic violence, native speakerism is predicated not only on the supposed flawlessness and 'purity' of a mythical archetype, but, as a corollary, also on the social construction of individuals that lack the characteristics associated with such an archetype. In fact, as 'non-natives', we are the emblem of 'failure' both for what we 'lack' and for what we have, for what we do not do and for what we do, or, in any case, for who we are not and for who we are. This seems to be readily detected by Respondent C, who hits the nail on the head suggesting that neither herself, nor the researcher or anyone else should subject her English to constant evaluation, insofar as her experience as a practitioner should be enough to render her authoritative, which, we argue, is all the more convincing a reason considering that she is a certified teacher abiding by the Brazilian legislation.

Respondent C's vexed comment also speaks to our own skepticism regarding a repeated attempt by several scholars in the Brazilian foreign language teaching context (cf. Consolo & Teixeira da Silva, 2014) to design and, ultimately, officially enforce a Brazilian standardized test to 'measure' teacher proficiency, namely, Proficiency Exam for Foreign Language Teachers.[1] The stated concern with diagnosing the level of proficiency of school teachers of English in order to ensure 'quality education' can be understood as a by-product of a system that keeps reconfiguring its mechanisms in order to guarantee the cultural capital of a 'special' group.

'Authenticity'

Standardized language tests such as the TOEFL, Cambridge Exams (FCE, CAE, CPE, etc), IELTS and teaching tests (Cambridge TKT, DELTA, ICELT) also showed up in responses mostly inscribed in the ideology of 'authenticism', though a great many teachers also raise questions about the validity of these instruments in a Latin American context. This resonates Khan's (2009) view that standardized tests (ST) strengthen the hegemony of Inner-Circle countries in addition to offering rather narrow cultural representations. Moreover, the reductionist interactional pattern assumed by ST, i.e. one that always involves the 'native-speaker' as the sole interlocutor of anyone learning English, has long been challenged by scholars within Applied Linguistics.

Among those who have taken ST (50% of the Questionnaire respondents), the reasons range from *recruiting pre-requisite* (64%), *career development* (22%) and/or *self-development/'diagnosis'* (12%). Working in commercial language schools was detected as a significant variable both in the importance attributed to ST and in the attitude towards tests as an important 'seal' of validation. 75% of student-teachers mentioned taking the Toefl ITP, which is part of macropolitical initiatives for placement purposes, stemming from the Brazilian Ministry of Education's program *English Without Borders*,[2] created to promote ELT as a way to foster the internationalization of Brazilian universities.

> The Toefl ITP was compulsory for English undergrads interested in teaching English as trainees in the English Without Borders program and to study English as an extra-curricular activity. Honestly, I don't think it really measures my proficiency: it's mechanicist and feels like a straight-jacket you have to put on and take off while the clock is ticking. (Questionnaire Respondent D)

Questionnaire Respondent D gives away that she only took the ST because it is a compulsory pre-requisite to take part in the trainee program and evaluates it negatively. When asked about ST, most respondents either seemed indifferent (15%) to the utility of the Toefl ITP; critical of it (10%), were credulous (75%) in its validation or even enthusiastic. Our remarks about ST, in this chapter, are less a critique than an attempt to carefully situate teachers' attitude to international validation within the conceptual category of 'authenticity', especially in its inter-relatedness with the power that institutions (educational and professional institutions alike) exert in consecrating the symbolic capital associated with them. As Pinner (2016) argues, the notion of 'authenticity' also includes the idea of authority, which, in the case of ST, can be seen in terms of institutional authority in validating selection, cleavage and, thus, exclusion, according to arbitrary standards.

With regard to the internationalization of the university, my own experience as former coordinator of the BA in English and member of the Department of Languages Committee for the elaboration of Linguistic Policies at the Federal University of Espírito Santo, the adoption of standardized tests from the USA, the use of imported materials and the flexibilization for the entrance of English-speaking international students with no necessary counter-offer on the part of universities from English-speaking countries for our Brazilian students render the neocolonial slant of the process obvious. As a seal of supposed excellence, authenticism manifests itself in academic practices that erase cultural differences and totemize the US and Europe thus producing attitudes towards internationalization similar to those discussed by Speciale (this volume) with regard to globalization: inequality is accepted and naturalized as the price to pay for it.

Included in participants' responses, discourses on teaching materials are also vectorial to the spread of authenticism, with direct commercial implications for an industry with the main publishing houses located in the UK and the US. Therefore, account always needs to be taken of the vested commercial interests in disseminating discourses inscribing the supposed inefficiency of the public school system while also affirming the putative inevitability of sending kids to commercial language schools. In Brazil, while public schools still adopt nationally-produced, state-financed textbooks,[3] i.e. designed by Brazilian scholars, chosen by the schools themselves with no extra cost to students, private schools and commercial language courses, in turn, privilege imported publications.

While referring to teaching materials, participants do not seem to subscribe to the commonsensical view widespread with the advent of Communicative Language Teaching, according to which authenticity relates to texts used by 'native-speakers' in 'real' situations (only 18% express this view). Rather, they by and large incorporate the perspective that authenticity lies beyond a supposedly inherent property of the material or language use, as put forward by van Lier (1996), but includes a range of enunciation situations, as Brazilian scholar Almeida Filho also proposes (2002). However, 50% of textbooks are reported by participants as coming either from the UK or the US, i.e. the adoption of materials that embody value systems largely representative of these nations is pervasive in commercial and private language schools. (cf. Rajagopalan, 2012, for a discussion of 'pedagogic imperialism' through materials).

> I'd rather work with a textbook produced for Brazilian learners. It would make more sense, especially considering the topics to discuss. We end up focusing too much on issues that are not specific to our local context, which impacts motivation and also the view we end up building that our own stories, problems don't matter. (Interview response: Teacher from a private school)

Putting forward opinions that counter naturalized views of teaching resources is paramount to deconstructing native speakerism/authenticism. Authenticism also featured in 68% of the references to the BA in English language and literature at the local university, namely: (1) the use of English as a means of communication both inside and outside the classroom, etc; (2) the prevalence of anglo-American literary works and authors in literature research topics; and (3) the weight of American English as a 'default' variety in the program. As the only local public university, UFES plays a crucial role in the construction of discourses on what constitutes good teaching, which authors should be read, the topics that merit scientific investigation, to mention some of the values that are disseminated through curricular and extra-curricular practices, albeit in an unformulated, tacit form. While the relationship between points (2) and (3) with authenticism may be self evident,[4] I would like to briefly comment on point (1).

> We need to speak English as much as possible at UFES, after all, we must to develop a very good level of proficiency in order to teach. But that doesn't mean it should be done everywhere. It embarrasses me that some people speak English in the hallway, when students from other programs feel awkward as if we were talking behind their back. It's just rude. (Questionnaire respondent E)

> Of course, there is a whole prestige thing connected with speaking only English inside and outside of the class. Once I invited my aunt who raised me to attend my end-of-course research paper presentation on Ebonics. It was in English and I told her about it. But I was shocked that the session was entirely carried out in English, including professors' greetings, instructions and comments. What's the point? Undergraduates were being evaluated, okay, but, what about the audience? Too much is taken for granted about who can or is welcome to attend the sessions. People may feel humiliated for not speaking English. (Interview response – State public school teacher)

Both excerpts suggest the direct relationship between the notion of authenticity as connected with people's representations regarding one's capacity to use English spontaneously outside the classroom. The meaning ascribed to our language practices (in this case, that it is okay to use only English even when people around us may not have access to it) perpetuates hegemonic cultural capital institutionally. The institution's capacity to raise awareness of symbolic violence through research discussion does not, of necessity, exclude participation in its infliction.

Closing Remarks

While the empirical survey data is limited in providing an in-depth account of native speakerism and authenticism at the local level, they nevertheless give us a glimpse of the potential mechanisms that have ensured reproduction of exclusionary boundaries, as well as teachers' general perceptions and attitude towards the problems we have raised. Although they are in many ways resisted and challenged by teachers, these mechanisms, ingrained practices and beliefs constitute the native speakerist habitus through which pedagogical action is performed. For instance, standardized tests adopted by the Brazilian government and educational institutions; curriculum content and academic culture that reinforce the elusive American/British dichotomy in ELT as discussed in reference to the BA in English at the local university; educational policies inscribed in principles of selectedness (Bourdieu & Passeron, 1990: 73); the English-only ideology that strengthens authenticism while also preventing local language and culture from playing a role in foreign language education; the adoption of imported textbooks by private schools; recruiting policies by commercial language schools as well as the advertisements that circulate through mass media in which 'native likeness' features as central in the sales rhetoric; the pressure that the industry of English language teaching puts on government and on social organizations to maintain anglo-American hegemony; the omnipresence of American and British agencies (The British Council and American Fulbright, for instance) as neocolonial domination tactics in the educational field and, last but not least, the neglect or obliteration of poverty are mechanisms through which symbolic violence is naturalized, inflicted and reproduced.

By and large, participants perceive themselves as inscribed in a socially unequal and ideologically charged field. This applies both to their general view of themselves as professionals in an industry fuelled by native speakerist discourse, and in relation to their students. Despite this awareness, inequality is seldom addressed in terms of its inherent socioeconomic nature. This problem is synthesized in one of the interviews, when an undergraduate criticized what she calls 'an over-emphasis on race and gender at the expense of poverty' in curricula and research at the University. She says 'People want to discuss gender in critical literacy? Fine, but do they know the woman who suffers the most is the poor black one?' Saviani (2011) criticizes the theory of cultural reproduction on grounds of teachers' supposed incapacity to intervene in social reality regardless of whether they are able to identify discourses and mechanisms, such as native speakerism, that produce inequality. While we take issue with that criticism and respond to it below, we nevertheless reverberate Saviani's concern with the role of education in a broader plan of social change. A plan that comprises, among other things, the educational system as a mechanism (or, as he puts it, 'an instrument', 2011: 60) to overcome class society. Language practices will feature as determining constituents of this process.

Attempts to counter native speakerism have been made heretofore in English language teaching and research (Braine, 2010; Kiczkowiak, 2017 among other works). For instance, the TEFL Equity[5] campaign is an initiative against 'native speaker bias in ELT and for equal employment opportunities for "native" and "non-native" teachers'. With the slogan 'build bridges, not moats' proponents promote webinars, make publications on the topic available, publish lists with links to anti-native speakerism statements issued by several organizations, as well as lesson plans and other resources for 'non-native' teachers. Relevant though the campaign definitely is, its anti-native speakerism perspective is largely focused on fighting discrimination with little attention drawn to the systemic nature of the problem, which renders initiatives such as this highly commodifiable. I am pointing this case out as an example to stress that focusing on acts of discrimination rather than on inherent discriminatory conditions reinforces a logic of exclusion through the belief that symbolic violence is always enacted in the same way, i.e. by neglecting its metamorphic nature.

Although critics of Bourdieu's theory of practice consider it a framework that supposedly leaves no room for political agency on grounds that the notion of reproduction presupposes an ever passive teacher, his notion of 'heterodoxy' may be resorted to as a less deterministic stance. As the emergence of discourses and practices that counter the misrecognition of arbitrary social processes and structures that produce symbolic violence, heterodoxy will ultimately depend on social agents' capacity not only to recognize and become aware of native speakerism and authenticism as symbolic violence, but, more importantly, to engage with the production of competing discourses, which requires both, an epistemic break (Kumaravadivelu, 2012) and political action, in a constant dialectic relationship.

Notes

(1) The Proficiency Exam for Foreign Language Teachers (EPPLE) is a sophisticated instrument with appealing affordances in the linguistic market. Its underlying rationale seems predicated on two myths, namely, that English cannot be taught in public schools (cf. problematization of this fallacy in Lima, 2011) and that Brazilian teachers'

command of English is insufficient. The commercial slant of the proposal is reflected in a liberal view of teacher competence focused exclusively on individual merit and career development.
(2) *English Without Borders* is a Brazilian Government policy targeted at university students, faculty and staff. Its online platform, *My English Online is* designed by two multinational companies. In addition to adopting an American standardized test for placement and for proficiency certification, the program is associated with other American agencies and companies.
(3) Cf. National Textbook Program (Plano Nacional do Livro Didático, Brasil, 2017) http://portal.mec.gov.br/index.php?option=com_content&view=article&id=12391&
(4) British and American literature have always featured as compulsory curriculum components (cf. UFES, http://letras.ufes.br/matriz-curricular-3). Over the years, American Embassy's book donations and provision of webinars, scholarships, grants, coupled with the establishment of Regional English Language Officers and Fulbright English Teaching Assistant programs in virtually all educational spheres in Brazil have worked as mechanisms to ensure cultural domination (cf. Phillipson, 1992) *through* education. The elusive dichotomy British/American that hinders a broader understanding of English as a language for transnational communication resists despite individual teacher's initiatives to de-centralize the teaching of literature, for example, by including 'periphery' authors in their programs, putting together reading projects, etc.
(5) http://teflequityadvocates.com/about/our-goals/).

References

Almeida Filho, J.C.P. (2002) *Dimensões comunicativas no ensino de línguas* (3rd edn) Campinas, São Paulo: Pontes.
Bourdieu P. and Passeron, J.C. (1990) *Reproduction in Education, Society, and Culture.* Translated by Richard Nice. London, Newbury Park, CA: Sage.
Bourdieu, P. (1991) *Language and symbolic power.* Translated by Gino Raymond and Matthew Adamson. Polity Press.
Braine, G. (2010) *Nonnative Speaker English Teachers: Research, Pedagogy and Professional Growth.* New York and London: Routledge.
Brasil (1998) *Parâmetros Curriculares Nacionais*: Terceiro e quarto ciclos do ensino fundamental. Língua estrangeira. Secretaria de Educação Fundamental. Brasília.
Busnardi, B. and Fernandes, A.M. (2011) *Avaliação da proficiência do futuro professor de língua estrangeira e implicações para os cursos de formação de professores no Brasil.* Revista Vertentes. UFSJ. V. 19, n. 1.
Consolo, D.A. and Teixeira da Silva, V.L. (2014) Em defesa de uma formação linguística de qualidade para professores de línguas estrangeiras: O exame EPPLE. *Horizontes de Linguística Aplicada,* ano 13, n. 1. pp. 63–87.
Cox, M.I.P. and Assis-Peterson, A.A. (1999) Critical pedagogy in ELT: Images of Brazilian Teachers of English. *TESOL Quarterly* v. 33, n. 3, pp. 433–452.
Davies, A. (2003) *The Native Speaker: Myth and Reality.* Clevedon, USA: Multilingual Matters.
Grenfell, M. (2008) (ed.) *Pierre Bourdieu – Key Concepts.* London: Acumen.
Holliday, A. (2006) Native speakerism. *ELT Journal* 60 (4) 385–387.
Holliday, A. (2015) Taking the concept forward and achieving cultural belief. In A. Swan, P. Aboshiha and A. Holliday (eds) *(En)countering Native-Speakerism: Global Perspectives* (pp. 11–25). Palgrave Macmillan.
Kachru, B.B. (1997) Culture and argumentative writing in world Englishes, In L. Smith and M. Forman (eds) *World Englishes 2000* (pp. 48–67). University of Hawaii Press.
Khan, S.Z. (2009) Imperialism of international tests: An EIL perspective. In F. Sharifian (ed.) *English as an International Language, Perspective and Pedagogical Issues* (pp. 190–208). Bristol: Multilingual Matters.

Kiczkowiak, M. (2017) Confronting native speakerism in the ELT classroom: Practical awareness-raising activities. *The European Journal of Applied Linguistics and TEFL* 16 (1).

Kumaravadivelu, B. (2012) Individual identity, cultural globalization and teaching English as an international language: The case for an epistemic break. In L. Alsagoff, W. Renandya, G. Hu, and S. McKay (eds) *Teaching English as an International Language: Principles and Practices* (pp. 9–27). New York: Routledge

Lima, D.C. (2011) *Inglês em escolas públicas não funciona? Uma questão, múltiplos olhares*. São Paulo: Parábola.

Modiano, M. (2009) EIL, native speakerism and the failure of European ELT. In F. Sharifian (ed.) *English as an International Language: Perspectives and Pedagogical Issues* (pp. 58–77). Bristol: Multilingual Matters.

O'Regan, J.P. (2014) English as a lingua franca: An immanent critique. *Applied Linguistics* 35 (5), 533–552.

Passeron, J.C. (1995) Hegel ou o passageiro clandestino: A reprodução social e a história. In *O raciocínio sociológico: O espaço não-popperiano do raciocínio natural*. Petrópolis, RJ: Vozes.

Petrić, B. (2009) I thought I was an Easterner; it turns out I am a Westerner!: EIL migrant teacher identities. In F. Sharifian (ed.) *English as an International Language: Perspectives and Pedagogical Issues* (pp. 135–150). Bristol: Multilingual Matters.

Phillipson, Robert (1992) *Linguistic Imperialism*. Oxford: Oxford University Press.

Pinner, R.S. (2016) *Reconceptualizing Authenticity for English as a Global Language*.

Rajagopalan, K. (2007) Revisiting the nativity scene: Review of 'The Native Speaker: Myth and Reality' by Alan Davies. *Studies in Language*, vol. 31, pp. 193–205.

Rajagopalan, K. (2012) O papel eminentemente político dos materiais didáticos de inglês como língua estrangeira. In D. Scheyerl & S. SIQUEIRA, S. (ed.) *Materiais didáticos para o ensino de línguas na contemporaneidade: Contestações e proposições*. (1st edn.) (pp. 57–82) Salvador-BA: EDUFBA, v.

Ramanathan, V. and Morgan, B. (2009) Global warning: West-based TESOL, class-blindness and the challenge for critical pedagogies. In F. Sharifian (ed.) *English as an International Language: Perspectives and Pedagogical Issues* (pp. 153–168). Bristol: Multilingual Matters.

Rampton, B., Harry, R., Collins, J. and Blommaert, J. (2006) Language, class and education. In. S. May and N. Hornberger (eds) *Encyclopedia of Language and Education:* 2nd Education. Vol 1. Heidelberg: Kluwer.

Saviani D. (2008) *Escola e Democracia*. Campinas: Autores Associados.

Saviani D. (2011) *Pedagogia Histórico-crítica: Primeiras aproximações*. (11ª ed. Revisada). Campinas: Autores Associados.

Schubert, J.D. (2008) Suffering/symbolic violence. In M. Grenfell (ed.) *Pierre Bourdieu – Key Concepts*. London: Acumen.

Seidlhofer, B. (2011) *Understanding English as a Lingua Franca*. Oxford: Oxford University Press.

Sharifian, F. (2009) (ed.) *English as an International Language: Perspectives and Pedagogical Issues*. Bristol: Multilingual Matters.

Van Lier, L. (1996) *Interaction in the Language Curriculum: Awareness, Autonomy and Authenticity*. London: Longman.

Zaidan, J.C.S.M. (2013) *Por um inglês menor: A desterritorialização da grande língua*. PhD thesis. Instituto de Estudos da Linguagem, Universidade Estadual de Campinas, São Paulo.

7 Knowledge Politics, Language and Inequality in Educational Publishing

Maria do Socorro Alencar Nunes Macedo, Daniele Alves Ribeiro, Euclides de Freitas Couto and André Luan Nunes Macedo

This chapter draws from a study that asks: What strategies does a Brazilian academic journal use to consolidate prestige in the field of education? How do the criteria for excellence in Brazilian publishing reflect global language inequalities? Our object of study is the journal *Educação em Revista*, produced by the Graduate Program in Education of Federal University of Minas Gerais (UFMG). UFMG, located in the comparatively wealthy southeast region of Brazil, is considered one of the best public universities in the country. We seek to understand how the Coordination for the Improvement of Higher Education Personnel (CAPES) evaluation policy shapes the ways that journals position themselves, and how those strategies for position reflect inequalities in language and knowledge production (see also Ribeiro *et al.*, 2016).

In Brazil, professors' and graduate students' levels of research productivity are evaluated by CAPES every four years, and this evaluation figures heavily in the score ascribed to graduate programs (measured on a scale from 3 to 7) – and thus their ability to maintain status, attract funding, and attract top students. In an attempt to make this evaluation more objective, CAPES establishes criteria that stratify journals based on their 'quality' through the *Qualis* journals system. Since 1998, *Qualis* has evaluated journals in order to classify them in strata ranging from local to national to international range.

In this chapter, we stress how the emphasis on national and, especially, international impact end up reproducing colonial knowledge politics and reinforcing material and linguistic inequalities. First, we argue that the emphasis on international impact privileges theoretical references that derive from Europe and the United States. Second, we show how social networks benefited the journal's consolidation of privileged status. Third, we show how the journal had to delocalize in order to consolidate prestige. Finally, we demonstrate how the emphasis on international impact privileges the production of materials in 'global' languages like English. As Windle (2017) points out, 'the foregrounding of the politics of power and knowledge provides a valuable way of reflecting on the epistemological dimensions of unequal global relations in academic predution' (2017: 20). From this point of view, this single case provides evidence on global inequalities that involve linguistic, social, cultural and economic boundaries.

The data for this chapter were collected through interviews with editors and analysis of the editorials since its first edition. Two editors were interviewed: Magda Soares, one of the founders of the journal, and Geraldo Leão Magela, the editor at the time of data collection. We also analyzed CAPES documents pertinent to the evaluation of journals.

To analyze the strategies of the journal to achieve a high status, the larger project considered its trajectory across three stages that correspond temporally to the development of the CAPES policies used to evaluate graduate studies in Brazil over the last three decades: initial development, consolidation, and maintenance. In this chapter, we focus on the initial phase and consolidation processes. The first stage involves the first 15 years of the journal (Volume 1–30). The consolidation phase comprises the period between 2000 and 2010 (from Volume 31 through Volume 26, issue number 3[1]) and it ends with the journal achieving an A rating, which is considered an 'international' rank.

The Journal *Educação em Revista*: Creation and Consolidation in the Brazilian Field of Education

Knowledge politics

Interviews with journal editors showed how notions of quality were intertwined with conceptual frames and theoretical traditions emanating from Europe and (to a lesser degree) the United States.

In its earliest days, the journal depended upon work produced by scholars associated with UFMG. Magda Soares, the first editor, explained that, when the journal was established in the 1980s, 'almost all, if not all of the professors in the education area' in her college had attended graduate programs abroad, bringing advanced experiences in the academic field regarding editing and publishing processes. From the earliest days, notions of quality were linked directly to engagement with discussions and debates abroad. Thus, the contributions of scholars who had the linguistic capital and who secured financial support to study outside Brazil were heavily valued. According to Geraldo Magela:

> It's impossible to separate the quality of a journal from the group of researchers who are involved in that institution. So, [...] it's not just

about the journal having good publicity. [You must have] researchers who are in graduate school, in college, who dialogue with this production, right, who do this exchange in the academic field. (Interview with Geraldo Magela, 2014)

In later years, the editors increasingly emphasized the publication of pieces by scholars *beyond* the home institution. The search for exchanges with foreign researchers has become fundamental for the acquisition of prestige and legitimacy in the international field, a strategy widely used by the hard sciences journals.

Social capital, social networks

In its earliest days, there was no systematic public funding for the publication of periodicals in the field of human sciences. The *Letter to the Editors of Education Journals* highlights the quest for solutions to some problems, 'especially those regarding financing of publishing, distribution and marketing of education journals...' (*Educação em Revista*, 1988: 105). Financial difficulties were also highlighted during the interview by Professor Magda Soares: 'there was no money, the school had no conditions' (Interview, 2014).

The Document of the II Conference of Editors registers that the participants decided to send requests to several organs, among them the National Institute of Studies and Educational Research (Inep), requesting changes in the financing programs; and to CNPq and Finep, requesting the inclusion of the journals of Human Sciences in the funding.

To survive, those affiliated with the journal used personal contacts to seek advertisement revenues. In issue number 2, 2 December 1985, there is an acknowledgment to the National Bank and also on the same page of issue number 3, of June 1986, a full page advertisement of the same bank. Although she did not clearly remember that announcement, Magda Soares pointed out that this was part of the discussions: '[...] I remember that we'd discussed the possibility of seeking sponsorship, support, through advertising ... whatever, right? But announcement of the National Bank, I really can't remember...' (Interview, 2014).

To overcome these limitations, those involved with the journal sought to build social networks of support. In issue number 2 of the journal (1985: 88), a paper titled *Encontro de Revistas (Conference of Journals)* reports on an event held by the Center for Educational Sciences of the Federal University of Santa Catarina (UFSC) and the *Perspectiva* (of the same institution) with the support of CNPq (National Council for Research and Technological Development). The paper highlights the 'atmosphere of cooperation and solidarity' and the objective of 'discussing and seeking solutions to the problems related to the production and dissemination of printed information regarding education.' Three other similar records were found: *Letter to the Editors of Education Periodicals*, issue number 3, June 1986; *Concluding Document of the II Conference of Brazilian Journals in Education*, which included the participation of 28 journals and representatives of financing agencies, in issue number 4, December 1986; and *Concluding Document of the III Conference of Brazilian Journals in Education*, promoted by *Educação em Revista* and *AMAE-Educando* (*Educação em Revista*, 1988).

These records confirm the involvement with other groups that studied the creation and the adequacy of the periodicals to the academic field. This strategy is similar to what we see today in the discussions among editors, especially in Fepae (Forum of Editors of Academic Journals in Education) and events of institutions such as ABEC (Brazilian Association of Scientific Editors).

The conferences of Brazilian education journals created a spirit of cooperation among the editors for the exchange of articles, due to the difficulty in obtaining publishable material only with the professors of the faculty of education. As Magda Soares recalls, there was 'this effort to exchange, with other journals that emerged at the time, the authorships, so as not to keep the so-called endogenous practices' (Interview, 2014).

Capturing papers by invitation was another strategy to complete the first few numbers. Therefore, the personal relations of the editorial commission contributed to the publication of quality journals. Capitalizing on lecture texts or talks given by visitors was another strategy for acquiring publishable products. The editorial committee not only focused on works with specific scientific papers formats, with well-defined objects and coherent results; they also published transcriptions of lectures. Soares points out: 'We used this strategy a lot, the person came to give a lecture, a conference, we had to ask for the text, ask for authorization to publish in the journal' (Interview, 2014). The texts were published in Portuguese. Thus, editors had to rely heavily on social capital and personal networks to recruit articles for the journal in the early years.

Expanding social capital helps to sustain the status of the journal. According to Magela,

> if you have a person who by their merit as a researcher is nominated for the National Education Council, to be part of the CNPq Evaluation Committee, the board of Anped [... or is] part of international research groups, it offers reference to the institution that provides for the journal. When a person, rather than an institution, becomes better known, they will carry the journal itself with them. (Interview with Geraldo Magela, 2014)

Thus, we note that the recognition of the journal is linked to the institution it belongs to, to the place occupied by the graduate program to which it is linked, and to the academic profile of the editor and editorial board. This recognition even interferes in relations with development agencies that, in order to sponsor the production of knowledge, opt to invest in journals already legitimized by the field. As one editor said:

> I think the institutional is also linked to these development agencies; since we have a graduate program, we have a well-evaluated production. With the inclusion in the recognized area, we also have the recognition of these agencies as a periodical that deserves to be financed. I think all of this contributes to this process of a good evaluation. (Interview with Geraldo Magela, 2014)

Delocalization and 'visibility'

Further, as it developed, the journal responded to CAPES demands that they secure wider 'visibility' by moving beyond the local institution. CAPES sought evidence of increasingly broad impact. Editors responded with several strategies. One was to 'seek to be inserted in more national and international indexes' (Interview, 2014). Scielo is the main indexing base for Brazilian journals in the human and social sciences and has clear criteria for indexing: Articles must contain title, abstract and keywords in the original language of the text and in the English language; regularity in the publication; peer evaluation; international editorial board, among others (see Packer, 2011). The decision to include the abstract and keywords in English represented an effort to reach a broader audience. However, there was no requirement that texts should be published in Portuguese and English, which certainly imposed limits on the dissemination of scientific knowledge outside the country.

A second strategy was to publish authors from different institutions. Editors began to

> seek productions from different parts of the country, institutions, and abroad as well, and incorporate topics that haven't been incorporated yet. That is to say, there's a proactive policy of the editorial committee, right, which is to try to ensure the quality and comprehensiveness of the journal, and the quality of the final production. (Interview, 2014)

As reflected here, notions of quality were bound up with notions of becoming more comprehensive and more national, if not international.

A third strategy to delocalize involved the addition of extra-institutional members to the editorial board. The events that were held in the Faculty of Education constituted exceptional opportunities to diversify the council institutionally. That is, researchers from other institutions were invited to join the editorial board, until then composed mainly by professors from UFMG itself. Currently the editorial board is composed by researchers of 19 institutions, seven of them from countries such as Portugal, Spain, Switzerland, France, Mexico and the United States.

Since 2000, with the redefinition of *Qualis* criteria, *Educação em Revista* underwent deep adjustments, which were put into practice in subsequent volumes. There were modifications in the graphic design, in the sections, as well as in the structure of the evaluation of the papers to be published. Evaluation by peers and the inclusion of articles that represent institutions from the countries and regions, as well as the regularity of the publication, were well established. These features represent the adaptation of the journal to the new evaluation standard of periodicals that began to take effect in Brazil in 1998. Notably, publication in more than one language still was not used as a quality evaluation criterion for journals.

One of the most important strategies developed since 1998 and the new evaluation standard was the elaboration of thematic dossiers, which further contributed to the rating of the publication as International (Stratification A). Between 2000 and 2003, dossiers were coordinated by members of research groups who invited other groups to discuss the proposed topics. After 2006, dossiers began to go through peer evaluation; they were still coordinated by members of research groups that organized the publications, received papers from several researchers and followed the procedure of processing these texts. The publication of dossiers was a strategy to promote the journal's visibility and increase its circulation. As Geraldo Leão explained:

> The dossier is a strategy of consolidation of periodicals. [It allows] a more consistent discussion on a particular topic and also gives the journal more visibility because people won't look for the journal because it brings one article that matters. They are going to get the journal because in that edition, in that issue, a certain theme has been approached. So the researchers in the field, they will get the journal as a source, and this has a very significant impact on these journals [...] that's why so many journals have opted for dossiers because it brings this visibility, this status to the journal. (Interview, 2014)

The visibility and status that the dossier can provide is justified by the greater disclosure, access and citation of the journal in the academic environment in which it is inserted.

The dossiers were also seen as a global tendency whose adoption benefited the cosmopolitan journal. In the issue of 31 June 2000, the editorial commission highlighted the dossiers that would be published, affirming the international character of this strategy:

> By incorporating the dossier into its editorial project, *Educação em Revista* now takes part in an international trend in the area of journals, a trend that undoubtedly allows a greater identification and affirmation of our editorial project. (*Educação em Revista*, 2000: 5)

Each dossier was coordinated by a different researcher, usually associated with a research group related to the proposed theme, who signed the submission of each dossier. Besides providing information about the area and content of the papers, the introductions explained the process of choosing the papers to be published. For example, regarding the presentation of the *Youth and Adult Education* dossier, in December 2000, Soares explains: 'We requested contributions from eight groups from different regions of the country, six of whom sent their papers' (2000: 137). In the June 2001 edition, Oliveira and Fidalgo, from the Group of Studies on Work and Education (NETE), relate the dossiers to this group and its importance to the 'Faculty of Education and to the development of this thematic field at the national range' (2001: 125).

The journal searched for the most up-to-date content in each thematic area, publishing groups already recognized and legitimized in graduate studies. The publication started to aggregate symbolic value, technical and social capital, and gained legitimacy (see Bourdieu, 1983) since it began to circulate among Brazil's graduate programs, as the dossiers comprised a great variability of institutions and regions. Thus, the Qualis/CAPES criteria of circulation within the field and the institutional variety of authors were met.

The pressure to delocalize and circulate in ever wider circles led directly to an emphasis on internationalization. In the July 2003 edition, the *Teachers' Work* dossier made a leap towards internationalization, being the first of Latin American-wide scope. According to the editorial, 'this dossier brings a picture of a small part of the vast production in going research on teaching work in Latin America today' (Oliveira & Teixeira, 2003: 120). Two articles of foreign researchers were published in Portuguese – one from Argentina and another from Mexico. Publishing international authors enhanced the institutional variability in the international scenario, circulation and visibility of the journal outside of the country. Only in volume 39, in 2004, after two decades, the first text in a foreign language (Spanish) was published.

Internationalization

Between issues 39 and 43, a period of three years, no dossiers were published. In issue 44 (December of 2006), the editorial committee revived the thematic dossiers, which were submitted to the peer review process. This measure meets the strategies of seeking legitimacy, since in the academic field, legitimacy, as well as the recognition of an agent, necessarily passes through the peer evaluation. The editorial committee highlighted the return of the dossiers and justifies:

> The dossiers have played an important role in the area of education by offering an alternative to collections of thematic articles published in the form of books. The fact that the articles published in dossiers are submitted to the same peer review processes (...) may improve the quality

of this type of publication, without giving up the contribution that the format brings to the area. By ensuring the thematic unity and the diversity of perspectives, the dossiers allow an interesting balance between research reports and essays, consolidated results and controversial incursions on a given topic. (Mortimer, 2006: 7)

Once peer review was instituted, dossiers were no longer produced by research groups, and the tendency towards 'internationalization' gained more space. The coordination of the dossiers continued to be carried out by invited researchers, 'who act as editors, inviting the authors and coordinating the arbitration process of the selected articles' (Mortimer, 2007: 9). Thus, the social networks of the individual editor predominanted in the process of curating dossiers.

Publications in European languages other than Portuguese are framed as 'international'; research done outside of Brazil is often portrayed as universal, and yet studies done within Brazil are not granted that same status. Nowadays, English is considered the primary language of world science (see Santin *et al*., 2016). The use of that language has a direct influence on the internationalization of publishing and reinforces the hypothesis that there is a clear relationship between the use of English language in scientific production and its global visibility. The use of English is essential not only to the articles published in foreign journals, but also to the Brazilian journals that intend to obtain international reach.

It is interesting to note that the dossier of issue 45 incorporated an interview with the English-speaking researcher Ivor Goodson. The interview, in Portuguese, was not produced for the issue, but the editor justified it by saying, 'the themes covered in it are in tune with what was dealt with in it' (2007: 10). These dossiers continued to follow this model in issues 46 (July–December 2007) and 47 (January–June 2008). After this issue, they began to appear in issues here and there, but not with the same intensity as previously.

In addition to the publication of dossiers, the journal was indexed in the Scielo Program[2] database, a strategy that contributed to the journal's prestige, visibility, and accessibility. The criteria for inclusion in Scielo periodically undergo updates. According to Fapesp, these criteria:

> evaluate the scientific nature of the journal, compliance with technical standards, acceptance rate of manuscripts, number of original papers published, periodicity, punctuality, performance in terms of citations received, and the institutional and geographical representativeness of the editorial staff. (2011)

Thus, to maintain the prestige of indexing, the journal needed to recruit papers that will be highly cited and maintain geographical representativeness, among other things. This strategy anticipates one of the decisive issues in the processes of internationalization of science, which is the partnership with international researchers.

Being indexed in Scielo faciliated a move from national to international status. In other words, it is a strategy that affords symbolic capital (see Bourdieu, 1983) and, consequently, allows the journal to obtain financial investment from the national funding agencies. A periodical that is part of the collection has its value recognized. 'So you already have an evaluation that keeps going on [by] all the agencies that are involved, all these institutions, development agencies and indexers, especially the indexers,' points out Geraldo Magela, referring to recognition relations by other indexers that also recognize the value of the publications displayed in Scielo.

By 2010, the journal achieved an 'A' rating in the evaluation Qualis/CAPES. This consolidation had already been crowned in the words of the editorial of issue number 46, which celebrates the 'triple success of the Faculty of Education of UFMG': the entry in Scielo, the rating of the journal by Anped (National Association of Research and Graduate Studies in Education) and Qualis/CAPES as a level A journal and the evaluation of the graduate program in education as an international program.

Discussion: Language, Inequality and Power Relations

The journal *Educação em Revista* has done well over the years. But that success reveals a number of contradictions and inequalities in academic publishing in the field of education in Brazil.

First, the expectation that journals produce knowledge that is widely recognized and widely cited has the effect of privileging work that engages with European theoretical models and conceptual debates. In the early years of the journal, as one strategy to establish 'quality,' the journal relied on research produced by scholars who had, generally, studied abroad before beginning their academic positions.

Second, the history of this journal shows how those editors, boards, and institutions with greater social capital were well positioned to recruit articles and, eventually, dossiers from other, similarly positioned institutions. In the days before public financial support, these social networks were essential.

Third, the expectation that journals demonstrate broad impact by increasing citations and diversifying topics and institutional affiliations of authors led to delocalization and, ultimately, an emphasis on internationalization. This trend has the unfortunate consequence of overvaluing research produced outside of Brazil and in European languages other than Portuguese.

There are also downsides to the way that impact is measured. The exhortation to 'internationalize' privileges readers of the centers of intellectual culture in the academic division of labor. In this sense, one of the main limitations of the journal relates to its medium of publication, allowing access primarily in the national territory, and only timidly in Latin America and Portugal. Internationalization encourages journals to seek recognition or permanence in multiple and legitimate systems of international standards. It also encourages the recruitment of foreign scholars for its editorial board. But that did not mean the publication of articles in a foreign language until recently. Publication in Spanish started earlier, with a more significant presence since 2009 in which one or two papers per volume were translated into Spanish. Only in 2016, after more than three decades of existence and a decade of international indexing, did some of the papers begin to be published in Portuguese and English.

Internationalization relies on an unstated center/periphery boundary. The researchers and intellectuals of these countries provide the main theoretical and methodological references in human sciences, forcing the peripheral countries to use English as the main language in the academic field. This tendency imposes on Brazil and its intellectuals the condition of subordinated producers of internationalized scientific knowledge.

The boundaries faced by this journal show, therefore, the contradictions and structural inequalities of the broader international academic environment. For the journal to demonstrate impact and position itself as an important player on the international educational field, the studies must be published not only in Portuguese, but also in English or other European languages. In the contemporary world, the scientific production of intellectuals from peripheral countries does not have impact if not written in or translated to the English language. It is certainly possible to conduct innovative research. However, if the product only circulates in its native language – in this case, Portuguese – it will not accrue the same measure of impact, however relevant it may be.

Conclusion

Considering that classifying journals is a way of supposedly objectifying their quality – i.e. qualifying professors' and students' graduate production – we conclude that the internal and permanent evaluation of a journal is a *sine qua non* condition for its quality.

According to Packer (2011), Brazilian journals have been progressively creating the conditions to publish in English. An increasing number of journals from hard sciences publish exclusively in English; they pay for specialized services for the translation and improvement of English. Some publish parts (e.g. titles and abstracts) in Portuguese, English and Spanish. Human sciences are less likely to make this abrupt shift: In 2009, only 10% of the articles in English language published in Brazilian journals indexed in the Scielo were from human sciences.

English articles experience an advantage in terms of visibility and legitimacy. For example, articles written in English are more quoted than those in Portuguese in the Brazilian journals indexed into the WoS platform. In 2007, with 34 indexed titles, the English articles were 30% more quoted than the ones in Portuguese; in 2009, with 129 journals, the English articles were 50% more cited. The increase of the number of articles in Portuguese indexed in 2009 may explain this difference. The lower performance of Portuguese publishing is relevant in the impact of Brazilian scientific production. To have more impact, Brazilian scholars and journals must spend scarce resources to publish in English or bilingual Portuguese-English in the national journals.

This research allowed us to understand part of a complex system of evaluation that involves the Brazilian journals, whose importance increased as the graduate studies grew in the country. The chapter shows how, even though CAPES does not value publishing in English for education journals, the measures of quality prioritize impact in a way that promotes delocalization and internationalization.

The chapter raises urgent questions that deserve further discussion: What are the expectations of the so-called 'internationalization of knowledge' in Brazilian educational research? For whom, and for what purpose, do we investigate and write our studies? How do questions of knowledge politics, language, and inequality influence what sort of research is conducted, published, and read? The ways we answer these questions will continue to exercise impact across global academia.

Notes

(1) The change in the numbering of the editions was due to adjustments experienced by scientific journals. This context will be explained in the analysis.
(2) The Scielo (Scientific Electronic Library Online) Program arose from an initiative of São Paulo Research Foundation (Fapesp) in 1997 as a pilot project and became operational in 1998. 'Maintained by FAPESP, Scielo Program [is supported by] CNPq and has its institutional facilities located in Federal University of São Paulo (UNIFESP) through the UNIFESP Supporting Foundation (FAPUNIFESP)'.

References

Bourdieu, P. (1983) O campo científico. In R. Ortiz (Org.) *Pierre Bourdieu – Sociologia*. São Paulo: Ática.
Cirino, S., Galvão, A., Leão, G., Sales, J., David, M. and Versiani, Z. (2000) Editorial. *Educação em Revista*, Belo Horizonte, , v. 29, n. 4, pp. 13–16, dez. 2013. Disponível em: < http://educa.fcc.org.br/scielo.php?script=sci_issuetoc&pid=0102-469820130004&lng=pt&nrm=iso>. Acesso em: 5 nov. 2014.
Comissão Editorial (2000) Editorial. *Educação em Revista*, Belo Horizonte, n. 31, p. 5. Disponível em <http://educa.fcc.org.br/scielo.php?script=sci_issuetoc&pid=0102-469820000001&lng=pt&nrm=iso>. Acesso em: 7 nov. 2014.
Comissão Editorial (2004) Editorial. *Educação em Revista*, Belo Horizonte, n. 39, p. 5, jul. Disponível em: <http://educa.fcc.org.br/scielo.php?script=sci_issuetoc&pid=0102-469820040001&lng=pt&nrm=iso>. Acesso em: 8 nov. 2014.

Comissão Editorial (2008) Editorial. *Educação em Revista*, Belo Horizonte, n. 48, pp. 11–14, jul./dez.. Disponível em: <http://educa.fcc.org.br/scielo.php?script=sci_issuetoc&pid=0102-469820080002&lng=pt&nrm=iso>. Acesso em: 8 nov. 2014.

Educação em Revista (1985) Belo Horizonte: UFMG, n. 2, dez.

Educação em Revista (1986a) Belo Horizonte: UFMG, n. 3, jun.

Educação em Revista (1986b) Belo Horizonte: UFMG, n. 4, dez.

Educação em Revista (1988) Belo Horizonte: UFMG, n. 8, dez.

Mortimer, E.F. (2006) *Educação em Revista*, Belo Horizonte, n. 44, pp. 7–10, dez. Disponível em: <http://educa.fcc.org.br/scielo.php?script=sci_issuetoc&pid=0102-469820060002&lng=pt&nrm=iso>. Acesso em: 15 set. 2014.

Mortimer, E.F. (2007) *Educação em Revista*, Belo Horizonte, n. 45, pp. 7–10, jan./jun. Disponível em: <http://educa.fcc.org.br/scielo.php?script=sci_issuetoc&pid=0102-469820070001&lng=pt&nrm=iso>. Acesso em: 15 set. 2014.

Oliveira, D.A. and Fidalgo, F. (2001) Apresentação. *Educação em Revista*, Belo Horizonte, n. 33, pp. 125–127, jun. de. Disponível em: <http://educa.fcc.org.br/scielo.php?script=sci_issuetoc&pid=0102-469820010001&lng=pt&nrm=iso>. Acesso em: 15 set. 2014.

Oliveira, D.A. and Teixeira, I.A.C. (2003) Apresentação. *Educação em Revista*, Belo Horizonte, n. 37, pp. 137–138. Disponível em: <http://educa.fcc.org.br/scielo.php?script=sci_issuetoc&pid=0102-469820030001&lng=pt&nrm=iso>. Acesso em: 15 set. 2014.

Packer, A.L. (2011) Os periódicos brasileiros e a comunicação da pesquisa nacional. REVISTA USP, São Paulo, n. 89, pp. 26–61, março/maio.

Peixoto, M. do C. de L. (2002) Apresentação. *Educação em Revista*, Belo Horizonte, n. 35, pp. 91–92. Disponível em: <http://educa.fcc.org.br/scielo.php?script=sci_issuetoc&pid=0102-469820020001&lng=pt&nrm=iso>. Acesso em: 17 set 2014.

Ribeiro, Daniele, Macedo, Maria do Socorro A.N. and Couto, Euclides (2016) Critérios Qualis A1 da Educação: A avaliação sob a perspectiva da disputa acadêmica. Brasília: *Linhas Críticas*, vol. 22, núm. 47, janeiro-abril, pp. 229–248.

Santin, D. Maria, Vanz, Samile A.S. Stumpf, Ida R. Chittó (2016) Internationalization of Brazilian scientific output: Policies, strategies and assessment measures. RBPG, Brasília, v. 13, n. 30, pp. 81–100, jan./abr.

Soares, L. (2000) Apresentação. *Educação em Revista*, Belo Horizonte, n. 32, pp. 137–138, dez.

Windle, J.A. (2017) Hidden features in global knowledge production: (Re)positioning theory and practice in academic writing. *Revista Brasileira de Linguística Aplicada* 12 (2), 355–378.

Section 3: Transgression and Agency

8 Decoloniality and Language in Education: Transgressing Language Boundaries in South Africa

Carolyn McKinney

Introduction

> one of the most humiliating experiences was to be caught speaking Gikuyu in the vicinity of the school. The culprit was given corporal punishment – three to five strokes of the cane on bare buttocks – or was made to carry a metal plate around the neck with inscriptions such as I AM STUPID or I AM A DONKEY. Sometimes the culprits were fined money they could hardly afford. (…). (Ngũgĩ wa Thiong'o, 1986, 11–12)

> I remember being caught speaking Spanish at recess – that was good for three licks on the knuckles with a sharp ruler. I remember being sent to the corner of the classroom for 'talking back' to the Anglo teacher when all I was trying to do was to tell her how to pronounce my name (…). (Anzaldua, 1987: 75)

> … we can't speak own mother tongue. It's understandable during class hours, but during breaks we sit in fear that we must look out for a teacher, that a teacher may come while we are speaking our language. (Sans Souci Girls' student quoted in *Cape Times*, 16 September 2016)

The quotations above draw our attention to the disturbing experiences of being censured for using languages other than English in post-colonial schooling systems. While the first two reflect notorious experiences in Kenyan colonial and in USA schooling, the third report of a student not being able to speak her own language is current. It should come as a shock to us that the physical and/or epistemic violence that Kenyan author Ngũgĩ wa Thiong'o and Chicano author Gloria Anzaldua so powerfully drew our attention to more than 30 years ago continues to be reproduced in present day South African education. Even more disturbing in the words of the unnamed protesting student from a high school in Cape Town, is her acceptance that she should not use her 'mother tongue' in the classroom, only asking for the freedom to use her familiar linguistic repertoire outside of class hours. The continuing subjugation of the language practices of students from non-dominant groups in education is made possible by powerful monolingual or monoglossic as well as Anglonormative language ideologies. While monoglossic ideologies promote the myth that the typical child is a monolingual speaker of a single 'standard' language, Anglonormativity refers to the expectation that people will be and should be proficient in English, and are deficient, even deviant, if they are not (McKinney, 2017[1]).

I argue that both the monolingual myth and the dominance of English are a product of coloniality, defined by Maldonado-Torres (2007) as the 'long-standing patterns of power that emerged as a result of colonialism, but that define culture, labor, intersubjective relations, and knowledge production well beyond the strict limits of colonial administrations' (Maldonado-Torres, 2007: 243). In short coloniality is that which 'survives colonialism' (Maldonado-Torres, 2007). The power of coloniality in shaping what count as legitimate language practices in South African education as well as how we might interrupt colonial language ideologies informing language in education are of central concern to this chapter. Ngũgĩ wa Thiong'o argued that 'language was the most important vehicle through which that [colonial] power fascinated and held the soul prisoner. The bullet was the means of the physical subjugation. Language was the means of the spiritual subjugation' (1986: 3). It can be argued that the continued acceptance of a schooling system that continuously fails African language speaking children in South Africa is a legacy of such spiritual subjugation. In Ngugi's view colonialism had

> the effect of a cultural bomb [...] annihilat[ing] a people's belief in their names, in their languages, in their environment, in their heritage of struggle, in their unity, in their capacities and ultimately in themselves. (1986: 3)

Today South African parents largely accept the myth that African languages cannot be used for learning and knowledge production, and that any kind of education in English is superior. We accept that our children should transition to English as a language of learning and teaching as soon as possible, but at least from year 4 and that children after only a few hours of exposure to English language learning in years 1 to 3 of school should follow the same curriculum using the same monolingual English textbooks and writing the same monolingual English assessments as their English home language peers. Teachers largely accept that they should hide their bi/multilingualism from education officials and view their innovative bilingual language practices as deficient.

Drawing on the perspective of coloniality and language ideologies, in this chapter I will provide a brief overview and analysis from the perspective of coloniality and language ideologies of the current language in education policy in South Africa. I want to pay specific attention to the colonial conception of language that informs this policy and its implementation. I will argue that in education policymaking and in the case of the prescribed South African curriculum and its revisions, a monolingual habitus has informed the approach to language and literacy. 'Who' informs curriculum decisions, especially in terms of their own language resources, histories and social class, as well as racial positionings, matters. From my perpsective, the lack of recognition of (mostly Black) children's linguistic resources due to the dominance of English and of monolingual ideologies in South Africa and other post-colonial contexts is a form of racism and one of the most pernicious ways in which coloniality continues to shape the schooling system and its deeply unequal outcomes. Following the policy discussion, I will present a case study of language and literacy pedagogy that proceeds from multilingualism as the norm and that takes up a dynamic bilingual approach. The case study offers an example of a pedagogical approach that develops powerful users of language and literacy resources in an established translanguaging space (García & Li Wei, 2014).

Post-apartheid Language in Education Policy in South Africa

In 1997, the first democratic government in South Africa launched a much-celebrated language in education policy. Taking its cue from the 1996 South African constitution, which recognised 11 official languages, the policy clearly stated its goal as 'to promote multilingualism, the development of the official languages, and respect for all languages used in the country' (DoE, 1997, Preamble 1). The underlying principle of 'additive bi/multilingualism' defined as 'to maintain home language(s) while providing access to and the effective acquisition of additional language(s)' was put forward as 'the normal orientation of our language-in-education policy' (Preamble 5). However, even in the idealism of early post-apartheid policy, the idea of 'maintaining' home language while learning additional languages, rather than developing and extending home language knowledge is present. There is also a reproduction of the idea of separate named languages in silos with no recognition of variation within a language, or of the potential gaps between languages named in the constitution and everyday language use, which involves elements of more than one, frequently multiple in urban areas, named languages. Though the widely used practice of moving across named languages in spoken discourse, often called codeswitching in the literature, is common in classrooms where there is a mismatch between teachers and learners' home language and the language of learning and teaching, it is not referred to, either as a bi/multilingual norm or as a potential strategy in the language policy.

Despite the 'multilingual' ethos of the preamble to the 1997 policy, what was legally required was only that learners study and pass one language for the first two years of schooling and a further language as 'first additional language' (FAL) or second language, from grade three. While there is an extensive and valuable literature on lack of implementation of a multilingual policy in South African schools,[2] missing in this research is the consideration of how language itself is conceptualized in the policy, i.e. the ideologies of language informing the policy. The most significant ideology informing both apartheid and post-apartheid language policy and its implementation is the conception of languages as stable, bounded entities clearly differentiated from one another, i.e. a monoglossic conception of language. And following this, ideas about what schools should be doing in implementing the language policy are profoundly shaped by monoglot ideologies which construct the ideal learner or normal child not as multilingual but as monolingual, and the simultaneous use of multiple language resources (or linguistic boundary crossing) as problematic and deviant. There are thus significant continuities between apartheid and post-apartheid language in education policies as well as conceptions of what language is and of what counts as (or does not count as) linguistic competence and capital. This means that in practice the same children who were racially and linguistically privileged during apartheid schooling, a numerical minority of home language speakers of mainstream varieties of English and Afrikaans, continue to be privileged. While policy foregrounds the fact of 'multilingualism' as a norm, it prescribes monolingual practices in a single home/first language, and single Second language (named First Additional Language, FAL, in the policy). It maintains strict boundaries between 'named languages' despite the highly heteroglossic nature of language practices in and out of schools in daily life (e.g. McKinney, 2014; Probyn, 2015).

New language policy through the back door

The Curriculum and Assessment Policy Statements (CAPS), introduced to schools in 2010 and currently in place, makes it mandatory that children take and pass two languages as subjects from Grade 1, using the terminology of the curriculum, one as a 'Home Language' and another as a 'First Additional Language' (and not from Grade 3 as previously mandated). This document in effect introduces a new language in education policy, overriding the 1997 document. While there is now a requirement for earlier introduction of an additional language and for an expansion of time spent on that language as a subject, there is, however, no change in the conception of language, or ideologies of language, informing the curriculum. This change to language in education policy via the back door was accompanied by a document on the national Department of Basic Education's website titled 'Frequently asked questions about LOLT/Language of Learning and Teaching' (DoBE, 2010). Although not an official policy, the one page document nevertheless produced authoritative answers to particular questions on language policy for schools from the government's perspective, and constructs very clear language ideologies. I would like to focus on the last of five points answering the question, 'Is it correct that foundation phase learners now have to have their mother tongue as their LOLT and one additional language? Do schools have to offer more than two languages?'

- (5th point) 'Learners who are taught in their mother tongue perform better than those learners for whom the LOLT is a second or foreign language. At the same time learners learn English as a subject to develop basic language competence in English and so increase its utility as a LOLT later on (from Grade 4).'

While neither the 1997 policy nor the current CAPS curriculum states officially that children should switch from HL instruction to English after the first three years of school, i.e. in Grade 4, this so-called early exit model of bilingualism (Walter, 2008) is widespread policy in primary schools (Probyn, 2005; Department of Basic Education, 2010). In the bullet list, however we see in a few words written in parentheses at the end of bullet point 5, '(from Grade 4)' that this is indeed expected practice. And provincial education departments do not supply textbooks, assessments or learning support in any form in any of the 9 official indigenous African languages. The idea that one can change the language of learning and teaching in a classroom entirely from one day to the next (that is from the final day of Grade 3 to the first day in the new year of Grade 4) is questionnable and is likely never to occur in this way in practice, except in cases where the Grade 4 teacher has only monolingual competence in English (very unusual in the schools where an African language is home language and LOLT in years 1–3). This notion of sudden switch in LOLT thus only makes sense if one is working with a monoglossic ideology of languages as discrete and clearly bounded entities. Additionally, the idea that one can learn a language sufficiently through exposure in a few hours of language as a subject over the course of a week in order to be able to then learn exclusively through that language depends on the social 'construction of language in general as a stable, contextless individual mental object' (Blommaert, 2006: 512). The curriculum in English as a subject is furthermore not designed to teach learners the kind of language they need to use in other areas of the curriculum such as Mathematics or Social Science.

Bearing this in mind, one wonders how the two claims can be made alongside each other as in the fifth bullet cited above – firstly that learners 'perform better' when taught in their mother tongue and secondly that they should learn English simultaneously but separately in English as a subject 'to increase its utility as a LOLT ... (from Grade 4).' It is also specified that learners learn 'English as a subject to develop basic language competence', yet 'basic language competence' is insufficient when language is the most significant tool for a child to access the curriculum. There is no doubt that middle-class parents of English- and Afrikaans-speaking children who begin schooling in these named languages and continue to develop and learn through these languages throughout their schooling would never accept their children moving in to Grade 4 with only 'basic competence' in the language of instruction. In an early exit and sudden transition bilingual model[3] such as is widely implemented in South Africa and in post-colonial contexts elsewhere, the majority of children will be deprived of the opportunity to use their linguistic repertoires as resources for meaning-making. It is difficult not to draw the conclusion that these children are not expected to become successful meaning-makers who can engage critically and creatively with knowledge.

The dilemmas dicussed above will be familiar to many contexts other than South Africa where learners are multilingual but policy and curricula are informed by monoglossic orientations to language. Parallel monolingualism rather than heteroglossia[4] characterizes multilingual education policy globally, yet there is little recognition of this (but see Creese & Blackledge, 2010; Martin-Jones, 2007). Monoglossic ideologies deriving from coloniality underlying language policy and curricula, I argue, are thus a central factor in the recontextualising of African children's linguistic resources as problems and deficiencies on their entry to schooling. With a monoglossic orientation to language, only monolingual language users with a single home language can be imagined as the ideal or normative learner in such policy. And English monolinguals whose home language matches the Language of learning and teaching from entry to school are constructed as the 'ideal' learners causing the least 'problems' for schools.

From Monoglossia to Heteroglossia: Mother Tongue Instruction and Dynamic Bilingualism

Critique of the practice of attempting to educate children in postcolonial countries through a foreign language is not new. But such critique is usually framed by the debate on the merits of mother tongue medium of instruction versus foreign language/English medium of instruction. This debate which pits one clearly bounded language against another is not constructive in a world where multilingualism is the norm and where everyday language practices are heteroglossic, constantly transgressing socially constructed 'language' boundaries. The notion of 'mother tongue' or a single dominant language in the home is also problematic.

In the laudable interests of access to quality education, UNESCO has advocated mother tongue language of instruction for all children as a basic requirement of quality education since 1953 (UNESCO, 1953, 2003). But as Ag and Jørgensen (2013) have pointed out, 'the belief that every person must have a particularly close relationship to one "language", almost invariably the "mother tongue" of the person' is also a consequence of a monolingual ideology (2013: 527, see also Makoni & Meinhof, 2003; Sebba, 2000; Winkler, 1997). In other words, the notion of mother tongue, and the idea that all children/adults have a single dominant language that is learned from birth, (re)produces the monolingual child as normative. The notion of mother tongue also aligns with language as object, and invokes a single standard language, denying the heteroglossic nature of language and multiple varieties of named languages. Related to this is the concern that for many African children in urban contexts characterized historically by migration, urban vernaculars vary greatly from the standard forms of languages named in the South African constitution that informs language in education policy (Makoni *et al.*, 2010). In such cases, it is the concept of mother tongue itself that can deny these learners access to learning through the linguistic repertoire and practices which are most familiar to them and which they bring with them to formal schooling.

A further concern is with the politicized use historically of mother tongue education to prevent access to English in British colonial contexts. De Klerk (2002) shows the historical relationship between mother tongue education and the apartheid-mandated inferior Bantu education. Bantu education enforced mother tongue medium of instruction initially for the duration of primary schooling (to Grade 8) and then later to Grade 4, with a sudden transition thereafter to English or Afrikaans language of instruction. Mother tongue education thus came to be associated with restricting learners' access to English.[5] As Makoni (1999) has pointed out, the legacy of the colonial invention of African languages in South Africa lives on powerfully through post-apartheid language rights in the constitution. While attempting to undermine the dominance of Afrikaans and English through the inclusion of nine indigenous languages as official, the clause, continues the ethnolinguistic categories used to divide and rule African people during apartheid. These official named languages inform and constrain what is considered legitimate as a language that can be used and studied as subject in education (Makoni, 1999, 2003). Colonial constructions of indigenous languages have in many cases nevertheless become sedimented into people's linguistic repertoires. And, despite their colonial construction, many people have strong attachments to or investments in the official South African named languages.

From Monoglossia to Heteroglossia: Principles for Dynamic Bilingualism in Practice

Having provided an analysis of the monoglossic ideologies underpinning language in education policy and its implementation in a post-colonial context as well as limitations of 'mother tongue' only education, I would now like to make a case for an alternative conception of language and literacy pedagogies that aim to delink from coloniality. Such pedagogy proceeds from heteroglossia as the norm and repositions learners from non-dominant backgrounds as resourceful and as legitimate learners. It aims to interrupt the dominant monolingual approach in language education, and specifically to disrupt Anglonormativity, as well as to disrupt the boundaries that are constructed or the borders between named languages. That is they interrupt the expectation that all learners will be proficient in and exclusively make use of a particular prestige variety of standard English as well as the expectation that only one 'pure' language should be used in a particular activity and space. In my view, pedagogies that work to shift the deficit positioning of African and other non-dominant students and their linguistic resources need to include at least two orientations:

- firstly, a focus on relationships between language and power, and particularly on how languages other than mainstream or 'standard' English are marginalised in the language and literacy class, and in schooling more broadly (Critical Language Awareness);
- and secondly enabling students to draw freely and creatively on their full linguistic and multimodal repertoires in order to learn, not only in language and literacy classes, but across the curriculum.

In relation to the first focus on language and power, we need to engage students and teachers in developing their understanding of what language is, what language ideologies are and how these work to advantage some and disadvantage others (e.g. through linguistic profiling). I am arguing for engaging teachers and students explicitly in critical language awareness in order to counter the language ideologies that inform Anglonormativity and monoglossic orientations to language. The process of enabling students to draw on their full linguistic repertoires and expanding what counts as legitimate language use in schools, the second focus, requires a shift in the language ideologies that are largely hegemonic in schools, educational policies and curricula. Ideally, transgressive language pedagogies will take seriously both of these foci. However, Anglonormative ideologies can be countered both through heteroglossic language practices and heteroglossic discourses about language. This is because the use of non-English and non-standard/mainstream English linguistic resources in the classroom in itself legitimises and increases the status of these resources. Thus countering Anglonormativity can happen explicitly, through critical language awareness work that counters hegemonic language ideologies, and implicitly through making visible, embracing and enabling the use of students' full linguistic repertoires.

A heteroglossic concept that has recently gained traction in pedagogical contexts of increasing linguistic diversity in North America and the United Kingdom is that of translanguaging. In contrast to the ideologies which cast monolingualism as normative and languages as clearly bounded objects, the concept of translanguaging proceeds from multilingual languaging as the norm (Blackledge & Creese, 2017; García, 2009; García & Li Wei, 2014; Makalela, 2015). Translanguaging has been defined in a number of ways with emphasis on the description of communicative practices involving a wide range of linguistic and semiotic resources, as well as on the ideological dimension of disrupting a monoglossic and monomodal understanding of language. Blackledge and Creese (2017) also foreground the ways in which people 'bring into contact different biographies, histories and linguistic backgrounds' as they translanguage. In our own take up of translanguaging in South African pedagogical contexts (e.g. Guzula *et al.*, 2016), my focus has been on translanguaging:

- as a normative communicative practice among bi/multilinguals;
- as an ideological position which resists the notion of named languages as autonomous, bounded objects; and
- as a descriptive term which incorporates semiotic modes beyond language.

Case Study: Developing Biliteracy Among 10-12 Year Olds in Rural Eastern Cape, South Africa

The case-study that I present here reports on the *Phemba Mfundi* (Fire learners) residential writing camps initiative of the Nelson Mandela Institute for Rural Education and Development (NMI) based at the University of Fort Hare in the Eastern Cape, South Africa. This initiative has been running for some time and my descriptions are drawn from the third writing camp of the year 2014 which was held at the Nelson Mandela Museum complex in Madiba's birthplace, Qunu, and which I attended. The writing camps were started as demonstration workshops for teachers in isolated rural schools who complained that the strategies that they were exposed to during in-service teacher training workshops were not viable in their own classroom settings and with their particular students. The NMI team were thus explicitly challenging the deficit positioning of rural children in schools with the goal of showing teachers what these children were capable of accomplishing. The camps, taking place over 2–3 days, are arranged around three public holidays on the annual South African calendar: Freedom Day (the anniversary of the first democratic elections), Women's Day (celebrating women's contribution to the anti-apartheid struggle), and Heritage Day. The public holidays provide thematic content for the workshops. In the Heritage Day camp that I focus on here, 60 children from primary school years 4–6 attended, and were divided into four groups of 15 children each. The workshops are facilitated by staff of the NMI as well as a team of volunteers recruited mainly from students at the nearby University of Fort Hare. All of the volunteer facilitators are themselves passionate about writing and about inspiring and supporting younger generations to become readers and writers, while a number of them are published poets and/or performance artists themselves. Teachers from learners' schools attend the daily sessions, participating in the activities and supporting learners in the individual writing sessions.

While the specific activities and sessions vary at different writing camps, they roughly follow a format where the first day begins with children arriving early for breakfast and then coming together for an energetic session of circle games, action songs and rhymes. Facilitators spontaneously take turns to lead different songs and games with some being in isiXhosa, some in English while others are hybrid drawing on the resources of both languages. From the outset, the Phemba Mfundi space is constructed as a bilingual space where both isiXhosa and English resources are valued and where children are positioned as bilingual and biliterate. The last song/game involves children dividing into four groups and following their facilitators into their different venues. Songs and games are used throughout the day in the small groups to energise children when attention is flagging and to inject fun and play into the day. The small group session continues with individual introductions. Following this, input sessions on different written genres such as personal narratives, poetry, and revising drafts are facilitated at different times. These are interspersed with individual writing sessions where children work in small groups at tables and can draw on assistance from facilitators and teachers. Individual writing sessions are followed by a communal session where children volunteer to read what they have written, or to tell stories, and receive feedback from peers and facilitators. At different points over the camp, the whole group of children come together for 'Jamboree' sessions. In one kind of Jamboree, children are treated to guest performances from visiting poets, storytellers and musicians, and/or performances by the volunteer facilitators. Another kind of Jamboree is performed by the children themselves. In their groups, children prepare performances of their poetry, stories, spoken word poems and plays for the whole group. These performances as well as the publication of selected pieces of writing in the annual Phemba Mfundi journal ensure that the children have a real audience for the writing they are producing. Apart from the input sessions run by facilitators, a number of resources are made available to the children throughout the camp. These include a range of published sources: stories, picture books, biographies and poetry anthologies in English and isiXhosa, as well as bilingual dictionaries; the Phemba Mfundi workshop notes compiled by NMI into a booklet for each child and including guidance on different genres; examples of the different genres; writing frames; and collaboratively generated notes from the session that are made on newsprint by facilitators and put up on the walls around the different venues for children to consult, such as in Figures 7.1 and 7.2 below.

The valuing of both the resources of isiXhosa and English is evident in the selection and production of learning materials. Published books are made available in isiXhosa and English, sometimes with the same book being available in both languages; the students' notes are bilingual with most of the instructional notes available in both isiXhosa and English and with both isiXhosa and English example texts provided for each of the genres covered in the notes. The newsprint notes collaboratively generated by facilitators and children (see Figures 7.1 and 7.2) feature translanguaging between isiXhosa and English with facilitators

Figure 7.1 Translation of Figure 7.1: 'Ground rules'/Imithetho: Umntu angabina ntloni/Don't be shy; Singahlekakani/We don't laugh at each other; Umntu makangazigqumi xa efunda/ Don't cover yourself [hold the book to close to your face] when you read; Phakamisa isandla xa efuna uthetho/Put your hand up when you want to talk; Masenze izinto ngexesha/ Let's work within the given time; Masimamele/Let us listen; Singaphazamisi xa kufundwa/Let's not disturb others when we are learning; Singahlebani/ We don't gossip about each other; Sibenexesha ladlala siphumle/we have time to play and rest; Sonwabe/We must have fun!!!

Figure 7.2

tending to record notes following the language that the child used in his/her input. Facilitators themselves move seamlessly across the resources of isiXhosa and English in their talk and children are free to draw on their full linguistic repertoires when they contribute to workshop sessions and tell or perform and write texts. Dynamic bilingualism and translanguaging is thus modeled as the norm in both spoken, performed and written texts. The examples of collaboratively generated ground rules in one group (Figure 7.1) reflect this natural use of language with the two ground rules generated and recorded in English 'No fighting' and 'Respect each other' sandwiched in between a number of rules expressed in isiXhosa. Similarly the newsprint example in Figure 7.2 recording goals, 'What are we doing here?' (Senzani Apha) and 'What we did at the previous camp' (Izinto besisenza kwinkampu endlulileyo) draws on isiXhosa and English resources with no strict separation between the languages, as seen in 4. of Figure 7.2 'Sibukele ne movie'/We watched a movie. Recording translanguaging in written text in this way models for the children the legitimacy of fluid language practices in the space. While translanguaging is common during classroom talk in South Africa, it is very unusual to see this in written form on the board.

I focus now on describing a few of the specific activities from the September 2014 Heritage Day camp. After the songs and circle games in the small group, the facilitator led the group in introductions, asking all to introduce themselves and to tell us about their clan names. This activity was explained and conducted in isiXhosa with some brief translanguaging into English. Through the facilitator's self-introduction in isiXhosa, the children were thus invited to value their families and their home language. The facilitator rounded off the session translanguaging across English and isiXhosa with a final message in English 'Thank you guys for sharing things we didn't know about you. [Now we can all feel] "This is my group and I am welcome here".' Following on the clan name introductions, the facilitator introduced the notion of 'heritage' and led a discussion using the resources of isiXhosa and English. Another of the NMI facilitators uses the topic to draw attention to language, and in this case isiXhosa, as part of one's heritage: 'language comes to my mind when I think of my heritage' ('something that we treasure something that we love'). In a rare moment where attention is explicitly drawn to the named language being used as medium of communication, the facilitator directs children to read aloud the English version of the text on 'Heritage, culture and identity' in their manuals. She justified her choice of the English text by explaining to the children that they often don't get enough opportunities to read English texts. She gets the children to take turns in reading paragraphs of the text and then at the end asks them to read the isiXhosa version silently and individually to reinforce the message. There is a subtle discursive positioning here of the children as more fluent in isiXhosa than English.

After a session of individual poetry writing, with some children supported in revising their draft poems by facilitators and teachers, the facilitator, Mihlali, drew children together for a group feedback session. She put two versions of a child's poem up on newsprint: a first draft and a revised draft and asked the group to look for differences between the two versions and to comment on the relative effectivenenss of the choices made by the author. The poem has been written in English and Mihlali herself speaks in English when she invites children to respond to the poem; children's freedom in choosing what language to respond in however is clear in the fact that different children make different choices and there is no attention drawn to what language resources children have chosen.

After lunch the children were treated to a Jamboree session with two performances by guests Zukiswa Wanner (author) and Dineo Pule (musician). Wanner performed her African retelling of the Rapunzel tale, *Refilwe*, in English and Dineo Pule performed second singing in isiXhosa and playing the *Uhadi* (traditional Xhosa mouth bow made from wood, a single string and a dried gourd). The audience were then invited to share their stories or poems. One child told two stories: the first in isiXhosa and the second in English. The English story was about a girl who leaves South Africa for the USA when she is five years old and learns only English. The dilemma presented is that on her return to her village in the Eastern Cape, she is unable to communicate with her grandmother and cousins in isiXhosa and feels excluded. While the narrator uses mainly English, he is able to communicate the exclusion of the girl through strategic use of isiXhosa highlighting the limitations of the girl's English-only linguistic resources, and her exclusion. I noticed that this theme had also been explored previously in a short story in the 2014 published *Phemba Mfundi* edited collection in which the experience of a child who is schooled at a suburban English only school in town loses her ability to speak isiXhosa and is similarly isolated from her grandmother and the other children on return to the family village. Such stories invert the discourses which exclusively privilege suburban English medium schooling and the dream of living in the USA. They provide evidence that the *Phemba Mfundi* children are internalizing the counter discourses to Anglonormativity circulating in the writing camps. Their performances and written pieces also provide evidence of the imaginative use of language and literacy resources as well as other modes in their meaning-making.

Despite the fluidity with which translanguaging, using isiXhosa and English, is used in the oral discussions, games, songs and input sessions at the workshops, the children tended to write their poems and stories in a single language, either English or isiXhosa. The same child might choose to write a poem in English and a narrative in isiXhosa or vice versa. At the end of the year when children are encouraged to submit their writing for inclusion in the annual *Phemba Mfundi* journal published by the NMI, they are asked to submit at least one piece in isiXhosa and one in English, though they can submit more. The published journal follows a similar bilingual approach to the camp manual or notes where sections are labeled and themes introduced in both languages, often running parallel to each other in a left hand and right hand column down the page. The creative writing itself is reproduced in the language in which it is written, thus only the editorial text is included in two languages. This is significant for two reasons. Firstly, while translanguaging, or fluidly drawing on the resources of isiXhosa and English is the norm in spoken, written and multimodal discourses during joint sessions at the camp, this does not mean that children and facilitators are unable to produce texts in a single language when they wish to or are required to do so. There is no doubt that for these children, isiXhosa is their dominant language, though they are becoming successfully bilingual and biliterate in English and isiXhosa through initiation into translanguaging practices at the writing camps.

Repositioning children as imaginative, enthusiastic and capable meaning-makers, the *Phemba Mfundi* camps illustrate transgressive pedagogy in a number of ways. Highly proficient bilingual facilitators constantly disrupt the monoglossic ideology that keeps languages in separate silos, modeling translanguaging through their spontaneous, and at times deliberate, use of all the resources in their linguistic repertoires. The fact that attention is most often not drawn to named languages means that translanguaging is constructed as a normative language practice in this context. The lack of attention drawn to named languages and lack of judgement of children's language use means that children are enabled to take risks in using English as emergent bilinguals. I was struck by the example of one boy who always chose to make his contributions in English, despite the fact that it would have been easier for him to speak in isiXhosa. Other children most frequently contributed orally in isiXhosa but produced written pieces in English. Freedom of choice regarding linguistic resources enabled children to exercise their agency in the writing camps. The discourses about language that are produced in the discussions further disrupt Anglonormativity by overtly valuing isiXhosa both as a current resource and as a significant part of the children's heritage. Children themselves reproduce these discourses in their own writing and performances, highlighting the inadequacy of others who are monolingual in English.

Conclusion

This chapter has drawn attention to the monolingualist orientation of the current South African curriculum and language policy as it is implemented in schools. I have argued that curriculum and policy enforce Anglonormativity, ignoring the language resources of the majority of South African children. The exclusive provision of monolingual English learning materials, assessments and curriculum not only flies in the face of children's constitutional right to receive education in their familiar languages but also ignores the heteroglossic ways in which language is used in daily life and the extensive research literature on dynamic bilingual approaches to teaching and learning. Language in education is thus a space in which the long shadow of coloniality (and its offshoot apartheid) is cast with dire consequences for African-language-speaking children and speakers of non-standardised varieties. There is no doubt that a review of the outdated 1997 Language in Education Policy and of the language provisioning in the current curriculum is urgent.

However, taking place outside of formal schooling, the learning and creating space of the Phemba Mfundi writing club is not shaped and constrained by the colonial language ideologies that saturate the schooling system. Learners are not restricted to the use of only one named language at a time and to the exclusive valuing of English as European language. While the construction of the named language isiXhosa recognised as one of the 11 official languages in the constitution can be seen as the product of missionary intervention, and thus a colonial construction, it has been appropriated as a resource by the children to design their own meanings outside of the constraints of Anglonormativty and imposed colonial ways of knowing and being. Unlike in their school classrooms, children are not expected to operate in one language (as if they were monolingual) but can draw on their full linguistic and semiotic repertoires. Written materials are produced bilingually showing the children how knowledge can be made and shared through the language resources of their ancestry and not exclusively through English and other European languages. The Phemba Mfundi (fire learners) children light a spark of hope that we can work against coloniality and embrace heteroglossia in language and literacy pedagogy in South African schools and beyond.

Notes

(1) Anglonormativity draws on the feminist-post-structuralist notion of heteronormativity which foregrounds the institutionalised normativity of heterosexuality and the far-reaching negative consequences for those who do not identify as heterosexual.
(2) Highlighted in this literature is the lack of an implementation plan for the policy; the fact that the new national curriculum was developed separately from the language policy thus indicating a lack of political will to promote multilingualism; as well as the common perception among parents that children will only develop advanced proficiency in English if they use it as a medium of instruction (see Banda, 2000; De Klerk, 2002; Heugh, 2013; Plüddeman, 2015; Probyn et al., 2002, 2005).
(3) Early exit model refers to the use of home language instruction for the first few years of schooling (1–3 years) with an early exit to English language of instruction thereafter; Sudden transition model refers to a sudden change in language of instruction from one year to the next (see Walter, 2008).
(4) Following Bakhtin (1981), heteroglossia can be defined as the complex, simultaneous use of a diverse range of registers, voices, named languages or codes, in our daily lives, but it also draws attention to the potential tension between different kinds of registers, and voices (Ivanov, 2000, see also Bailey, 2007).
(5) See Brutt Griffler (2002) on use of mother tongue medium of instruction in order to restrict access to English in the British colonies of Lesotho and Sri Lanka.

References

Ag, A. and Jorgenson, J.N. (2013) Ideologies, norms, and practices in youth polylanguaging. *International Journal of Bilingualism* 17 (4), 525–539.
Anzaldua, G. (1987) *Borderlands/La Frontera: The New Mestiza*. USA: Aunt Lute Books.
Bailey, B. (2007) Heteroglossia and boundaries. In M. Heller (ed.) *Bilingualism: A Social Approach*. Palgrave Macmillan
Bakhtin, M.M. (1981) Discourse in the Novel, in M. Holquist (ed.) *The Dialogic Imagination Four Essays*. Austin: University of Texas Press. (translated by C. Emerson and M. Holquist).
Banda, F. (2000) The dilemma of the mother tongue: Prospects for bilingual education in South Africa. *Language, Culture and Curriculum* 13 (1), 51–66.
Blackledge, A. and Creese, A. (2017) Translanguaging and the body. *International Journal of Multilingualism* 14 (3), 250–268.
Blommaert, J. (2006) Language ideology. In K. Brown (Editor-in-Chief) *Encyclopedia of Language & Linguistics*, Second Edition, volume 6, pp. 510–522. Oxford: Elsevier.
Brutt-Griffler, J. (2002) Class, ethnicity and language rights: An analysis of British colonial policy in Lesotho, Sri Lanka and some implications for language policy. *Journal of Language Identity and Education* 1 (3), 207–234.
Cape Times, Not allowed to speak Xhosa, 2 September 2017, page 1.

Creese, A. and Blackledge, A. (2010) Translanguaging in the bilingual classroom: A pedagogy for learning and teaching? *The Modern Language Journal* 94 (1), 103–115.

De Klerk, G. (2002) Mother tongue education in South Africa: The weight of history. *International Journal of the Sociology of Language* 154, 29–46.

Department of Basic Education (DBE). (2010) The status of the language of learning and teaching (LOLT) in South African Public Schools: A Quantitative Overview. Pretoria: DBE.

Department of Education (1997) Language in education policy, 14 July 1997. Pretoria: Department of Education.

García, O. (2009) *Bilingual Education in the 21st Century: A Global Perspective*. Malden and Oxford: Wiley Blackwell.

García, O. and Li Wei (2014) *Translanguaging: Language, Bilingualism and Education*. Palgrave Macmillan.

Guzula, X., McKinney, C. and Tyler, R. (2016) Languaging-for-learning: Legitimising translanguaging and enabling multimodal practices in third spaces. *Southern African Linguistics and Applied Language Studies* 34, 211–226.

Heugh, K. (2013) Multilingual Education Policy in South Africa Constrained by Theoretical and Historical Disconnections. *Annual Review of Applied Linguistics* 33, 215–237.

Ivanov, V. (2000) Heteroglossia. *Journal of Linguistic Anthropology* 9 (1–2), 100–102.

Kamwangamalu, N. (2007) One language, multi-layered identities: English in a society in transition, South Africa. *World Englishes* 26 (3), 263–275.

Makalela, L. (2015) Translanguaging as a vehicle for epistemic access: Cases for reading comprehension and multilingual interactions. *Per linguam* 31 (3), 15–29.

Makoni, S. (1999) African languages as Colonial scripts. Coetzee, C. and Nuttall. S. (eds) *Negotiating the Past*. Cape Town: Oxford University Press.

Makoni, S. and Meinhof, U. (2003) Introducing Applied Linguistics in Africa. *AILA Review* 16, 1–12.

Makoni, S, Makoni, B. and Rosenberg, A. (2010) The wordy worlds of popular music in Eastern and Southern Africa: Possible implications for language-in-education-policy. *Journal of Language, Identity and Education* 9 (1), 1–16.

Maldonado Torres, N. (2007) On the coloniality of being: Contributions to the development of a concept. *Cultural Studies* 21 (2–3), 240.

Martin-Jones, M. (2007) Bilingualism, education and the regulation of access to language resources. In M. Heller (ed.) *Bilingualism: A Social Approach*, Basingstoke and New York: Palgrave Macmillan.

McKinney, C. (2014) Moving between ekasi and the suburbs: The mobility of linguistic resources in a South African de(re)segregated school. In M. Prinsloo and C. Stroud (eds) *Educating for Language and Literacy Diversity* (pp. 97–115). Basingstoke: Palgrave MacMillan.

McKinney, C. (2017). *Language and Power in Post-colonial Schooling: Ideologies in Practice*. New York and London: Routledge.

Ngũgĩ wa Thiongo (1986) *Decolonising the Mind: The Politics of Language in African Literature*. London: James Currey.

Plüddeman, P. (2015) Unlocking the grid: Language in education policy realisation in post-apartheid South Africa. *Language and Education* 29 (3), 186–199.

Probyn, M. (2005) Language and the struggle to learn: The intersection of classroom realities, language policy, and neo-colonial and globalisation discourses in South African schools. In A. Lin and P. Martin (eds) *Decolonisation, Globalisation Language-in-Education Policy and Practice*. Clevedon: Multilingual Matters.

Probyn, M. (2015) Pedagogical translanguaging: Bridging discourses in South African science classrooms, *Language and Education* 29 (3), 218–234.

Probyn, M., Murray, S., Botha, L, Botya, P., Brooks, M and Westphal, V. (2001) Minding the gaps – an investigation into language policy and practice in four Eastern Cape Districts. *Perspectives in Education* 20 (1), 29–46.

Sebba, M. (2000) What is 'mother tongue'? Some problems posed by London Jamaican. In Acton, T. and Dalphinis. M. (eds) *Language, Blacks and Gypsies: Languages without a Written Tradition and Their Role in Education*. London: Whiting and Birch 109–121.

UNESCO (1953) *The Use of Vernacular Languages in Education*. Paris: UNESCO.

UNESCO (2003) Education in a multilingual world. UNESCO Education Position Paper. Paris: UNESCO.

Walter, S. (2008) The language of instruction issue: Framing an empirical perspective. In B. Spolsky and F. Hult (eds) *The Handbook of Educational Linguistics*. Malden, Blackwells (129–146).

Winkler, G. (1997) The Myth of the Mother Tongue: Evidence from Maryvale College, Johannesburg. *South African Journal of Applied Language Studies* 5 (1), 29–39.

9 Queering Literacy in Brazil's Higher Education: Questioning the Boundaries of the Normalized Body

Dánie de Jesus

Introduction

The aim of this chapter is to reflect on the ways I have dealt with gender issues within language teacher education in Brazil. This topic has not often been addressed in English Language Teaching (ELT), and one of the possible reasons is that language is still seen as a tool for communication, not as a socio-discursive practice that constructs our identities through different power relations which contribute to produce, reproduce or transform social realities. From a critical and queer theoretical perspective, I interpret the experiences of pre-service ELT teachers, understanding gender as the result of discursive conventions which may legitimize, reproduce, and/or question gender inequality. These experiences of gender are based on ideologies that support our perceptions on being male and female. These same ideologies help to reinforce social stereotypes, e.g. individuals interested in the same sex are promiscuous or a danger to the integrity of family and society.

In the Brazilian school environment, it is not unusual to find prejudiced attitudes against gay/lesbian/transgender students. Many teachers prefer to overlook the fact that certain students do not behave according to conventional norms. My analysis of this scenario is grounded in queer theory (Butler, 2006; Sedgwick, 1990/2008) as well as the product of my personal experience as a student who suffered symbolic violence (Bourdieu, 1998/2012) in an educational setting.

I begin my reflection by summarizing my theoretical approach, focusing on certain concepts that have developed around gender in educational settings. I then briefly outline notions from critical literacy related to gender studies, which I call critical queering literacy. Moreover, I describe some activities I have been using with my students so as to question the boundaries of the normalized body in my work environment. Lastly, I indicate some implications of gender-related issues for teacher education.

Contextualization

Over the last few years, I have been thinking about the relationship between gender and education within higher education, and its impact on the Brazilian educational system, particularly in ELT, whose curricula usually focus on communicative skills such as reading, writing, speaking, and listening, and on grammar sequences. This educational orientation tends to develop a linear perception of learning, avoiding the complexity of the issue of diversity. It is also based on a monolingual perspective and on the predominance of English as an artefact of colonialism (McKinney, this volume). Moreover, language is viewed as transparent, neglecting ideological components which conspire to construct our social realities. By contrast, I understand that language can be perceived as a set of discursive practices which collaborate to construct identities and power relationships. In this view, all texts are spoken or written by someone for a particular purpose, in a historical and political context (Janks, 2010).

The challenge of promoting a dialogue around queering issues in ELT goes beyond the educational context. According to an annual survey conducted by the *Grupo Gay da Bahia* (GGB) organization,[1] an LGBT person is brutally murdered every 25 hours in Brazil. This is not confirmed by government officials because crimes against the LGBT community are not reported in Brazil as having been motivated by victims' sexual identities. Moreover, the national school system has historically been a place of neglect of gender differences that strives to regulate and discipline students who may disturb hegemonic boundaries. A conservative wave has sought to avoid discussing gender in Brazilian schools, and as a result teachers have refused to address diversity with their students in spite of gender inequality. I observed this fact during a previous research study (Jesus, 2016), which showed teachers are often not adequately prepared to face diversity in their educational settings. The lack of discussion about gender, combined with bullying from colleagues and institutional oppression, have led many LGBT students to abandon school. Nevertheless, those who remain in the system are silenced and encouraged to adjust to conventions in order to be accepted.

On the other hand, when schools are pressed to talk about sexuality, the latter is always examined as a phenomenon based on a canonical perception of men and women, as well as of different-sex marriage.

Educators do not understand that the hegemonic discourse of masculinity and femininity is circumstantial, i.e. subject to change due to social, historical and cultural factors. Thus, female and male bodies have different silhouettes in specific times and cultures.

However, attitudes towards some LGBT rights have gradually changed. For instance, the Brazilian Supreme Court has passed a law which benefits transgender people by enabling them to use their preferred names without the need to present a medical report, and there has been considerable media coverage of LGBT artists, such as the drag queen Pabllo Vittar, and gay singer Johnny Hooker. There is a contradiction at the heart of Brazilian society: on one side, a conservative group seeks to impose barriers to prevent LGBT rights, and on the other, LGBT culture is becoming popular across different social classes.

In my interaction with pre-service students, questions about how to teach language for diversity purposes have become increasingly common. Students usually do not know how to deal with prejudice and symbolic violence (Bourdieu, 1998/2012) in the classroom, the latter being understood as a set of unconscious violent actions which seek to regulate individuals according to hegemonic behaviour. This type of violence is a way of legitimizing heteronormative, monolingualist or racist discourses. One of the strategies of symbolic violence, for example, is to make gender/racial/linguistic/cultural dichotomies visible in order to reinforce the hegemonic position, and sanction conventional norms regarding gender, race, language and culture.

This strategy inspires the need to question such norms. I want to stress those four perspectives – gender, racial, linguistic, and cultural – as being inseparable aspects of language teaching and learning, in that they stem from a colonized view of education. In other words, we cannot ignore the fact that our syllabi are grounded in ideologies which construct our realities. In English language textbooks, for example, it is common to find women represented as housewives or receptionists and men as doctors or dentists. In terms of culture and race, textbooks tend to stimulate certain stereotypes.

Critical Queering Literacy

My position about what criticality is does not encapsulate the idea of objectivity, which strives to observe the object in a distant and contemplative way. Moreover, I do not perceive the subject as a reflection of social reality, the latter far from being an inevitable consequence of his/her actions. Additionally, I do not view criticality as an oppressive/oppressed binary, given that this stance, while seeking to emancipate subjects by revealing that reality is being masked, simplifies power relationships as synonyms of oppression, ignoring the social, historical and cultural context. Following Freire (2014), I understand criticality as a means to problematise practices that engage with difference in a process of resistance that pursues, in social contradictions, actions of critical agency in the world. Problematising practices are ways of questioning what is seen as truth by the modus operandi. This is not to say that I advocate a discursive relativism that attempts to explain human nature based only on discourse. Understanding how people present themselves in discourse allows me to perceive their locus of enunciation, i.e. why they speak, think or act in certain ways. This enables me to understand how power relations and their possible contradictions are established. From this interpretation, I can search for fissures in the social system, and change them as well.

My action as a teacher educator is therefore supported by a curriculum that embraces differences as being inseparable from human nature. I try to challenge deterministic notions of non-learning that collaborate to maintain a status quo which sustains the destitution of marginalized people. I achieve this by placing myself in a transgressive position that seeks to challenge the boundaries of normalization of bodies. As a transgressor, I adopt a political position that strives to establish a space for dialogue by viewing pre-established identities as contingent and unstable. Through this stance, the teacher education environment may enjoy moments of breaking the circle of normalization, while participants may perceive this moment as a place of criticality. This process needs to be learned in queering literacy practices in order for the social process of normalization of bodies to be apprehended. I use the word 'queer' so as to assign it with a meaning other than that which traditionally rendered it as an insult within the realm of binary systems.

Despite reflecting on teacher education through the lenses of queering literacy, I must confess that this process is not easy, for my students undergo their educational experiences with the notion of an imaginary language as a closed system, centered on the ideal of a native speaker. On the other hand, I have the opportunity to set myself the task of listening to and permanently problematising their statements. In this sense, Menezes de Souza (2008: 138-139, emphasis added) offers us this warning:

> [...] criticality lies not only in listening to the other in terms of their socio-historical context of production of meaning, but also in *listening to oneself while listening to others*. What results from this process of listening is the perception of the uselessness of wanting to impose on the other, to dominate him/her, to silence him/her or to reduce his/her difference to a likeness of our 'I'; careful and critical listening will help us realise that none of this will eliminate the difference between ourselves and the other, as well as encourage us to look for other forms of interaction.[2]

According to Menezes de Souza's view, I can only access critical lenses if I put myself in other people's shoes, hence allowing them to truly speak from their locus of enunciation. However, the locus of enunciation is also not absolute; it is directly tied with context. Thus, every social interaction is marked by conflict. The basic question is to understand why a given situation works in a certain way and not in another. In this sense, as an educator I am not the agent emanating knowledge, but the individual who creates and recreates conditions and the context for learning. Therefore, my professional skill does not consist in offering tools for a correct reading of a certain reality, but in generating instruments through which my students can produce their own readings of different cultural frameworks.

The reader may be thinking: from a practical point of view, how does one operate queering literacy practices when teaching English? In order to understand my line of reasoning, I will now describe four tasks I have used with a group of English language students within language teacher education. I must emphasise that all these activities were followed up by several others so as to help students develop their learning.

In the first task, students watch a video produced by the multinational toiletries brand Dove (www.youtube.com/watch?v=Ei6JvK0W60I), entitled *Beauty Pressure*, in pairs, and answer the following questions:

(1) Who is the possible target audience?
(2) Why did the advertisement choose a girl as the main character?
(3) What is the implication of casting a white girl in the video?
(4) Do you believe this type of advertisement helps women to feel better about themselves?
(5) Why should someone talk to his/her daughter before the beauty industry does?
(6) Do you really think Dove fights beauty stereotypes in the advertisement?

The purpose of these questions was to broaden students' critical perception on the notion of a universal beauty standard, confronting the global/local relationship. Students, in turn, were invited to think not only of the words themselves, but of the implications of lexical-grammatical and semiotic choices for the construction of meanings in the video.

In the second task, students presented life stories of people who were often not noticed at university, such as cleaners, security guards, transgender people, and garbage collectors. During this activity one of my students reported having realised that the cleaning ladies felt humiliated by their working conditions. Grounded on this perception, students debated the experiences of oppression inside the university campus and were able to problematise cleaners' position at university. Some students confessed that they had never paid attention to these people. From what I noticed, students sought to explain class differences without considering racial and gender differences. By realising that all cleaning workers involved were black, poor, and female, students expanded their critical-interpretative repertoire for understanding Brazilian society and its inequalities.

In the third task, students watched a video entitled *Men's Standards of Beauty Around the World* by online media outlet Buzzfeed (www.youtube.com/watch?v=tneKwarw1Yk) which described male beauty standards in different countries. They then had to classify as true or false sentences that summarized ideas about the video. After the listening comprehension task, students discussed in groups their perceptions of a universal masculine beauty and its social, political, and ethical consequences. In addition, they were invited to think about which other types of beauty were possible in addition to those presented in the video. We also questioned the way common sense tends to idealise men with European phenotypes.

In the fourth task, students in pairs had to consider their classmates and answer the following questions:

(1) Who do you classify as male or female? What criteria did you apply for defining them (sex organs, clothes, behaviour)?
(2) Did you need to see your classmates' genitals?

Following, students watched a video entitled Human Installation I, by artists Kyrahm and Julius Kaiser (https://www.youtube.com/watch?v=otqy2cmc9Y4) about gender obsolescence, focusing on an art performance by Kyrahm and Julius Kaiser which was awarded the Arte Laguna prize in Italy in 2009. The performance is a ritual which shows a variety of genders and describes the female-to-male transition. The bodies are naked but faces wear masks, and at the end of the performance there is a dressing-up rite. In groups, students discussed the following questions:

(1) How is gender presented?
(2) What do you feel when you see that some people are able to cross gender boundaries?
(3) What meanings do you assign to the bodies in the video?
(4) Do you think your criteria for defining male and female can be applied to the video?

In this task, students are invited to reflect on bodies and their cultural and moral effects in our society. At the beginning, the video may be provocative to some of them; however, given the fact that it is an artistic performance, a possible eroticism is completely dismissed. In my experience, this type of activity also makes students aware of their own bodies.

Conclusion

In this chapter I attempted to discuss, based on my academic and professional experiences, what I mean by queering literacy and its effects on teacher education. Without being prescriptive, I sought to illustrate this by presenting four activities I developed in one of my classes.

I realised there are few empirical reflections which can help ELT beginner teachers in rethinking curriculum-related perceptions,[3] particularly considering the evidence associated with the issue of 'queering' – involving cultural, racial, linguistic, and other factors beyond formal English language teaching.

As I have pointed out in this chapter, we need to become aware that many students are still unfamiliar with a critical perspective. Perhaps it is important to take into consideration that some of them may not wish to think critically in teacher education. They may wish to remain in a more comfortable position, teaching language through language. However, this should not be an impediment to the development of queering critical literacy.

It remains a fact that many queer students have been threatened with physical or symbolic violence, as the following excerpt shows:

> When I was a kid I always saw a cartoon called the 'X-men'. I loved this cartoon. I would wake up early and sit in front of the TV to watch my favorite cartoon. I always watched it with my sister. One day my sister asked me who I wanted to be. I said I wanted to be the 'Storm' [a female hero in the cartoon] and my mom heard it and hit me. (Jesus, 2016)

This text derives partly from my dissatisfaction with ELT teacher education in Brazil in relation to queer students. However, such dissatisfaction has become a stimulus for reflecting upon education and the issue of critical queering literacy in higher education. I know some teachers may feel insecure about dealing with issues related to queering, while others may be prejudiced or simply not interested. Perhaps as a result of teaching a culture which focuses on the rationality of homogenising our students, we cannot overlook diverse forms of human behaviour in view of the fact that they are a socially given, even when barriers are erected to normalize bodies.

Notes

(1) https://g1.globo.com/bahia/noticia/ba-tem-media-5-lgbts-assassinados-por-mes-em-2017-aponta grupo-gay.ghtml
(2) '[...] a criticidade está em não apenas escutar o outro em termos de seu contexto sócio-histórico de produção de significação, mas em também *se ouvir escutando o outro*. O que resulta desse processo de escutar é a percepção da inutilidade de querer se impor sobre o outro, dominá-lo, silenciá-lo ou reduzir sua diferença à semelhança de nosso "eu"; a escuta cuidadosa e crítica nos levará a perceber que nada disso eliminará

a diferença entre nós mesmos e o outro, e nos levará a procurar outras formas de interação'.
(3) Perception is not only a cognitive process in which one recognises and repeats sensory stimuli. In this paper, it is also understood as a social, cultural, and political representation of the world. In other words, our perception is not fixed, but changeable, and it is constructed in our daily social interactions.

References

Butler, J. (2006) *Gender Trouble: Feminism and the Subversion of Identity*. New York and London: Routledge Classics.

Buzzfeed (2015) Men's standards of beauty around the world.. Disponível em: <https://www.youtube.com/watch?v=tneKwarw1Yk&t=2s>. Acesso em: 07 out. 2017.

Freire, P. (2014) *Educação e mudança*. 36. ed. São Paulo: Paz e Terra.

Janks, H. (2010) *Literacy and Power*. New York: Routledge.

Jesus, D. (2016) Critical literacy for difference: teachers' perceptions of the English language curriculum in Brazil. *Polifonia* 23, 184–202.

Menezes de Souza (2011) L.M.T. Para uma redefinição de letramento crítico: conflito e produção de significação. In R.F., MACIEL, V.A. ARAÚJO (Org.). *Formação de professores de línguas*: ampliando perspectivas. Jundiaí: Paco, pp. 128–140.

Sedgwick, E.K. (1990/2008) *Epistemology of the Closet*. Berkeley/Los Angeles/London: University of California Press.

Unilever (2017) *Beauty Pressure* (2007) Disponível em: www.youtube.com/watch?v=Ei6JvK0W60I. Acesso em: 07 out.

10 'Saudi Women Are Finally Allowed to Sit Behind the Wheel': Initial Responses from TESOL Classrooms

Osman Z. Barnawi and Phan Le Ha

Foregrounding the Change

Recent happenings in Saudi Arabia offer a timely condition for us to examine the intersections of TESOL, empowerment and teachers' role to engage students for change in an under-researched context. While English has, to a certain extent, already penetrated into all aspects of life and has also enjoyed a privileged status in the Saudi context, recent changes have further leveraged the role of English as a language of the new economic reality in this nation. At the same time, English can serve as a language of political, social and gender empowerment more directly through incorporation of social justice pedagogies (Abednia & Izadinia, 2013; Kubota & Lin, 2009). Specifically, using decades of Saudi women's struggles on education and liberation as an analytical lens, we explore the ways in which two Saudi female Western-trained TESOL teachers responded to the new significant reality of their everyday life – '*women can drive*'. Classrooms are 'reflections of the societies in which they are located, so they are infused with the same injustice [gender and racial unrest, struggles] and restrictions afflicting the societies at large', and at the same time 'language and social life are inextricably linked' together in which language is always implicated in the quest for social justice (Khatib & Miri, 2016: 98). These understandings inform our study, as we shall elaborate in greater detail.

In what follows, we briefly re-evaluate over four decades of issues surrounding Saudi women education and liberation. We then address the ways in which the Saudi Economic Vision 2030 and its National

Transformation Plan (NTP) have paved the road towards neoliberal education policy agendas in general and English as a language of new economic reality in particular. We also demonstrate how Saudi female TESOL teachers seek to inject the victory of their decades long of struggles into their TESOL classrooms. We argue that long-term symptoms of oppressions stemmed from rigid cultural traditions and social norms/effects such as cultural stigmas, certain promoted interpretations of Islamic doctrines, every day judgments and parental pressures continue to obstruct Saudi women's enthusiasm to celebrate and make sense of political and social changes symbolized by removal of the driving ban for women. We, thus, argue nothing fuels Saudi women's enthusiasm to explore new pedagogies in their TESOL classrooms more than those historic symptoms of oppression and their own effects.

Women's Rights in Saudi Education: Complexities, Paradoxes and Multiple Realities

While Islam strongly acknowledges women's rights and wisdom long before now and always (e.g. Al Rawaf & Simmons, 1991; Alsuwaida, 2016), rigid cultural traditions and social norms being practiced in certain Muslim communities including Saudi Arabia tend to restrict women's freedom and deny their access to fundamental rights, including the type of education and profession they wish to pursue. As a result, women were not been allowed to receive any formal education in the Kingdom of Saudi Arabia (KSA) until 1956. They began to have access to formal education in the late 1950s only 'when a group of educated middle-class men petitioned the government to establish schools for girls' (Alsuwaida, 2016: 114). Specifically, the first state-run schools for girls were established in the country between 1960 and 1961. Then, women's education was fully controlled by the all-men Ministry of Education (MoE) and its sister organization, General Directorate of Girl's Education. Without inputs from the women's sides, men at the MoE were taking full control of the national policy, curricula and pedagogies which stemmed from Islamic conservative interpretations and local norms. As Barnawi, (2017: 55) shows, in those early days of women's education, the amount of time at school 'allocated to Islamic education ... was 30 per cent', as compared to '14 per cent in 2006–2007 for socio-political and economic reasons.' The primary purposes behind such practices were to ensure that women were educated according to the Islamic traditions, cultural values and social norms being promoted and practiced in the country. These sociocultural norms consider the main role of women as 'nurturing mothers', 'good housewives', and/or social workers (Al Rawaf & Simmons, 1991: 287). Such rituals of naming have also contributed to the sufferings of Saudi women and their social realties as well as educational endeavours until these days, as we show below.

Specifically, in the context of higher education (HE), 'not all degrees are offered in Saudi Arabia for women, which increases the burden on the [female] students who are willing to pursue' (Alamri, 2011: 90) their degrees in specializations such as engineering, banking, architectures, piloting, law, political sciences as well as sport sciences. Such restrictions on fundamental rights of women's education have led to the graduation of thousands of Saudi women with qualifications in social sciences and humanities (e.g. history, geography, and Islamic studies) as well as natural sciences (physics, biology, math, etc.) who then have to compete for very limited job opportunities. Consequently, teaching positions in urban cities have become highly competitive and even very difficult to get with the presence of thousands of female teachers specialized in religious studies, Arabic language, geography, history and the like. Worse even, those who could get government or private jobs as school teachers are paying a huge amount of their monthly incomes to male drivers in order to commute to their schools. Those who work at schools in remote villages far away from their home are now suffering from long commutes and fatal accidents caused by careless male drivers.

These challenges have caused many female teachers to give up their dreams, while others have experienced mental stress because they could not get permission from their male guardians to commute several hours long back and forth every day to teach in a village (e.g. Al-arabiyah, 2008). At the same time, women who had pursued their qualifications in nursing and other medical fields also found it hard to get married. This is because such professions are considered for men only, and it is rather too liberal for women to share offices with men and freely interact with them at workplaces such as hospitals or banks. For several decades until recently, activists who were vocal about gender inequalities and social injustice were aggressively suppressed by religious clerics whose doctrines were dominating the sociocultural environment of the country, including local newspapers, TV shows, dress code, and other public discourses.

Nevertheless, the events of 9/11 and its aftermath began to challenge over 40 years of rigid religious, ideological and epistemological beliefs rooted in the socio-cultural environment of Saudi Arabia. Concretely, since 9/11 international organizations from Western countries and those led by the US government have aggressively attacked the Saudi education system and its curricula. They have argued that the current Saudi education curricula impart doctrines of violence and intolerance against others, and promote abusive male guardian systems, and so on. As Karmani (2005) reports:

[The US] Congress (H. Con.Res, 432) concurred that the textbooks being used in Saudi educational curricula were focusing on what is described as a combination of intolerance, ignorance, anti-Semitic, anti-American, and anti-Western views in ways that posed a danger to the stability of the KSA, the Middle East region, and global security. (2005: 261)

This led the Saudi government to drastically restructure and transform its entire education policy, accompanied by the introduction of more English into its school curricula and specific steps to address gender issues. In 2004, the MoE, for the first time in the history of the country, allowed both boys and girls to study the same English textbook called *'Say It In English'*, developed by female Saudi TESOL teachers. Additionally, in 2004, 'the Saudi MoE allocated a budget worth millions of dollars, with Royal Decree No. 171 dated 14/08/2004 (corresponding to 27/6/1425 H)', to the implementation of English at primary schools, starting at grade 6 (Barnawi & Al-Hawsawi, 2017: 199). All these decisions caused heated debates among and between religious clerics and liberal Saudis. Some religious clerics raised their concerns about a conspiracy behind all those moves orchestrated to liberate women and to destroy Arabic, the national cultural identity as well as the Islamic heritage associated with it. Yet, senior Saudi officials argued that English was/is a national strategic choice in today's neoliberal globalized economy; thus, opponents need to reconsider their reactions (See Barnawi, 2017 for more accounts on these issues). While these debates were happening inside Saudi Arabia, international organizations such as Human Rights Watch continued to argue that women's rights violations were prevalent in Saudi Arabia despite the fact that the government had already established its National Human Rights Commission in 2004 in order to protect women from the abusive male guardian system. As seen in the Human Rights Watch Report released in 2004,

> Saudi women continue to face serious obstacles to their participation in the economy, politics, media, and society. Many foreign workers face exploitative working conditions; migrant women working as domestics often are subjected to round-the-clock confinement by their employers, making them vulnerable to sexual abuse and other mistreatment.[1]

The US Department of State in its 2004 report on Saudi women's liberation also expresses that

> Women may not legally drive motor vehicles and were restricted in their use of public facilities when men were present. Women must enter city buses by separate rear entrances and sit in specially designated sections. Women risked arrest by the Mutawwa'in for riding in a vehicle driven by a male who was not an employee or a close male relative.[2]

The last decade has witnessed drastic transformations on issues surrounding women's education and liberation in the KSA. The King Abdullah Scholarship Program (KASP) implemented in 2005 has allowed hundreds of Saudi females to travel overseas (e.g. the UK, Canada, Australia, USA, etc.) to pursue their qualifications in disciplines such as TESOL, engineering, nano-technology, media, political science, architecture, law and medicine. Under the government's will and direct support, local universities have also been aggressively internationalizing their academic programs by changing their school vision and vision statements, franchising their programs with international institutions and adopting English medium of instruction and the like (see Barnawi, 2017; Phan & Barnawi, 2015). Consequently, within the past 10 years, the demography of the country has dramatically changed with the increasing number of western-educated Saudi females.

The very presence of western-trained Saudi females, many of whom have become more vocal about their fundamental rights, has also attracted the attention of both local and global media outlets. Many Saudi females have begun to demand equal opportunities at work, custody of their children, physical education curricula at schools and gyms for women. They have also demanded the right to dress the way they want, to travel outside the country without permission from male relatives, and to enter and leave their university premises without restrictions or being asked to fill out a paper with their driver's details and guardian's signature. They have also demanded the government lift the ban on using their camera phones on campuses and put an end to violence caused by security supervisors on women's campuses across the country. In the midst of all this, the death of a female Saudi student caused by a heart attack, who did not receive timely medical treatment because the male paramedic had to wait for permission from the local authority to enter into the female campus, caused a huge uproar on Twitter and local media. Saudi females then organized many campaigns urging the government to meet their demands and at the same time to allow female drivers behind the wheel.

The year of 2013 in particular witnessed the peak in this campaign when several Saudi females attempted to drive in major cities such as Riyadh, Jeddah, Dammand and Al-Khubar. They had also gathered over 16,000 signatures via an online petition requesting that the government allow women to drive. Manal Al-Sharif, a public face of this campaign (dubbed October 26 driving for women), and other female activists were all imprisoned for over one week because such acts were considered 'public order offences and demoralisation'. Nevertheless, as one of us argues (Barnawi, 2017), 'the rapidly emerging socioeconomic and political challenges within the country and beyond' together with the international pressures over Saudi women's education and liberation forced the government to seriously evaluate the situation. Specifically,

> (1) a high unemployment rate among youth (aged between 15 and 29 years); (2) low economic participation by females; (3) the recent oil

crisis, which caused leading Saudi companies like Ben Ladin, Saudi Oger. Ltd. and Al-Mojil to declare bankruptcy; (4) the Arab Spring uprisings; (5) the birth of ISIS; and (6) the Yemen War (led by the KSA) have worsened the political and economic conditions of the country. (Barnawi, 2017: 47–48)

To address its national interests in the face of policy pressures domestically and internationally, the Saudi government in 2016 endorsed a comprehensive national reform backed by a series of policies, the 'Saudi Economic Vision 2030', which aims at moving the country from an oil-based economy to a knowledge based economy. We argue and demonstrate below that in the context of these national reforms further endorsed by this 'Saudi Economic Vision 2030', dominant neoliberal social imaginaries have added more value to English, positioning it as a language of new economy and social transformations in the country.

English as a Language of New Economy and Social Transformations in the KSA: Vision 2030 and NTP

With over 50 percent of our university graduates being female, we will continue to develop their talents, invest in their productive capabilities and enable them to strengthen their future and contribute to the development of our society and economy. (Saudi Vision 2030)[3]

The Saudi Economic Vision 2030 and its NTP released in April 2016, under a royal decree, has created a new spirit for the country, showing the highest commitment to participating and playing an ambitious role in the global market economy in all fields, including education. At the same time, the very language of the Vision 2030 not only plainly acknowledges the struggles of Saudi females, but also makes a promise to 'develop their talents, invest in their productive capabilities and enable them to strengthen their future' so that they can equally contribute to the human capital development of the country.

To fulfill its promise to empower females and liberate them from abusive male guardian systems, the Saudi government has implemented several radical initiatives that have disrupted the country's well-established social norms and cultural traditions. Following the spirit of the 2030 Vision, within two years (2016 and 2017), the Saudi government already lifted the ban on using camera phones on female campuses, removed the ban that used to forbid women to go to cinemas and movie theaters, allowed women to enter sport stadiums and to travel outside the country without permission from their male relatives, approved physical education programs in girls' schools, allowed females to enter and leave their university premises without restrictions, allowed women to be elected to municipal councils for the first time in the history of the country, and hosted the first concert of female performances in the history of the country as well. In a breakthrough, the Minister of Education appointed a female professor, Dr Sumaya Bint Sulaiman Al Sulaiman, as the first dean ever for a design college. A few months later, Dr Dalal Namnaqani also became the first woman dean of a medical university in charge of male and female faculties. It should be noted that except Princess Nourah Bint Abdul Rahman University, an exclusively for women university in the capital city, Saudi female professors had never enjoyed such leading positions in Saudi Arabia's history up to this point in 2016–2017.

While the Saudi society is still struggling to make sense of these collective shocks and deep-seated sociocultural transformations occurring in the country, the government has made an even more radical move: endorsing women's rights to drive by themselves. Truly, it is a reality that Saudi females are now free to sit behind the wheels. While this decisive move from the government has been supported with much solidarity and celebrations by local as well as international actors (e.g. Okaz, Alwatan, Riyadh Newspaper, Hollywood Stars, US State Department, Fox News, CNN, BBC, etc.), many religious clerics and conservative scholars have openly opposed the idea. They have condemned it as 'westernisation' and a 'conspiracy' from the US to destroy the cultural identity of the country. The US is 'a byword in traditionalist circles for anything distasteful or immoral – for being behind the campaign' (The Guardian News, 2017, n.p.). In opposing the decision to allow women to drive, for instance, a Saudi cleric has commented that

> If a woman drives a car that could have negative physiological impacts as … physiological and medical studies show that it automatically affects the ovaries and pushes the pelvis upwards.[4]

Another leading Saudi cleric, Saad Al-Hijri, has expressed a shockingly humiliating statement towards women and women driving,

> It is not their fault, but women lack intellect, do they not? 'Would you give a man with half an intellect a driving licence? So how would you give one to a woman when she has half an intellect?' And if they go out to the market this gets halved again! So they now have a quarter of an intellect.[5]

Indeed, such ridiculous, offensive and disgraceful statements went viral on social media such as Twitter and the like. For instance, an Arabic hashtag dubbed 'Al-Hijri-women-quarter-brain' was circulated 119,000 times within less than 24 hours criticizing the cleric and asking him to empirically substantiate his claims. In showing support for women and their rights to drive, a Saudi comedian, Hisham Fageeh, produced a new version of Bob Marley classic song 'No Woman, No Cry' and called it 'No Women, No Drive'. However, alongside this strong collective support was a hashtag with 20,000 tweets supporting Al-Hijri's position being simultaneously circulated. In response to all this, the Saudi officials have taken a firm action by suspending Al-Hijri from all religious activities, on the grounds that his insulting, dubious and naïve statements could easily spark controversies and tensions in the society, which in turn could hinder the government's endeavors to further modernize the country and to revert it to a moderate Islamic society.

At the same time, many Saudi women posted videos of themselves driving cars side by side with their male guardians, while others posted videos on social media driving alone. Unfortunately, in less than three months, several female drivers died in road accidents while learning to drive, thereby complicating the discourse and domestic fights regarding Saudi women's education and liberation.

In this very context, we argue that Saudi female educators, including those in TESOL, are at the forefront of these historic moments. They have been given the opportunity as well as tremendous challenges to navigate an over 40-year period of struggles filled with painful memories and die-hard stigmas. Saudi TESOL teachers/educators, together with teaching linguistic, functional and communicative knowledge and skills to students, can now incorporate the above spirit into language teaching and learning to address and discuss cultural stigmas, inequalities and power relations associated with gender. They also have every opportunity to devise socially situated classroom pedagogical practices that help raise female students' awareness, and proactively engage them with new realties occurring in the country (Kubota, 2011).

Specifically, in this chapter we present the accounts of two Saudi female Western-trained TESOL university teachers to help understand (1) how they responded to the official news of *'women can drive cars'*, and (2) what pedagogical means they have used to introduce this symbolic, economic, social and cultural victory into their TESOL classrooms. The accounts reported are from our multi-year project on international teachers of English in global contexts. This project consists of several sub studies investigating inter-related questions and phenomena; and each sub study has adopted its specific data collection methods. Our publications including Barnawi and Phan (2014) and Phan and Barnawi (2015, 2018/2019) are informed by this overall project as well. Our intention in this chapter is not to provide universalized classroom pedagogies to address varied social struggles experienced by female TESOL teachers; instead, we aim to realize potential and fundamental elements that help facilitate teachers' classroom pedagogical choices and practices in Saudi Arabia inspired and driven by their very specific symbolic moments of social and cultural transformations.

Three methods were used to collect data: (i) a semi-structured individual interview with the teachers, followed by (ii) a proposed lesson plan developed by each teacher respectively, and then (iii) a follow-up interview with each teacher. After the first interviews, we asked each participant to propose a lesson plan that could help her students understand how cultural stigmas, inequalities, and power relations regarding gender are embedded and negotiated in/through language. The follow-up interview with each participant was to obtain more insights into the pedagogical justifications that informed the design of the lesson plan. The interviews were conducted in English as well as in Arabic.

Getting to Know Ahlam (pseudonym)

Ahlam obtained her Master's and PhD degrees in TESOL from the United States of America. She also has a BA in English literature from Saudi Arabia. She has 10 years of experience teaching English academic writing courses to female undergraduate students at one of the leading universities in the capital city, Riyadh. Ahlam felt that her Western qualifications bestowed on her several forms of capital, including instrumental, cultural, social and institutional capital:

> My TESOL qualifications have offered me access to a prestigious job with a high pay at XXX University. Also, my research interests and expertise in the area of critical pedagogy have allowed me to help my students understand the cultural as well as the political aspects of the English language. I have also conducted several awareness workshops on the role of Saudi women in TESOL. For several times, I have been invited to speak about women issues in conferences and seminars across the country as well.

She describes the news of '*Saudi women can drive cars*' as being both emotional and painful. Emotional because she immediately remembered her 'best friend, Amani, who passed away in a fatal car accident' a few months earlier while commuting for three hours back and forth every day to teach English in XXX village outside Riyadh. It was painful because, as she narrated, 'it took [her] a year to convince [her] husband to teach [her] how to drive', while they were both studying in the United States. As she narrated, 'I could not sleep ... I could not eat ... I kept posting my US driver licence on Facebook and promising my friends that I would teach them how to drive no matter what it takes'. She also acknowledged that among her colleagues at XXX University, she had been known for being more vocal about women's rights and equalities. She recalled:

> I sent an email to my colleagues the next day asking them to spend the first 10 to 15 minutes of their classes discussing the news of 'women can now drive a car' with their students. I urged them to pay special

attention to different expressions and vocabularies used by students in the classroom to express their feelings. This is because expressions and vocabularies occurred on such an occasion are also signs of power and authority as well as social values that need to be taken seriously.

She also proposed the following pedagogical tasks, as part of her lesson plan, to transform such a historical and symbolic victory into her academic writing classroom:

Task 1: Engaging the learners
- I will ask students to gather different materials written in English that discuss the issue of 'Saudi women allowed to drive', in the form of glossary brochures, newspapers and the like.
- I will then negotiate, refine and select texts/materials that are more significant and can ignite dialogues and generate debates around the issue of women driving.
- The selected materials will then be given as a reading assignment for the following class.

Task 2: Reading assignment
- Prior to the next class, I will prepare several reading activities for the purpose of raising language as well as political/cultural awareness (e.g. tensions surrounding women's rights, past ideologies, tones, expressions, etc.)
- This assignment can be conducted through a variety of reading techniques such as scanning and skimming and subsequently allow students to make inferences and predictions while acquiring vocabulary relevant to the topic in question, and highlighting grammatical components, etc.

Task 3: Discussions
- I raise thought-provoking questions around the issue of *women allowed to drive* such as 'Should Saudi women be allowed to drive a car?' I then ask students to share their opinions through English. I will also encourage them to discuss the question of *'Should Saudi women be allowed to drive a car with their family members (e.g. parents, bothers, etc.)'?* While students are discussing the topic, I will draw their attention to different vocabularies, structures, and written expressions in the texts as well as inquire about the opinions of their family members.

Task 4: Writing an opinion essay
- I will introduce the structures of essay writing to the class: an introduction, a body of the essay, and a concluding paragraph.
- As a second step, I will ask each student to write her opinion about *'should be allowed to drive a car?'* using the essay structures discussed

in the classroom (e.g. introduction, general statement, thesis statement, etc.)
- The two previous steps will culminate into a feedback workshop through which I will ask students to read their essays in class and get feedback from peers.

Ahlam strongly believes that such pedagogical tasks will offer her students great opportunities to discuss challenges and address individual pedagogical needs, be they 'language, forms, structures, content, and so on'. In the follow-up interview, she justifies her proposed pedagogical tasks as follows:

> In the first task, I mainly want to encourage students to take part in the selection of teaching and learning materials. The second task tends to foster the culture of critical reading abilities among students so that they can make sense of written texts in a questioning fashion using wh-indicators like how, when, who, why and so on.

Importantly, such tasks suggest that, through textual analysis, students will learn how language arranges meaning and conveys a set of ideological beliefs and attitudes in a given discourse community, as Blommaert (2005) argues. Ahlam sees writing as a social activity in which

> students should be given freedom to express their voices in class and share their opinions with different audiences, including family members.

She elaborates on her pedagogical choices,

> Through in-classroom discussions, I want my students to see Saudi women's struggles in rather contradictory ways. They will learn tenses as well as lexis used by different writers to describe the event'. [In this fashion, while learning English], they will also become aware of the narrative of tensions as well as resistance between different groups both inside and outside classrooms.

> My students will not produce an imaginative piece of writing. [Instead,] they are more likely to express their opinions in an authentic manner.

Ahlam's views echo Breuch's (2002) argument that 'writing as an activity rather than a body of knowledge, our methods of teaching as indeterminate activities rather than exercises of mastery, and our communicative interactions with students as dialogic rather than monologic' (2002: 99). Through these pedagogical tasks, Ahlam wants to play the role of teachers as 'co-workers who actively collaborate with their students to help them through different communicative situations both inside and outside the university' (Kent, 1994: 166). Importantly, she hopes that her students will able to demonstrate their authorial presence in the text, voice their opinions, and develop internally persuasive positionalities in classrooms, the very position that has been well argued in Bakhtin (2004).

Getting to Know Tahani (pseudonym)

Tahani holds a Bachelor's degree in English Literature from Saudi Arabia and a Master's degree in English as Second Language (ESL) from the United States. While completing her MA program, she had the opportunity to teach ESL students at the language center affiliated to her university in the States. She described herself as being 'open minded' and 'internationally-minded woman' because of her family background. Her father worked as a diplomat and she lived with her family in Virginia for several years. Because she lived in a big city in America where commuting between schools, hospitals and shops by taxi was very expensive, she was forced to learn how to drive and become self-dependent. Another factor that motivated her to drive, as she narrated, was the fact that 'hundreds of Saudi families [in the US] were comfortably driving cars, including [her] mother's friends'. She learned to drive through 'XXX driving school in Virginia'. Her family – mother, brothers, sisters and father – offered her a medal to mark the event and took many pictures with her when she obtained her US driver's license. Unfortunately, after moving to Saudi Arabia, she ended up using the Uber car service, and at the same time had been fighting against incessant harassment of male drivers. Thus, when the government made it official that Saudi women can now drive cars on their own, she felt relieved and overwhelmed at the same time.

> A few minutes before going to bed, I checked my Twitter account and heard that Saudi women could now drive cars. I began to shout and scream unconsciously because I was tired for so long, tired of fighting against the harassment of male drivers, tired of spending a lot of money on drivers, and tired because I have the power and driving skills but cannot drive. I had a lot of snapshots that night. (Tahani)

She continued to recall,

> The following day, many of my students came to my office and congratulated me because I often discuss the suffering of Saudi women in the classroom.

Tahani celebrated the news with her students at the university by posting the statement 'Today is a historic day' on the board in her classrooms for an entire week. 'It is not about driving, it is about freedom, empowerment and basic rights. You, males, would not understand the impact of this news on day-to-day life,' expressed Tahani.

Tahani believes that the following classroom pedagogical practices would effectively connect the classroom with the students' social realities, facilitate learning processes, improve students' motivation, enhance their academic literacy and raise their political consciousness. She also argues that 'By the end of this lesson, students will be able to: (a) explore issues of unconscious bias and (b) practice ways to be more understanding 'empathetic'. Below is Tahani's lesson plan.

- *Learners' profile*
  - The English proficiency of learners ranged between A2–B2 levels based on The Common European Framework Reference for Languages: Learning, teaching, and assessment (CEFR).
- *Warm-up activities (8 to 10 minutes)*
  - Share a PowerPoint presentation showing random pictures of Saudi girls waiting for someone to pick them up, a driver with children, and girls subject to harassment on the street.
  - Ask learners if they can relate these pictures to their daily life.
  - To generate an open discussion, ask learners to imagine what it feels like to be in someone else's shoes: *How would I feel in this situation? What is the solution? How life would be easier if we had the right to drive our own car.*
  - Ask learners to write the name of some Saudi activists on the board: Manal Alsharif, Lujain Alhathlol, and Aziza Alyousif.
  - Ask learners to work in pairs in order to share any ideas they have about those females and their deeds in relation to women's struggle for freedom.
- *Activities for the main body of the lesson (50 minutes)*
  - Ask learners to explain: *why did I mention Saudi activists' names?*
    - Ask learners about their opinions regarding the means through which the right to drive was granted to them. Ask them about the possibility of leading their own struggle if they had the power and support and what they would avoid to conquer their rights. Here, the learners will be asked to use the proper forms such as *I agree* and *I disagree* to convey their opinions.
    - Ask learners to use the clip from the movie '*Suffragette*' to discuss the challenges women had to go through to win what a lot of people nowadays take for granted, and relate that to the importance of Saudi activists' struggle.
    - While listening, the teacher will introduce new vocabulary from the movie (e.g. *protest / driving bans / motorists / arrested / posting videos / public opinion / traffic / illegal /rights/ hiring a driver, etc.*). The teacher then asks students to surmise the meaning from the context.

- *Comprehension questions (7 minutes)*
  - The learners will be asked several comprehension questions about the movie such as *In what ways can we relate this movie to the struggles of Saudi women? What is Manal Alsharif's story? What is she campaigning for?* etc.
- *Lesson closing activities (10 minutes)*
  - **Exit slip:** The learners will write messages to Saudi activists on a sticky note and post it on the board while they leave the classroom.

Tahani felt that the warm-up activities, coupled with the listening and speaking tasks in the proposed lesson, aim at not only depicting 'the ground realties' faced and experienced by her students, but also at helping them 'understand the pains of others' in the classroom. Such pedagogical tasks will certainly foster a culture of solidarity and support in actual classroom settings. Importantly, they would help students acquire the ability, knowledge and skills to speak with confidence and authority. She further explained in the follow-up interview that vocabulary items such as 'protest/driving bans/motorists/arrested/posting/rights/videos/public opinion/traffic/illegal/hiring a driver' and the like presented in the lesson would help students 'negotiate power relations' and 'express their opinions'. 'The actors in the movie and the different events and expressions used throughout the movie would help female students to know the history of women struggles and successes around the world', elaborated Tahani.

Such arguments and justifications of pedagogical choices from Tahani are in line with Bourdieu's (1991: 7) position that linguistic expressions are inclined to 'specific social conditions in which they are used'. Tahani's proposed activities can enable 'the actual speakers … to embed sentences of expressions in practical strategies which have numerous functions and which are tacitly adjusted to the relations of power between speakers and hearers' (Bourdieu, 1991: 7). Indeed, language is never a neutral system in conveying messages; instead, it is a semiotic system that manifests certain social values and ideological effects in a given social and educational settings (Street, 1984). Thus, 'the sticky note' used by Tahani represents an apparatus of power negotiation and relation between the students and the status quo they want to disrupt. Students will have the freedom to write a short message to Saudi activists in order to maintain or revisit the existing distribution of power 'between men and women' in Saudi Arabia and internationally.

Concluding Remarks and Implications

This chapter thus far shows that female TESOL teachers can play a major role in addressing social injustice and inequalities in contexts like Saudi Arabia where issues of women's education and liberation have long been controversial. Under the Saudi Economic Vision 2030 market framework, English has become a language of advancement and job opportunities for both males and females. Symbolically, English has also become a language of social, political, educational, and cultural transformations centered on women's empowerment. We argue that language classrooms can also be utilized by teachers to address social injustice and inequalities through different pedagogical tasks, in addition to the issues of identities, power relations, ideologies and the cultural politics of the language itself. The pedagogical tasks proposed by Ahlam and Tahani in their TESOL classrooms are aimed at achieving the demands of decades long of women's struggles; liberating them from male guardian systems and offering them necessary language skills to pursue their dreams, including driving cars and education. Nevertheless, in our earlier work (Barnawi, 2017; Barnawi & Phan, 2014; Phan & Barnawi, 2015) we fully acknowledge that English and English medium instruction practices increasingly promoted by the Saudi government are not neutral and are all about empowerment. English and EMI also serve as a means of inequality, power (re)distribution and social (re)construction, as in many ways English and EMI 'decide which social and linguistic groups have access to political and economic opportunities, and which groups are disenfranchised' (Tollefson & Tsui, 2004: 2). Moreover, when English, power, culture and gender are interwoven, the degree of complexity is paramount and intensifies, as seen below.

Ahlam shocked us at the end of the follow-up interview with her when she suddenly stated, 'I am not going to drive cars because my mother would not accept it.' This answer was totally unexpected. It contradicted what she has committed to achieving throughout her proposed lesson plan. It contradicts her self-claimed image as a critical pedagogue. She responded to our confusion, speaking in both English and Arabic,

> I know Islam does not forbid women from driving but (الجنة تحت أقدام الامهات) (Paradise lies under the feet of your mother).

On the contrary, Tahani firmly stated that 'I am not going to buy a car now because of the male harassment and reckless drivers. But I will rent a car and begin to drive immediately.' We argue that many deep-seated rigid cultural traditions and social norms/effects, everyday social judgments and parental pressures resulted from particular interpretations of Islamic teaching have continued and will continue to prevent Saudi women from owning and taking initiatives to create new meanings of their new era. While nothing could fuel Saudi TESOL female teachers' enthusiasm to explore new pedagogies in their TESOL classroom more than those repeated experiences of oppression and their accompanying effects (troubles and displeasures) on women, these very experiences and fears are also gatekeepers – many of whom are family members and women themselves. We boldly propose that a way to move forward is for Saudi female TESOL teachers to critically and proactively engage with those experiences and fears and effects as analytical lenses to navigate their new era both inside and outside classrooms. Seen in this manner, TESOL classrooms in Saudi Arabia could be a productive site to nurture and enable these propositions to take shape and be sustained. We further argue that women driving and women's rights should not only be an integral part of the TESOL classroom dynamism, motto and spirit among female teachers and their students. They ought to transcend gender boundaries whereby male teachers and students also acknowledge, participate, and advocate for a better and more just society for women. While this great momentum surrounding women driving is still fresh, Saudi female TESOL teachers have a unique opportunity to inject this victory into official syllabi and textbooks as well as into the broader society.

Notes

(1) Human Rights Watch Report (2004). Saudi Arabia Events of 2004. Accessed 2 June 2018. www.hrw.org/world-report/2005/country-chapters/saudi-arabia.
(2) US Department of State Country Report on Human Rights Practices (2004). Saudi Arabia. Accessed 22 May 2018. www.state.gov/j/drl/rls/hrrpt/2004/41731.htm.
(3) Saudi Vision 2030 (2016). Accessed 3 May 2018. http://vision2030.gov.sa/en/node/8.
(4) Reuters (2013). Saudi cleric says women who drive risk damaging their ovaries. Accessed 12 Jun 2018. https://www.reuters.com/article/us-saudi-driving/saudi-cleric-says-women-who-drive-risk-damaging-their-ovaries-idUSBRE98S04B20130929.
(5) Ary News (2017). Saudi Arabia's ban on women driving must remain because they 'lack the intellect' of men, says leading cleric. Accessed 11 June 2018. https://www.arynews.tv/en/driving-ban-saudi-cleric-women-lack-intellect-men.

References

Al-arabiyah, N. (2008) Saudi study shows accidents involving female teachers on the rise. Retrieved from https://english.alarabiya.net/en/perspective/features/2015/08/22/Saudi-study-shows-accidents-involving-female-teachers-on-the-rise.html. Accessed 11 June 2018.
Abednia, A. and Izadinia, M. (2013) Critical pedagogy in ELT classroom: Exploring contributions of critical literacy to learners' critical consciousness. *Language Awareness* 22 (4), 338–352 DOI: 10.1080/09658416.2012.733400.
Alamri, M. (2011) Higher education in Saudi Arabia. *Journal of Higher Education Theory and Practice* 11 (4), 88–91.
Al Rawaf, H.S. and Simmons, C. (1991) The education of women in Saudi Arabia. *Comparative Education* 27 (3), 287–295.
Alsuwaida, N. (2016) Specifically women's education in Saudi Arabia. *Journal of International Education Research* 12 (4), 11–18.
Bakhtin, M.M. (2004) Dialogic origin and dialogic pedagogy of grammar. *Journal of Russian & East European Psychology* 4 (6), 12–49.
Barnawi, O. (2017) *Neoliberalism and English Language Education Policies in the Arabian Gulf*. London/New York: Routledge.
Barnawi, O. and Al-Hawsawi, S. (2017) English education policy in Saudi Arabia: English language education policy in the kingdom of Saudi Arabia: Current trends, issues and

challenges. In R. Kirkpatrick (ed.) *English Language Education Policy in the Middle East and North Africa* (pp. 199–222). Cham: Springer.

Barnawi, B. and Phan, L. (2014) From Western TESOL classrooms to home practice: 'Privileged' Saudi teachers critiquing, appropriating and transforming post-method pedagogy. *Critical Studies in Education* 56 (2), 259–276. doi:10.1080/17508487.2014.951949.

Black, I. (2017) Saudi Arabia's women hold day of action to change driving laws. Retrieved from www.theguardian.com/world/2013/oct/25/saudi-arabia-women-action-driving-laws The Guardian, Last accessed 18 June 2018.

Blommaert, J. (2005) *Discourse: A Critical Introduction*. Cambridge: Cambridge University Press.

Bourdieu, P. (1991) *Language and Symbolic Power* (John B. Thompson, ed.; transl. by Gino Raymond and Matthew Adamson) Cambridge: Polity Press.

Breuch, L.M (2002) Post-process 'pedagogy': A philosophical exercise. *A Journal of Composition Theory* 22 (1), 119–150.

Harkoun, M. (1994) *Rethinking Islam*. Oxford: Westview Press.

Karmani, S. (2005) 'English', 'Terror', and 'Islam.' *Applied Linguistics* 26 (2), 262–267.

Kent, T. (1994) Externalism and the production of discourse. In A. Gary, A. Olson and D. Sindey (eds) *Composition for the Postmodern Classroom* (pp. 295–312). Albany: State University of New York Press.

Khatib, M. and Miri, M. (2016) Cultivating multivocality in language classrooms: Contribution of critical pedagogy-informed teacher education. *Critical Inquiry in Language Studies* 13 (2), 98–131.

Kubota, R. (2011) Questioning linguistic instrumentalism: English, neoliberalism, and language tests in Japan. *Linguistics and Education* 22 (3), 248–260.

Kubota, R. and Lin, A. (2009 eds) *Race, Culture, and Identities in Second Language Education: Exploring Critically Engaged Practice*. New York/London: Routledge.

Phan, L.H. and Barnawi, O. (2015) Where English, neoliberalism, desire and internationalization are alive and kicking: Higher education in Saudi Arabia today. *Language and Education* 29 (6), 545–565 doi:10.1080/09500782.2015.1059436.

Street, B.V. (1984) *Literacy in Theory and Practice*. Cambridge: Cambridge University Press.

Tollefson, J.W. and Tsui, A. (2004) *Medium of Instruction Policies: Which Agenda? Whose Agenda?* London: Lawrence Erlbaum Associates.

Multilingual Abstracts

1. Across Linguistic Boundaries: Language as a Dimension of Power in the Colonization of the Brazilian Amazon

Dennys Silva-Reis and Marcos Bagno

Portuguese

Através das fronteiras lingüísticas: a linguagem como dimensão do poder na colonização da Amazônia brasileira

A tradunguagem como dimensão do poder na colonização da Amazônia brasileira internationalizationtests in Japan. y in the kingdom of Saudi Arabia: Current trends, issues and challenges. ld fuel Saudirick (ed.) nd will continue to prevent Saudi wome*l trad geral* de base tupi, uma espmensão do poder na colonização da Amazônia brasileira internationalizationtests in Japan. y in the kingdom of Saudi Arabia: Current trends, issues and challenges. ld fuel Skpatrick (ed.) nd will continue to prevent Saudi women uras, mas como produtora de novas realidades, essencialmente híbridas, características de territórios sob domínio colonial.

2. Navigating Soft and Hard Boundaries: Race and Educational Inequality at the Borderlands

Joel Windle and Kassandra Muniz

Portuguese

O lugar da linguagem em modelos teóricos de desigualdade educacional: Fronteiras suaves e duras

Este capítulo reflete sobre os modelos teóricos de analise das desigualdades educacionais em relação à linguagem que surgiram primeiramente nos países desenvolvidos nos anos seguintes à Segunda Guerra Mundial, quando as credenciais ganharam ligação mais estreita com os destinos profissionais e os sistemas escolares sofreram expansão em massa. Esses modelos trazem vestígios de peculiaridades nacionais e históricas, bem como um horizonte metodológico delimitado pelo Estado-nação. Uma segunda onda de teorização das desigualdades educacionais, influenciada por *métodos etnográficos,* enxergou as práticas linguísticas e culturais subalternas como tendo potencial de ganhar aceitação na escola através de novos conceitos de letramento e linguagem (Street, 1984; The New London Group, 1996). O foco nas relações microssociais e práticas locais, nos lares, nas comunidades e nas salas de aula, buscou exemplos positivos, alguns dos quais, como o hip-hop (Pennycook, 2007), foram teorizados como fenômenos globais. Assim como na primeira onda de teorização, o trabalho estruturado por teorias da globalização tem sido criticado por impor modelos que refletem as peculiaridades e histórias das nações desenvolvidas em que foram concebidos (Connell, 2007). O capítulo discute as críticas à falta de 'portabilidade' teorico com referência à educação na América Latina e, particularmente, no Brasil. Conclui apresentando um estudo sobre evoluções nas identificações raciais no Brasil e as possibilidades de uma formação de professores anti-racista que também afirme outras identidades marginalizadas.

3. Rural-Urban Divides and Digital Literacy in Mongolian Higher Education

Daariimaa Marav

Mongolian

Монголын оюутнуудын интернетийн хэрэглээ: Хөдөө, хотын ялгаа

Хураангуй: Бордьюгийн онолыг 'Literacy Studies'-ын судалгаанд хэрэглэн, тоон болон чанарын судалгааны аргуудыг ашигласан энэхүү судалгаагаараа англи хэлээр мэргэшиж буй монгол оюутнууд цахим технологи, ялангуяа интернетийг өдөр тутмын амьдралдаа хэрхэн ашигладаг талаар судлахыг зорьлоо. Оюутнуудын дунд тэдний нийгмийн гарал үүсэл, тухайлбал, хаана (хотын төв, хотын зах, хөдөө орон нутаг) амьдардаг, төгссөн дунд сургуулийн чанар зэргээс шалтгаалан англи хэл, цахим технологийн мэдлэгийн түвшин, хэрэглээний хувьд ялгаа байгааг судалгааны үр дүн харууллаа. Англи хэл, цахим технологийн хэрэглээний хувьд бусдаасаа давуу оюутнууд дээд боловсрол эзэмшихдээ бэрхшээл багатай, өөрсдийгөө хөгжүүлэх боломж илүүтэй байна. Цаашилбал, тэдний энэхүү давуу талууд нь нийгэмд эзлэх байр суурь, нэр хүнд, мэдлэгт нь нөлөөлж, нийгэм, соёл, эдийн засаг, бэлгэдлийн капиталаа хуримтлуулан, бэхжүүлэхэд нь тусалж байна. Эдгээр терлийн капитал нь судалгаанд оролцогчдын англи хэл, цахим технологийн хэрэглээнд нөлөөлж байсан төдийгүй улмаар тэдний ирээдүйд, ажил хөдөлмөр эрхлэхэд нь чухал үүрэгтэй нь харагдлаа.

4. A Cycle of Shame: How Shaming Perpetuates Language Inequalities in Dakar, Senegal

Teresa Speciale

Wolof

Gàcce gu dajal: Naka la jiiñaate saxalee lóomaate làkk yi ci Dakar, Senegal

Pàcc bii ñu awale ci yoonuw teggi-nooteel (decoloniality), li ko soxal mooy caytug taxawaayu bu lënt bi jam bi nit ku ñuul di jam boppam, te mu di lu lalu ci xelam ak xalaatinam ba yóbbe ko muy dëkk ci di foog ni làkki réewi Afrig yi ñoo féete suuf yu réewi tubaab yi, te wareesu leen a mën a jëfandikoo ci njàng ak njàngale / ci daara yi. Pàcc bi nag jël na niki misaalu gëstu jenn daara, ci Ndakaaru (Senegaal), ju njàngale ma di jaar ci farañse ak àngale te ñu tere fa njëfandikoom làkki réewi Afrig yi ci anam bu fés. Ña ŋànk daara ja ak ndongo ya, ñoom ñépp damoo nañu tëralinu làkk woowu, jàpp ni lu baax la luy tax ba ndongo yi doon ay way-dëkkey àddina su booloo, te loolu nekk lu mënul a ñàkk ci ñoom ngir seen ëllëg mën a àntu. Laaj bi pàcc bi bëgg a leeral mooy ndax tëralin yooyu ñuy nëpp-nëppal – te ñu juddoo ci jam-sa-bopp ak tolluwaay bu tane bi ndongo yi nekk, moo xam ci alal la mbaa ci pénc – duñu wéy di suuqat idewolosi yi, toftale yi ak gënale yi làkki yees dooleel yi di sukkandiku ngir gën a dëggal ak a gën a yoonal seen bopp.

5. The Role of Shame in Drawing Social Boundaries for Empowerment: ELT in Kiribati

Indika Liyanage and Suresh Canagarajah

Sinhala

කිරිබස්හි (Kiribati) ඉංග්‍රීසි භාෂා ප්‍රවර්ධනය හා සාමාජීය සීමාවන් නංවාලීම

ඉංග්‍රීසි භාෂාව ඉගෙනීම හා භාවිතය පිළිබඳව කිරිබස්වාසීන්ගේ හැසිරීම් සහ ආකල්ප රටාවන් හා විදේශිකයන්ගේ ඒ පිළිබඳව ඇති පුද්ගලිකත්වය හා භෞතිකත්වය මත පදනම් වූ සාමාජ විශ්වාසයන් එකිනෙකට ප්‍රතිවිරුද්ධ බවක් දක්වයි. කිරිබස්වාසීන් විසින් ලැජ්ජාව හා බිය සාමාජීය එකමුතුවක් සඳහා වූ හා සංස්කෘතික වෙනස්කම් පාලනය කොට බහු භාෂා භාවිතය ප්‍රවර්ධනය කිරීම සඳහා වූ ඇති යාන්ත්‍රනයක් ලෙස සලකති. ජාත්‍යන්තර සංවර්ධන විශේෂඥයන් විසින් එය සාමාජීය පසුගමනයක් ඇතිකිරීමට දිරිගන්වන්නාක් සේ සලකා දේශීයයන් ඉංග්‍රීසි භාෂාව ඉගෙන ගැනීමටත් හැසිරවීමටත් දිරිමත් කරවති.

මෙහිදී අප විසින් ඉංග්‍රීසි භාෂාව ඉගෙනීම කෙරෙහි සාමාජීය වශයෙන් ඇති ලැජ්ජාව හා බිය විශ්ලේෂනය කොට එය දේශීය වටිනාකම් හා අවශ්‍යතාවන් අවප්‍රමාන නොකොට හැදෑරීමට අවශ්‍යවන්නාවූ වැවස්ථා ප්‍රතිපදාන හා ඉගැන්වීම් ක්‍රමවේදයන් පිළිබඳව සාකච්ඡා කරන්නෙමු.

6. Native-speakerism and Symbolic Violence in Constructions of Teacher Competence

Junia C.S. Mattos Zaidan

Portuguese

Nativismo e Violência Simbólica na Formação de Professores de Inglês no Brasil

Baseando-no em dados empíricos do context brasileiro de ensino de inglês e relativos à formação em Letras inglês em nível de graduação, discutimos reprodução cultural e violência simbólica (Bourdieu & Passeron, 1990) a partir dos construtos 'autenticidade' e 'nativismo'. Os efeitos materiais das referências anglo-estadunidense na pedagogia de língua incluem tanto a avaliação negativa que as professoras de inglês tendem a desenvolver sobre si mesmas – conclusão a que Braine (2010) também chega em relação ao contexto asiático – e a desigualdade social, detectável nas práticas de contratação de pessoal. Apesar do avanço nas pesquisas brasileiras e em iniciativas que resultaram na consolidação de discursos afirmativos em favor de perspectivas 'não-nativas' (cf. Parâmetros Curriculares Nacionais, 1998; Cox & Assis-Peterson, 1999; Rajagopalan, 2007, 2012), argumentamos que o discurso nativista concorrente ainda prevalece (cf. Holliday, 2015), escamoteando processos de resistência e de 'apropriação e transformação' da língua inglesa, como propõem os Parâmetros Curriculares Nacionais. Em última análise, defendemos que o discurso nativista, inscrito como é em uma lógica de opressão e dominação, demanda que se considerem a estratificação de classe e a pobreza para compreender sua dinâmica, argumento que também reclama atenção para o fato de que até o discurso anti-nativista é potencialmente comoditizável e, portanto, facilmente capturado como forma de manutenção da estrutura social.

7. Knowledge Politics, Language and Inequality in Educational Publishing

Maria do Socorro Alencar Nunes Macedo, Daniele Alves Ribeiro, Euclides de Freitas Couto and André Luan Nunes Macedo

Portuguese

Este capítulo baseia-se num estudo cujas perguntas centrais são: quais estratégias usadas por um periódico brasileiro para se consolidar e obter prestígio no campo da educação? Como os critérios de excelência na avaliação da publicação científica refletem desigualdades no uso da língua? Nosso objeto de estudo é o periódico *Educação em Revista* do programa de pós-graduação em educação da Universidade Federal de Minas Gerais. Ressaltamos como a ênfase na 'internacionalização' tem como consequência a reprodução de uma política colonial e reforça as desigualdades linguísticas. Os dados foram coletados por meio de entrevistas com editores e análise de editoriais desde a primeira edição. Partimos do pressuposto de que a internacionalização baseia-se na divisão não declarada centro-/periferia. Do ponto de vista das nações periféricas produtoras de conhecimento como o Brasil, a internacionalização relaciona-se diretamente com a produção científica dos países centrais do capitalismo, tais como França, Inglaterra e Estados Unidos.

Os dados evidenciam que as barreiras enfrentadas pelo periódico em questão mostram as contradições e desigualdades estruturais presentes no ambiente acadêmico mais amplo. Para que um periódico demonstre impacto e se coloque como um importante player no cenário internacional, seus artigos devem ser publicados não apenas em Português, mas também em Inglês.

8. Decoloniality and Language in Education: Transgressing Language Boundaries in South Africa

Carolyn McKinney

Afrikaans

Dekolonialiteit en taal in onderwys: Oorskryding van taalgrense in Suid Afrika

Hierdie hoofstuk gebruik die teorie van Dekolonialiteit om te wys hoe taal in Suid-Afrikaanse onderwysbeleid nog steeds deur 'n 'colonial matrix of power' gevorm word (Mignolo, 2009). Dit lei daartoe dat kinders wat sprekers is van Afrika tale die stilte opgelê word en dat hulle uitgesluit word van onderwys van hoë gehalte. Die hoof argument van die hoofstuk is dat oorskryding van sosiaal-opgelegde taalgrense en ontwrigting van eentalige taalideologieë van sentrale belang is vir die herposisionering van taal as 'n hulpbron in die leerproses in Suid-Afrikaanse skole. Die eerste deel van die hoofstuk analiseer die taalideologieë wat die basis vorm van taal in die onderwysbeleid en kurrikulum in Suid-Afrika. Die analise sal wys hoe *Anglonormativiteit/Anglonormativity* (die verwagting dat mense vaardig is of vaardig behoort te wees in Engels en dat hulle 'n groot gebrek toon, of selfs afwykend is, as hulle nie vaardig is nie) en eentalige ideologieë vorm gee aan die huidige implementering van taalbeleid in Suid-Afrikaanse skole. Die tweede deel van die hoofstuk bied 'n gevalle-studie van dekoloniale taal- en geletterdheidspedagogiek wat taalgrense oorskry en wat dit moontlik maak vir kinders om gebruik te maak van hulle volle taal-repertoire wanneer hulle betekenis gee.

9. Queering Literacy in Brazilian Higher Education: Questioning the Boundaries of the Normalized Body

Dánie de Jesus

Portuguese

Letramento Queer na Educação Superior no Brasil: Questionando os Limites do Corpo Normalizado

No Brasil, uma onda conservadora tenta evitar a discussão sobre gênero na escola e, como resultado, professores tem dificuldade em discutir questão a cerca de diversidade com seus alunos, apesar da desigualdade de gênero. Eu observei esse fato durante uma pesquisa anterior (Jesus, 2016), que mostrou que docentes não estavam adequadamente preparados para enfrentar a diversidade em suas configurações educacionais. Em vista deste contexto, neste capítulo, discuto como procuro implementar e fomentar a questão sobre gênero na formação de professores de línguas em uma universidade brasileira, com a finalidade de promover resistência contra a desigualdade de gênero.

10. 'Saudi Women Are Finally Allowed to Sit Behind the Wheel': Initial Responses from TESOL Classrooms

Osman Z. Barnawi and Phan Le Ha

Vietnamese

'Cuối Cùng Thì Phụ nữ Ả Rập Cũng Được Phép Tự Lái Xe': Các Phản Hồi Ban Đầu Từ Lớp Học TESOL

Tóm tắt

Hàng loạt các cuộc cải cách lớn của Ả Rập Xê Út kể từ sau khủng bố 11 tháng 9, và gần đây nhất là 'Tầm nhìn Kinh tế Saudi 2030' công bố năm 2016, đã phản ánh mạnh mẽ những khát vọng thay đổi xã hội ở mọi cấp độ. Những khát vọng này đã khởi xướng một loạt động thái căn bản nhằm giải phóng phụ nữ Saudi khỏi hệ thống giám hộ của nam giới đã ăn sâu bám rễ vào đời sống nơi đây. Việc những cải cách này thường bị thôi thúc bởi trí tưởng tưởng về một xã hội vận hành theo xu hướng cởi mở và không cực đoan về mặt tôn giáo cũng làm tăng thêm các đặc quyền dành cho tiếng Anh và việc dạy tiếng Anh vốn đã được ưu ái ở Ả Rập Xê Út. Đồng thời, những cải cách này cũng gắn cho tiếng Anh vai trò là ngôn ngữ của nền kinh tế mới và của những biến đổi xã hội. Việc cho phép phụ nữ được vào sân vận động xem thể thao, được vào rạp chiếu phim, và cuối cùng là được tự lái xe mà không cần có sự giám sát hay bảo hộ của nam giới được coi là những thay đổi xã hội có tính bước ngoặt. Những thay đổi và cải cách này nhận được phản ứng nhiều chiều cả trong và ngoài nước, từ nhiều thành phần xã hội, và từ chính những người phụ nữ. Trong bối cảnh này, chúng tôi thực hiện một đề tài nghiên cứu quy mô nhỏ với hai nữ giáo viên Saudi chuyên ngành TESOL được đào tạo ở phương Tây để xem xét cách họ ứng xử và tiếp nhận ra sao việc phụ nữ được cho phép tự lái xe. Chúng tôi muốn tìm hiểu xem khoảnh khắc 'chiến thắng' này có tác động như thế nào đối với việc dạy học trên lớp của hai giáo viên, và liệu những lớp học tiếng Anh có thể đóng vai trò gì trong việc thúc đẩy những thay đổi và tiến bộ xã hội, đặc biệt là bình đẳng và quyền tự do cho người phụ nữ trong xã hội Saudi. Trong bài viết này chúng tôi đã sử dụng hàng thập kỷ đấu tranh cho quyền giáo dục và tự do của phụ nữ Saudi như một lăng kính phân tích. Chúng tôi cho rằng các triệu chứng dài hạn của việc bị áp bức vẫn tiếp tục cản trở sự nhiệt tình của phụ nữ Saudi trong việc tiếp nhận và ứng xử với sự thay đổi rất lớn có tính xã hội và chính trị đang diễn ra trong đời sống hàng ngày của họ - đó là việc bỏ lệnh cấm lái xe với phụ nữ. Những áp bức họ phải chịu có nguyên nhân từ các truyền thống văn hoá và quy tắc xã hội cứng nhắc, ví dụ như những định kiến mang tính văn hoá bất lợi cho nữ, một số giáo lý Hồi giáo nhất định được xã hội thúc đẩy, áp lực từ cha mẹ, và các đánh giá về người phụ nữ từ xã hội. Vì vậy, chúng tôi cho rằng những áp bức có tính lịch sử lâu dài và Ảnh hưởng sâu sắc của chúng đối với cuộc sống hàng ngày của phụ nữ Saudi chính là động lực mạnh mẽ nhất, thúc đẩy sự nhiệt tình của giáo viên TESOL trong việc tìm tòi khám phá các phương pháp sư phạm có thể làm thay đổi xã hội ngay trong lớp học của họ.

Arabic

أخيراً .. المرأة السعودية خلف عجلة القيادة،

ردود أفعال أولية من داخل القاعات الدراسية المخصصة لتدريس اللغة الإنجليزية لغير الناطقين بها

عثمان زكريا برناوي

الملخص

إن سلسلة الإصلاحات الرائدة التي شرعت في تنفيذها المملكة العربية السعودية منذ الحادي عشر من سبتمبر، والتي تلتها الرؤية الطموحة «الرؤية الاقتصادية السعودية ٢٠٣٠»، التي انطلقت عام ٢٠١٦ ، لتعكس تطلعات مستقبلية كبرى من أجل إحداث التغييرات والتحولات الاجتماعية على كافة المستويات. وقد شرعت تلك التطلعات في إحداث نقلات جوهرية لتحرير المرأة السعودية من نظام الوصاية الذكورية الذي يضرب أطنابه في المجتمع السعودي. كما اقترنت هذه الإصلاحات بتصورات اجتماعية نبعت من خلال الليبرالية الجديدة ، حيث كان للكثير من تلك التصورات تأثيراً إيجابياً واضحاً في المكانة المتميزة التي تبوأتها اللغة الإنجليزية سواء على صعيد التدريس أو استخدام اللغة في البلاد بشكل عام. وفي الوقت نفسه ، توّج هذه الإصلاحات اللغة الإنجليزية كلغة للاقتصاد الحديث والتحولات الاجتماعية الجديدة.

وإذا ما سلطنا الضوء على عقود طويلة خلت، ظلت المرأة السعودية خلالها تناضل من أجل الحصول على حقها في التعليم والتحرر، ففي هذا البحث -وبأسلوب دراسة الحالة- فإننا سنكتشف الأسباب الكامنة وراء تفاعل مدرستين سعوديتين حصلتا - في العالم الغربي - على الدراسات العليا في مجال تدريس اللغة الإنجليزية لغير الناطقين بها، مع الواقع الجديد بالغ الأهمية في حياتهن اليومية - «النساء يمكنهن القيادة».

ونحن هنا نزعم بأن دلائل الاضطهاد التي ظهرت على المدى الطويل نبعت من خلال التقاليد الثقافية الصارمة والأعراف/التأثيرات الاجتماعية مثل الوصمات الثقافية ، وبعض التأويلات المروّجة للمذاهب الإسلامية ، والقرارات والضغوطات اليومية التي تمارس من قبل الأهل والتي ما زالت تقف حجر عثرة أمام حماس المرأة السعودية لاستيعاب والاحتفال بالتغييرات السياسية والاجتماعية التي تتمثل في تبديد فكرة حظر القيادة على النساء.

وبالتالي ، فنحن نؤكد بأنه ليس ثمة شيء يشعل حماس النساء السعوديات لاستكشاف طرق تدريسية جديدة في القاعات الدراسية المخصصة لتدريس اللغة الإنجليزية أكثر من تلك الدلائل التاريخية للاضطهاد والآثار المترتبة على ذلك.

Index

Academic publishing xvi, 100–113
Affect theory 61, 63–64, 73
Amazon region xii, xiv, 3–23
Anglonormativity 116, 122, 123, 129
Authenticism 84–85, 89, 90, 93–96

Bilingual schools xv, 61–62, 64–65, 68, 117, 119–120, 125
Boundaries/borderlands xi–xii, xiv, 3–4, 6–7, 13, 20, 24–41, 44–46, 48–49, 51, 54–55, 68, 71–82, 85, 87, 96, 101, 109, 118, 120, 122, 134, 136, 138, 156
Bourdieu xv, 27–28, 46, 48, 61, 63, 84–89, 97, 106, 108, 135, 154
Brazil xii, 24–41, 135, 138, 139, 84, 100–114, 133–140

Capital: institutional, cultural, social, symbolic, linguistic 44, 46–47, 49–54, 63–64, 66–69, 75, 78, 84, 87, 91, 93–94, 96, 101–103, 106, 108, 118, 149
Capitalism 6, 39, 86
Coloniality and colonialism xii, 3–21, 24–41, 61–62, 64–66, 68, 75, 77, 79–80, 94, 96, 100, 115–117, 120–122, 129, 130, 134
Critical literacy 30, 96, 134, 139
Criticality 135, 136
Curriculum xiii, 4, 30–33, 35, 39–40, 80, 85, 90, 116–120, 129, 136, 139

Decoloniality and decolonial theory xvi, 61, 63, 68, 115, 117
Digital divide xv, 44–59
Digital literacies xv, 30, 44–59
Dimensions of power 4, 12, 14–16, 29–31, 47–49, 63 –68, 88–94, 101–110, 115–122, 133–139, 148–156
Dynamic bilingualism 117, 122, 125, 129

Examination systems 27–28, 32, 93–99, 116, 118, 129
English language teaching xiii, xv, 139, 71–83, 84–99, 141–157
Equivalence (translational) 14–15

Feminism xvi, 130, 141–156

Gender 133, 135, 137, 138

Heteroglossia 118, 120, 122, 123, 130
Higher education 24–25, 32–41, 44, 100–113

Identity 5, 28, 32–33, 40, 72–74, 77–78, 80–82, 144, 147
I-Kiribati 72–81
Indigenous languages xii, 3–21, 119, 121
Interpreting 3–21

Kiribati xv, 71–83

Language awareness 122–123
Language contact 13–14, 16, 18–21, 28, 72
Language ideology xiii, 8, 24–26, 28, 31, 67, 84, 85, 93, 96, 116, 117, 119, 122, 128
LGBTQI+ 133–139
Língua Geral 3–21
Linguistic diversity 7, 18, 20, 30, 40, 87, 123
Linguistic ideology (see language ideology)
Linguistic inequality xi–xii, xvi, 40, 84, 100
Literacy 31, 33, 74–75, 117, 122–123, 128, 130, 133, 135, 136, 139
Locus of enunciation 34–40, 136, 137

Marxism 84, 88, 89
Mongolia 44–56
Monoglossia 119, 120, 122, 128
Monolingualism 116–117, 120, 129, 134–135

'Mother' tongue 73, 84, 115–116, 120–121
Multilingualism 73, 79, 117–118, 120, 130

Native-speakerism 36, 64, 67, 74, 76, 80, 84–97, 96, 136
New Literacy Studies 29–32, 44–59

Pedagogy 4, 27, 30, 35, 37, 71, 73–74, 79–80, 82, 87–88, 95–96, 117, 122–123, 128, 130, 141–142, 148–151, 153–155

Queer theory 37, 133–139

Race xv, 24–41, 96, 117–118, 135, 138–139, 141
Renaming 14–15
Rural-urban divides 44–56

Senegal xv, 61–70
Shame/shaming xv, 29, 50–51, 61–70, 71–82, 86, 91–92
Social class 6, 10, 25–29, 77, 84, 86–89, 97, 117, 120, 137
Saudi Arabia 141–156
South Africa 115–130
Symbolic violence 3, 54–55, 84–98, 133, 135, 139

Teacher education (and teacher training) 32–41, 123–124, 133–139
Translanguaging 117, 123, 125, 126, 127, 128
Translation 3–21, 54, 79, 109

For Product Safety Concerns and Information please contact our EU Authorised Representative:

Easy Access System Europe

Mustamäe tee 50

10621 Tallinn

Estonia

gpsr.requests@easproject.com

www.ingramcontent.com/pod-product-compliance
Ingram Content Group UK Ltd.
Pitfield, Milton Keynes, MK11 3LW, UK
UKHW021943200326
4879IPUK00004B/67